QUEER NIGHTLIFE

TRIANGULATIONS

Lesbian/Gay/Queer ▲ Theater/Drama/Performance

RECENT TITLES IN THE SERIES:

Queer Nightlife Edited by Kemi Adeyemi, Kareem Khubchandani, and Ramón H. Rivera-Servera

Translocas: The Politics of Puerto Rican Drag and Trans Performance by Lawrence La Fountain-Stokes

Prismatic Performances: Queer South Africa and the Fragmentation of the Rainbow Nation by April Sizemore-Barber

Ishtyle: Accenting Gay Indian Nightlife by Kareem Khubchandani

The Bodies of Others: Drag Dances and Their Afterlives by Selby Wynn Schwartz

Charles Ludlam Lives! Charles Busch, Bradford Louryk, Taylor Mac, and the Queer Legacy of the Ridiculous Theatrical Company by Sean F. Edgecomb

Memories of the Revolution: The First Ten Years of the WOW Café Theater edited by Holly Hughes, Carmelita Tropicana, and Jill Dolan

Murder Most Queer: The Homicidal Homosexual in the American Theater by Jordan Schildcrout

Butch Queens Up in Pumps: Gender, Performance, and Ballroom Culture in Detroit by Marlon M. Bailey

Acts of Gaiety: LGBT Performance and the Politics of Pleasure by Sara Warner

Performing Queer Latinidad: Dance, Sexuality, Politics by Ramón H. Rivera-Servera

A Menopausal Gentleman: The Solo Performances of Peggy Shaw edited by Jill Dolan

Lady Dicks and Lesbian Brothers: Staging the Unimaginable at the WOW Café Theatre by Kate Davy

Bulldaggers, Pansies, and Chocolate Babies: Performance, Race, and Sexuality in the Harlem Renaissance by James F. Wilson

Queering Mestizaje: Transculturation and Performance by Alicia Arrizón

Queer Nightlife

Edited by
Kemi Adeyemi, Kareem Khubchandani, Ramón H. Rivera-Servera

University of Michigan Press
Ann Arbor

For questions or permissions, please contact um.press.perms@umich.edu

Published in the United States of America by the
University of Michigan Press
Manufactured in the United States of America
Printed on acid-free paper
First published May 2021

A CIP catalog record for this book is available from the British Library.

Library of Congress Cataloging-in-Publication Data

Names: Adeyemi, Kemi, 1985– editor. | Khubchandani, Kareem, 1982– editor. | Rivera-Servera, Ramón H., 1973– editor.
Title: Queer nightlife / edited by Kemi Adeyemi, Kareem Khubchandani, Ramón H. Rivera-Servera.
Description: Ann Arbor : University of Michigan Press, 2021. | Includes bibliographical references and index.
Identifiers: LCCN 2021003605 (print) | LCCN 2021003606 (ebook) | ISBN 9780472074785 (Hardcover : acid-free paper) | ISBN 9780472054787 (Paperback : acid-free paper) | ISBN 9780472128587 (eBook)
Subjects: LCSH: Nightlife. | Sexual minority culture. | Performance art. | Racism. | Sexism. | Sexual minorities—Social conditions. | Communication and sex. | Ethnology—Fieldwork.
Classification: LCC GT3408 .Q84 2021 (print) | LCC GT3408 (ebook) | DDC 307.76—dc23
LC record available at https://lccn.loc.gov/2021003605
LC ebook record available at https://lccn.loc.gov/2021003606

Contents

Digital materials related to this title can be found on the Fulcrum platform via the following citable URL: https://doi.org/10.3998/mpub.11700274

Introduction

Kemi Adeyemi, Kareem Khubchandani, and Ramón H. Rivera-Servera

THE PAT DOWN

Much of this book was completed in travel—it is as much a travelogue as it is a theorization of queer nightlife in motion. Mapping the movements to and from queer nightlife destinations (and the movements within them) evidences the variegated routes, and obstacles, the sensual and social bliss offered by queer leisure after dark. Following a "Queer Nightlife" symposium we hosted in Evanston, Illinois, we subsequently received a grant from the American Society for Theatre Research to convene a global cohort of scholars and performers around the same theme in Atlanta and San Diego, and the three of us then gathered in San Juan, Puerto Rico to compile this volume. Our weeklong tour through the bars of San Juan in autumn 2018 reminded us of the sensations, pleasures, affects, and possibilities that draw each of us to study queer nightlife. We each continually seek that feeling of being swept up in spaces and communities that make us believe in our bodies and affirm our desires, and we sought as much together when we traveled to San Juan to compile this volume. In San Juan, we were also reminded of the many forms of surveillance staged within queer nightlife settings that can limit the forms and expressions of desires and bodies—and how this often starts at the door. Ramón and Kareem had been patted down at every gay bar they'd been to that week. When door staff saw Kemi, however, they simply waved her in with barely a second glance. Nobody paid her any mind inside, either: not a second glance in Circo, the glossy video bar where she lost multiple rounds of drag bingo before go-go boys smelling of poppers took to the poles; she was ignored at Sex, where lap dances disappeared behind closed doors or down a dark hallway that she was kindly asked to steer clear of because it was for men only; she was acknowledged at Tia María's, but only because there were so few people inside. She vacillated between the dull annoyance that comes from being categorically ignored and the routine boredom that accompanies being a queer, woman-identified, female-bodied person in spaces predominated by gay men.

When Kemi saw that the doorman of the Bear Tavern wasn't asking Ramón for ID but was about to pat him down, though, she jumped in line, thinking that tonight might prove more exciting. She was looking especially handsome with her braids set under a fitted baseball hat, the deliberate shapelessness of her tan Willy Chavarria set covering her bound chest. The masc look calmed her nerves about entering what had always felt like the least accessible gay space, the bear bar, where she didn't know what to expect or how to interact with the older white gay men inhabitants (the only people she thought frequented bear bars). She also thought the look provided enough cover for her to be patted down, a process that she had now twisted into an event necessary to her feeling actually included in these bars, and she was curious about the crisis of intimacy that might erupt upon the doorman's experience of her physical body.

Her turn came, and she stepped up close to the 350-pound doorman so that he could tip forward to run his hands down her sides, along her waist through her knees and down to her ankles. He was just about to begin when Kemi's smiling announcement of "My turn!"—voice not all that high, not all that low—froze his hands midair, and he jerked his eyes upward. She saw his confusion bleed into that form of irritation that quickly tips into anger. Arms wide and feet still spread, she looked herself up and down and said "Come. On." as much to encourage him as to settle into her own resignation that this pat down would not, in fact, be happening. They continued to lock eyes as he swatted Kemi's left hip with a flick of his wrist, swishing her pants more than touching her body, a move meant mostly to push her into the bar. "I'm not gonna touch her tits," he grunted, as she walked in. Playfully dejected, Kemi entered the empty bar and took to the dance floor with Ramón and Kareem, dancing to a mix of Top 40 pop and pop-rap hits from the early 2000s, the three of them laughing about her failed attempt at passing into a bar where nobody would see her anyway.

The essays and interviews collected together in *Queer Nightlife* do not reproduce the false narrative that queer nightlife or queer subject positions are inherently or necessarily utopian formations. For LGBTQI+ people whose desires, pleasures, bodies, and/or existences are invalidated in the propriety of daytime, the night does often offer an alternative set of rules with which we can know ourselves and one another. But for all of the ways that queer nightlife spaces can provide refuge and play, they can also be sites of alienation that are circumscribed by normative modes of exclusion. Our account of entry protocols in Puerto Rico illustrates how the night, seemingly loose and free for purposes of leisure that complement the laborious day, is in fact deeply regulated by curfews, last calls, the closure of public transportation, the vigilance of door staff and the police alike, school hours, and the work bell. Who then comes out at night, capitalizes on its flexibility and ambiguity, and risks the surveillance that penetrates darkness? What does it mean to live your life, or more specifically, to "get your life" at night? The writers collected together in *Queer Nightlife* center the labor of queer people who apprehend the risky medium of the night to explore, know, and stage their bodies, genders, and sexualities in the face of systemic and social negation.

The writers do so by paying rich attention to the ways that bodies are crafted in conversation with one another, within nightlife sites, and against the broader landscapes that contextualize them. Though the contributors herein hail from a variety of disciplines and knowledge practices, they all draw on performance as method, optic, or object in order to capture the social politics of the night. From elaborate onstage shows to gestures that travel across empires and decades, the authors witness and describe performance carefully to extrapolate how bodies hold and repurpose history. Interviews with bar-goers and performers, field notes taken in the dark, and poetic autoethnography evidence the necessity of the body as an instrument of research in nightlife studies. Seeing nightlife *as* performance allows for beautiful analyses of mundane acts of waiting, worshiping, and wondering what to wear.

What we describe in this volume as "queer nightlife" is staged in the variety of permanent, temporary, static, and mobile sites that queer people congregate in to get relief from the pressures of everyday life. These include sites such as the Bear Tavern or other nightclubs, bathhouses, and monthly parties, but also living rooms, street corners, and public parks. This queer nightlife is inextricable from the spaces that surround nightlife excursions, and the writers in the volume engage the bathrooms in which people prepare themselves; the circuits of train rides, walks, and taxi cabs that route them to the function; the parking lots partygoers spill out onto once the venue closes; and the bedrooms/couches/sidewalks they lay down on—alone and with others—as the night ends. These sites of queer nightlife are inseparable from the oftentimes violent political economies within which they emerge. Indeed, the emptiness of the Bear Tavern mirrored a lot of the empty queer nightlife scenes we had encountered throughout San Juan, which was still rebuilding after the devastating blow of Hurricane María exactly one year and three months prior. The subsequent collapse of the electrical grid left the majority of the population in the dark for what amounted to the longest blackout in US history, the length of which reflected the ongoing infrastructural, political, and economic contributions to the island's deepening financial crisis. The effects of María contributed to the ongoing precariousness of Puerto Rico's queer community, which saw its diaspora, many of them escapees from the accelerating economic crisis, violently attacked at the 2016 Pulse massacre in Orlando, Florida. The essays in *Queer Nightlife* situate the rich context of queer nightlife formations within such macropolitical and global frames as settler colonialism, ongoing imperialisms and warfare, racial capitalism, border securitization, and anti-Black violence, highlighting the experiences of Indigenous, migrant, enslaved, colonized, and displaced people within and beyond the Americas.

Queer Nightlife is organized to track the trajectories of the night ("Before," "Inside," "Show," and "After"), capturing the range of movements and sentiments engaged from when the sun goes down to when it rises anew. The writers often disrupt this even linearity as they move the reader across time and borders. Authors bear witness to a diversity of scenes from across the globe, and queer nightlife necessarily becomes many things across the volume. In each section of the book, we include an interview with people who work in nightlife, allowing them to theorize in their own voices the contributions they make to the worlds documented here. Rather than reify any notion of what queer, night, or life should look like, the contributors to this volume bring specificity to their archives and field sites in order to build a more capacious vision of queer nightlife.

DISCIPLINING QUEER NIGHTLIFE

Through this volume, we convene an interdisciplinary body of scholarship that attends to how gender and sexual minorities, made marginal if not criminal by state and society, forge pleasure, sociality, and creativity after dark. Our contributors attend to people who inhabit categories such as "lesbian," "gay," and "trans," but whose lives often refuse to be captured by the many demarcations those terms invoke. You'll see throughout this volume, then, variations of the acronym LGBTQ, representing the distinct communities and politics *Queer Nightlife*'s contributors engage, and signaling the diversity of life that always exceeds attempts at shorthand. We consolidate these projects under the rubric of "queer nightlife" in an acknowledgment of the ways that academic disciplines have also marginalized this scholarship. The essays and interviews reflect the long-standing and ongoing scholarly and creative labor to document queer and trans creativity, resilience, loss, and subjugation, and they recall work by so many scholars who have often worked alone in their disciplines and their departments to invest in minoritarian practices that are deemed fickle, trivial, or escapist. Below we discuss conversations and contributions in queer nightlife that have been staged across gender and sexuality studies, historical and literary research, sociology and anthropology, theater and dance analysis, and area studies. As scholars trained in performance studies, we have curated *Queer Nightlife* with an eye toward the ways that performance knits these diverse fields together and provides an essential method for sensing, analyzing, and querying the multiple expressions of queer nightlife.

We have also been intentional in grounding *Queer Nightlife* in queer of color criticism, an analytic framework that considers how modes of governance make particular bodies, genders, sexualities, and desires nonnormative and thus subject to scrutiny and violence (C. Cohen 1997). Under racial capitalism, gender and sexuality are managed for the purposes of labor extraction; as people become surplus, so too do their bodies, desires, and aesthetics become excessive (Ferguson 2004; Vargas 2014). Seeming aberrance from Euro-Western genders and sexualities has justified colonial settlement and militarized invasions to supposedly save Brown people from their own perversions (Puar 2007; Reddy 2011), and it continues to justify violence against people who exist across the spectrum of lesbian, gay, bisexual, trans, queer, and intersex identities. Queer nightlife contexts allow us to see how racial capitalism has predetermined the value of bodies and continues to shape the intimacies, erotics, and desires that emanate from them (McBride 2005; Pérez 2015; A. Wilson 2004), and, moreover, how queer life, set at night or otherwise, continues to be a site of violence.

Indeed, queer nightlife venues have often been the target of police raids meant to manage aberrant bodies and desires, and gentrification efforts meant to "clean up" neighborhoods to make way for allegedly normative people and revenue streams. Infamous incidents such as the 1981 raid of bathhouses in Toronto, the 1966 Compton's Cafeteria riots in San Francisco, and arrests made on the Queen Boat in Cairo in 2001 remind us of the specific nexus that racialized queer genders and sexualities, labor, criminality, and nightlife occupy (L. Cohen 2007). Modes of policing difference in nightlife settings have often operated through the criminalization or disallowance of gender nonconformity (Chauncey 2008; Shahani 2008)—and the criminalization of sex work, in particular—to justify city-sanctioned efforts to "clean up" queer and trans enclaves. The criminalization and displacement of sex workers paves the way for the transformation of their spaces of work, habitation, and leisure into tourist venues and residential neighborhoods (Crawford 2014; Berlant and Warner 1998; Delany 1999; Hanhardt 2013). Overtures in favor of gentrification are not necessarily explicitly grounded in anxieties over the presence of queer bodies and labor systems; city managers, administrators, police, and community alliances have used sex and drug panics and stripped or revised zoning regulations to generate occupancy turnover, and they have enforced cabaret licenses, noise ordinances, and dance permits to regulate queer spaces (Hae 2012; Morcom 2013; Siegel 2001). These regulations are unevenly distributed. As British and North American news media debate the survival of gay bars under gentrification, online dating, and post-identity politics, scholarship shows that US queer bars seeing the highest rate of closure are those serving women, queer people of color, and gay cruising (Mattson 2019).

But studies that focus primarily on commercial establishments and neighborhoods miss the multiplicity of ways that queer nightlife is practiced. While bars, nightclubs, parties, and dance fundraisers have long served as venues for activist organizing and political subject formation, the relationship between nightlife and politics is almost always narrated through the uprisings at New York's Stonewall Inn in 1969. This narrative's centering of New York, the United States, and white gay men has been critiqued for its metronormativity (Manalansan 1995; Herring 2010) and necessarily reimagined (Tourmaline and Wortzel 2018). Further, queer scholars offer us other geopolitical frames to imagine queer and trans collective creativity, such as the rural, suburban, archipelagic, and regional (Gray 2009; Tongson 2011; Gill 2018; David 2018; Gopinath 2018). In *Queer Nightlife*, we certainly find ourselves in New York, Chicago, and San Francisco, but we also locate nightlife's political import in underresearched and unexpected places: the US South, rural Maine, Havana's outskirts, Andean Indigenous festivals, Mumbai police stations, and Beirut drag balls.

Considering the systemic racism in gay bars and neighborhoods that are predominated by gay men, and in hostile municipalities, women, trans folks, and queer people of color have long been throwing parties in nonqueer bars (Adeyemi 2019), finding collectivity on "ladies' night" (Strey 2017), and hosting parties at home (Thorpe 1996). For these reasons, *Queer Nightlife* contributes to more capacious geographies of queer nightlife that look to the café instead of the nightclub (Merabet 2004), that cruise the suburbs in cars rather than walk the city on foot (Tongson 2011), that shift even as we drift from room to room (Livermon 2014). We might even trouble the notion of "going out" altogether. For young queer people who can't get into bars, online venues such as Tumblr become spaces to hone queer of color politics and aesthetics (Cho 2018; Gray 2009). When the bar's cover charge, distance from home, and microaggressions take too much of a toll, house parties, rent parties, and *stokvels* offer alternatives that render going out a domestic affair (Thorpe 1996; J. Wilson 2010; Livermon 2014). As Summer Kim Lee (2019) offers in her critique of "coming out" and "going out" as inevitable queer teleologies, one can "stay in" even when out at the concert or club through embodiment and affectation. Her turn to performance and embodiment recalls queer of color critiques of "coming out" that complicate the timeline of queerness and articulate multiple and more tacit modes of practicing queer visibility (Decena 2011; Manalansan 2003; Ross 2005; Han 2015).

Indeed, performance has been a critical optic to studies of nightlife that depend on the aesthetics and sensorial data of the night—from the music played to the lighting to the ways that people move together and apart, reading bodies as they perform against the visual, sonic, and kinesthetic landscapes that surround them—to make sense of the ways that individual and collective identities are felt and negotiated. The "bright lights" of some club spaces work as beacons of gay modernity or even ominous warnings in the postcolonial city (Benedicto 2014), and the dim lighting of others can both create a sexy mood and hide architectural flaws (Grazian 2008). Sometimes the absence of windows altogether allows clubgoers to forget their relationship to hetero-capitalist time (Buckland 2002; Halberstam 2005), and luxurious velvet ropes segmenting entryways make waiting outside under street lamps feel worthwhile (Munuera 2017). Glowing video screens in queer bars perform their own pedagogies, offering dancers gendered and racialized gestures to dance like a diva or Bollywood hero (Griffin 2008; Peterson 2011; Dudrah 2006). The nightlife practices shaped among and conversant with these architectures are always political, and negotiations of how, where, and with whom you dance are particularly fruitful sites for understanding this (Bollen 2001; Buckland 2002; Thornton 1996). Club dance can of course accrue sexiness and pleasure alongside sartorial choices (Cvetkovich 2001), or through the introduction of differently racialized music genres (Rivera-Servera 2016). With all these tools at hand, David Román (2003, ix) recounts how dancing in queer nightlife was "a way for me to begin choreographing my own movements through the world as an openly gay man," alongside narrating the critical role of dance parties in raising funds for HIV/AIDS activism (Buckland 2002).

Just as dancing queerly in the club becomes its own "choreography of protest" (Rivera-Servera 2012; Foster 2003), the long reach of queer nightlife beyond the boundaries of the bar incubates political subjectivities that are continually redefined through other systems of movement. Lesbian bars allowed for the rehearsal and consolidation of butch/femme aesthetics (Kennedy and Davis 1993; Case 1988), and drag performance has provided an accessible entry point for some trans people to experiment with gender (Vaid-Menon 2018). Indeed, Judith Butler's (1990a) ubiquitous theory of gender performativity is explained through the figure of the drag queen, though abstracted from her home in the nightclub. With more specificity, Marlon Bailey (2013) explains the relationships between gender, subjectivity, and performance by describing how the distinctive gender matrix of Detroit's Black ball culture is constituted through "communal performance labor." Drag performance and ballroom scenes have in fact captured an especially outsized amount of attention in scholarly conversation and popular culture alike. Queer nightlife studies have tracked their significant impact on global popular culture, fostering fashion, movement, and sound that now feels mainstream, doing particularly important work to historicize and contextualize the importance of disco music and culture in the late sixties and early seventies. Scholars variously consider disco's mechanically produced sound, the ways it initiated and encouraged individualized dancing in nightclubs, its capacity to invoke collectivity, its Black and queer origins, the erasure of Black and queer artists particularly by *Saturday Night Fever* and the Bee Gees, and homophobic, misogynist, and racist backlash against the music and dance (Echols 2010; Lawrence 2011; Dyer 1979; Nyong'o 2008). Micah E. Salkind (2019) importantly demonstrates how house music and dance emerging out of Chicago's queer of color communities and now globally popular extends disco's contested personality.

Harlem's Black and Latinx ball cultures, which blossomed in the late seventies and directly and indirectly conversed with disco, have had global influence (and contested circulation) in forms like Madonna's 1990 song "Vogue," Jennie Livingston's 1990 documentary *Paris Is Burning*, the 2016 documentary *Kiki*, and the TV show *Pose*, which premiered in 2018 on FX (Regnault 2011). *Paris* in particular has been an important though controversial cultural phenomenon, spurring discussions about the dominance of whiteness in queer imaginations (hooks 1992), the inscrutability and opacity of Black queer dance (Nyong'o 2015), the spread of voguing into the Midwest (Bailey 2013), and the political economic conditions for making queer kinship under neoliberalism (Reddy 1998). The overwhelming success of the reality TV drag queen competition *RuPaul's Drag Race* (2009–), which incessantly quotes *Paris*, is another export of queer nightlife's aesthetics into the mainstream; the show has spawned spin-offs and imitations in the United Kingdom, Canada, Thailand, Mexico, Holland, and Chile.

Queer Nightlife works alongside the heightened fabulousness of enactments of drag and ball cultures, understanding, as Madison Moore (2018) has demonstrated, that the fabulous need not always be reduced to labels and narcissism, to attend to those moments, bodies, gestures, and choreographies that are more difficult to track, or that can't easily fit into normative protocols of queerness that circulate in mainstream culture. We return to the optic of the night as a site for understanding the many ways that minoritarian life is governed by time, and for understanding how queer subjects utilize, if not wield, the night in order to reorganize their relationships to time and space alike. Nightlife is restricted by the limited time meted out for leisure, from the offshoring of US and European labor, which brings work and leisure, day and night, into closer proximity east of the Greenwich Meridian (Khubchandani 2020), to the limited permission that enslaved Black folk were given for evening dances (Hartman 1997), to the enforcement of a "closing time" that folded Harlem's revelers back into heteronormativity (Vogel 2009). But the many improvisations possible in nightlife allow us to examine how time is practiced such that even paltry permissions for pleasure have expansive and long-lasting possibilities. Setting up tables and decorating in anticipation of the revelry of the ball is essential "kin labor" that forges bonds between people that flourish when the pageantry begins (Bailey 2013). When the party starts, Black queer women's slowing music and dance down swims against the current of gentrification (Adeyemi 2019), and the *puro pedo* temporality of the cantina remains defiantly old-fashioned in the face of modernizing musical impulses (Vargas 2013). Nightlife's ephemera, whether hangovers, wrist stamps, or good or bad feelings, extend its pleasures, politics, and possibilities well "after the party" and into the world at large (Chambers-Letson 2018; Muñoz 1996, 2009). Dance's ability to conjure the past and "drag" history through the body reorganizes time (Freeman 2010; Hamera 2007), producing a gestural archive for future worldmaking (Rivera-Servera 2017), manifesting intergenerational homespace (Khubchandani 2020; Salkind 2019), and even taking us to church (E. P. Johnson 1998; McCune 2004).

As queer nightlife studies think deeply about the consequences of how and where minoritarian bodies come together in space, the essays in this book also think deeply about how we might generate more ethical practices of being together in the process—of thinking together, to be sure, but also of moving together and feeling one another when we find each other in the queer night. Queer nightlife surely comprises sites to be investigated; *Queer Nightlife* asks after methodological-cum-ethical strategies for doing this. Nightlife scholarship requires innovative methods: digital ethnography (Dasgupta 2014), memoir (Seymour 2008), collaborative interview (M. Moore 2018), and curation (Qureshi 2018), but ultimately it might also be its own method altogether. In Roderick A. Ferguson's *Aberrations in Black* (2004) a "black drag-queen prostitute" becomes a cipher for theorizing relationships between capitalism, gender, sexuality, and race. In a fictional encounter between a Black drag queen on Chicago's South Side and University of Chicago sociologist Conrad Bentzen in the 1930s, the former says to herself, "Oh there goes another white boy tourist come to slum with the faggots" (Ferguson 31). The racialization of sexual and gender difference cultivates sexual tourisms across national borders (Boone 1995; Mitchell 2016), as well as across urban geographies (Heap 2009; Orne 2017; Vogel 2009). But Bentzen's academic tourism, which produced his 1938 "Notes on the Homosexual in Chicago," might well count as one of the first scholarly accounts of queer nightlife. Ferguson's speculative Black drag queen offers us a way to disidentify with the legacy of this scholarship, and to use nightlife *as a method* by studying nightlife from the position of the person being studied. For many of our contributors, nightlife is far from tourism: it is a place where they too make and are made. Their writing evidences how they are seduced by beauty, performance, sound, gesture, and movement.

Yet queer nightlife does not need the perceived legitimacy of scholarship to be legible or to thrive. It is a nimble world that shifts into the daytime to accommodate older and younger folks, moves to backyard potlucks to welcome people with disabilities or those who can't afford covers, hides in plain sight through unmarked doors, cruisy glances, and colored bandanas, slows down the music to invite other genders to the dance floor. But as scholars of queer and trans life, culture, and criticism, we need queer nightlife because it teaches us to be nimble thinkers, moving with bodies, history, money, and aesthetics. We need this world because it archives politics (elsewhere undocumented) through gesture, memory, DJing techniques, promotional fliers, architecture. We need this world because, as the root and incubator of other kinds of politics and culture that feel more mainstream, urgent, serious, or researchable, it tells a fuller story. With so many forces at work, studying nightlife asks us to bring our fullest selves—body, sensation, subjectivity, desire, criticism, artistry—to our research, to wear our "best informant's dress" as it were, ready for a romance with our work (Newton 1993).

BEFORE

Nightlife begins well before sundown. It begins with embodied anticipation for a "night out" constituted by desire, boredom, work, and loneliness. It begins with decisions about what to wear, requests to take off work the next day, WhatsApp group messages coordinating a destination, and even resolutions to "stay in." The before of nightlife is also the political histories that dictate when, how, and where we find queer pleasure and community. The before of nightlife includes the memories, lore, and fairy tales that sustain nightlife's affective charge. Nostalgia is central to making and foreclosing nightlife's capacious possibilities. The nightclub can be a place to dance again with the ghosts of friends lost to AIDS (Buckland 2002), or to pay pilgrimage to the activisms of queer and trans ancestors. But in increasingly gentrified urban conditions, there are more places that people cannot return to, as city ordinances zone where we commune, dance, and fuck. Martin F. Manalansan IV's essay on queer fabulations of Jackson Heights gestures to the productively slippery memories of the neighborhood's erotic zones. The intimate possibilities of queer knowledge and memory also appear in AB Brown's essay, in which they consider the generativity of intergenerational spaces at a queer party in Cape Town. In an interview with Kareem Khubchandani, DJ Rekha describes their journey to DJing and party planning, and in particular the way that the sounds they play are informed by the radical activism that preceded their music career. Karen Jaime attends to how music calls history into the present in ways that conjure and queer time, examining how disco invites a different audience and copresence to Nowhere Bar in Brooklyn.

Writing from her standpoint as a bouncer at Nowhere, Jaime brings another before into relief: the bar's threshold. While the inside is replete with contestations over space, hierarchies of class, race, and cultural difference become apparent before entering the club: in the apartment where one anticipates company, encounters on the commute to the bar, the parking lot and strip malls that function as sites of surveillance and refuge, or the thrill of travel to a sexy destination. Caleb Luna's deliberation on how to dress their fat Brown body for a queer night out calls attention to the specificity of style in queer nightlife, and the compromises and risks they take in pursuit of pleasure and safety moving through queer San Francisco. Locating the party is its own challenge and adventure, as Brown shows, and Emily R. Bock meditates on the critical relations that develop in the time spent waiting for a ball to begin. Sometimes the club is not the destination at all. Sometimes the threshold of the bar is too expensive, or too classed to cross. Sometimes the risky pleasures of public sex offer intimacies not found in the bar. In his ethnography of queer Mumbai, Brian A. Horton explores the messy erotics of public sex and police entrapment as safer-sex education workshops in the daytime intertwine with nighttime escapades of public sex.

INSIDE

As Ramón has argued in *Performing Queer Latinidad* (2012), entering the club does not grant immediate access to the pleasures and community popularly imagined inside. While bouncers and other gatekeepers regulate access to the interior, socialities inside the nightclub are regulated by the aesthetics and architecture of the space, as well as by patrons and workers. Patrons judge one another based on what they wear, how they move, and who they dance with. The utopian possibilities of the inside, the capacity for creativity and community to imagine alternative futures for minoritarian subjects, depend on the physical and figurative room we leave for invention and improvisation on the social dance floor, how "loose" or "tight" such spaces are (Vogel 2009). As a space of improvisation and play, the inside is predictable and unpredictable, and patrons are attracted to both these conditions of being with others, the comfort of kinship as well as the fantasy of escape. The sensory, affective, and kinesthetic conditions of the night produced in the confluence of media, performance, and community have the potential to transport us to unexpected worlds.

The aesthetic qualities of queer nightlife guide us on how to behave inside. As Eddie Gamboa demonstrates, light, or more exactly dark, is especially instructive for queer subjects: darkness teaches their interlocutors how to be with one another in an unnamed bar in Chicago. Music too calls forth particular articulations of the body; dancehall music, as Sabia McCoy-Torres demonstrates, very literally prompts dancers to assume gendered and sexual relations. Her careful analysis of Paws Ambush's improvisations demonstrates how Caribbean women comply with and refuse the pedagogy of dancehall music. Sable Elyse Smith further meditates on dance, on its psycho-corporeal capacity to give life to minoritarian subjects, what she calls "ecstatic resilience," which she tells us "is not an escape."

Indeed, while many of our authors describe the fabulous possibilities of nightlife, they attend carefully to the material context of the night, and to the safety, labor, and activism inside. Sisters, a now-closed lesbian bar in

Maine, functioned as a home, a refuge even, for queer women living in a rural context. In her essay on the bar, Clare Forstie maps the uneven gender landscape of the lesbian bar, in which a butch white gender dominated, while femmes and transmasculine folk remained marginal. In Mexico City, where lesbians and trans women are exceptionally harassed and disenfranchised by the state, the "lesbotransfeminista" space La Gozadera provided refuge as well. Jennifer Tyburczy's reflection on La Gozadera demonstrates the co-constitutive nature of "sex and social justice" in a place where lesbians and trans folks could make art and make out.

In addition to being a sanctuary, the bar is also a site of work: barbacks, bouncers, light technicians, and go-go dancers are employed by the bar, and dealers and sex workers use the bar to meet clients. Thinking through the labors of sex work and burlesque performance, Ms. Briq House describes in an interview with Kemi Adeyemi her interventions in racialized queer histories of Seattle and beyond. In La Hueca, a queer bar in Chicago's Mexican neighborhood Little Village, trans Latinas arrive at the bar ready to work. However, as Andrea Bolivar shows in her ethnography of this long-standing bar, the work these women do goes well beyond sex work, and she points to the intergenerational care work and spiritual labor that her interlocutors engage in inside.

SHOW

Queer nightlife is often synonymous with drag shows, particularly those featuring hyperfeminine drag queens, but we need more expansive rubrics to think about theatricality in nightlife. For those who don't have access to nightclubs—such as underage folks and rural queers—sometimes the aisles of Walmart are their catwalks and stages (Gray 2009). At balls and pageants, the show is the whole night and not just a break from the DJ's set (Bailey 2013; Ochoa 2014). Sometimes the show makes queer nightlife feel more like a Filipino Catholic festival (Manalansan 2003), Black church service (E. P. Johnson 1998), or Mexican family-friendly gathering (Carrillo 2004) than the cosmopolitan nowhere. Club kids who never take the stage but circulate through the crowd in spectacular and strange outfits recraft the space through their style. In Thai go-go bars, the show is only a prelude to sex work, performers take the stage to show off their bodies so that they may be booked for more intimate and private work (A. Wilson 2004). But we would be remiss to not consider the critical work of theatrical performance in the nightclub. As José Esteban Muñoz's (2009, 78) corpus of work shows, queer of color performers such as Vaginal Davis, Carmelita Tropicana, and Kevin Aviance use spectacular aesthetics to perform critiques and conjure affects so that the crowd can "see and experience the feelings they do not permit themselves to let in." The affective force and pedagogical structure of the show allows the crowd to be together in the present, but sometimes also to do the mournful memory work "of crossing over or back into communities long left" (Parédez 2009, 185).

In this volume, scholars writing about drag and pageantry map new geographies of performance, escorting us out of the nightclub to witness the show elsewhere. They show us how repertoires of nightlife performance—sexiness, humor, glamour—are retooled for new audiences. We follow Matthew Leslie Santana to the outskirts of Havana, where working-class Black drag kings rechoreograph Black Cuban masculinities through rumba, reggaeton, and *son* in their living room. At a Zapotec *vela* (celebration) at which a Muxe is crowned queen of the festivities, Noé López draws our attention to the walls that surround her dance, and the land she dances on, to bear witness to histories of colonialism, displacement, and migration that make necessary such scenes of community, that *require* queer diasporic Indigenous cultures. Enzo E. Vasquez Toral demonstrates how the Bolivian drag collective La Familia Galán cultivates syncretic aesthetics as its members' performances move from the irreverent stages of nightclubs and pride marches to the repertoire-based dance-dramas of folkloric festivals.

These shows in living rooms, religious festivals, and community celebrations evidence how nightclub aesthetics, especially those of the show, filter into other aspects of everyday life: nightlife inspires other kinds of theatrical performance, such as the works of queer Black choreographer Trajal Harrell. In her essay on Harrell's *Antigone Sr.*, Clare Croft explores how nightlife's aesthetics, particularly the runway walks, poses, and "slashing grace" of Black queer ball culture, are deployed in the choreography, unlikely but necessary arrivals at the elite Judson Church venue. Nightlife's fashionability is capitalized on by sex workers in Rio de Janeiro, as Gregory Mitchell shows; the fashion show for Daspu, a line of clothing designed and modeled by sex workers, layers the nightclub, street, and catwalk to draw attention to many creative labors of Brazil's prostitutes. In conversation with Meiver De la Cruz, Alexandre Paulikevitch talks about the material contexts of life in Beirut to explain the efficacy of dance, nightlife, and collectivity, whether onstage performing *Baladi* dance or at makeshift voguing balls.

AFTER

As the aesthetics of the nightclub bleed into and layer onto the everyday, so too do its politics. The longevity of nightlife's possibilities, its utopian gesture, its ephemeral persistence, is perhaps one of nightlife scholarship's most seductive offerings. The extended scholarly conversation on queer futurity is certainly concerned with the distribution of queer resources, life, and pleasure to those made most precarious—young queer and trans people of color—through the party, nightclub, and sex (Allen 2009; Rodríguez 2014; Chambers-Letson 2018). But the club must always close, and "closing time" works to inscribe revelers back into hetero-capitalist temporal order (Vogel 2009, 112). However, closing has more severe connotations when we think about the shutting down of so many queer spaces and forms of intimate life under neoliberal projects of "urban renewal" and homonormative gentrification in Chicago, New York, San Francisco, and Washington, DC.

In this section on after, our contributors explore the afterlife of nightlife's time: when the doors close for the night, when they are shut forever, or when they reopen as new bourgie straight venues wiped of all *suciedad* (dirt). While nightlife is narrated as an ephemeral site of performance and politics, select films serve as important documentations that extend the reach of the night: *The Queen* (Frank Simon, 1968), *Wildness* (Wu Tsang, 2012), and of course *Paris Is Burning* (Jennie Livingston, 1991). Jih-Fei Cheng's analysis traces the ways that gestures captured in *Paris* travel across oceans, betwixt empires, and amid health crises to allow intimacies between Black and Brown subjects in Harlem and Hawai'i. Cheng's focus on the intergenerational transmission of gesture from older to younger queens leads us to an interview with Puerto Rican indie musician Eduardo Alegría conducted by Ramón H. Rivera-Servera and José Álvarez-Colón. Alegría's interview remembers the scenes and space where he cultivated his life and practice as a queer performer in San Juan's experimental dance and performance scenes.

Where do we go when the bar has closed? In E. Patrick Johnson's memoir-history of Black queer southern nightlife, we bear witness to the closure of bars and the rise of new forms of nightlife. The shifts of Black gay dance cultures over a century that Johnson describes, as well as his gesture toward new forms of queer nightlife, remind us that there will be many afters. Xandra Ibarra's ritualistic performance tours her audience-participants to the queer Latinx spaces that have been wiped out by the forces of gentrification. Juana María Rodríguez's analysis of Ibarra's performance names the macropolitical forces that work to eradicate Indigenous, queer, poor, and other minoritarian life by attending to the sites (including digital sites) of the performance. At the same time, Rodríguez makes evident the possibility of queer nightlife performance, even performance that cannot go back into the club, in restoring bodies and life.

TRAVELOGUES OF DESIRE

Before, inside, show, and after frame the spatiotemporal coordinates of a traveled phenomena reliant on political economies of global circulation (of goods, people, data) but grounded in the embodied microsociologies of the senses. Touch, sight, sound, smell, and even taste open up the possible elevations of the quotidian into the glittery opacity of the night. But the senses are organized into majoritarian systems of power. Moving through the cracks of the normative while acknowledging the rough surfaces and structural limitations en route to pleasure allows for a choreography of nightlife that indulges in the performance of possibility, sustained in the myriad repertoires from theatrical to quotidian cataloged in this volume. It is our hope that you the reader will travel along with a similarly playful disposition while remaining responsive to the economic and sociological contingencies that elevate the ethics of relation emergent in queer nightlife into a politics of life.

Before

That Magical Touch

Migrant Nocturnal Stories in Queer Jackson Heights

Martin F. Manalansan IV

> The idea of "night life" comes to mind, with its promising associations: pleasure, escape from the everyday, secret get-aways. It would be tempting, delightful and only too easy to write about this "night life," to craft garish, colourful phrases, paint image of the "intoxication of the night." We will talk about night life, but night in the big city has other dimensions. It is worth digging deeper, questioning clichés and stereotypical images: the riches of the night do not disclose themselves at first glance, but lie buried in little-known sources, texts and stories.
>
> —Joachim Schlör, *Nights in the Big City*

Nightlife is a set of hidden stories about auras and ecologies, modern times and spaces, feelings and desires, bodies and things. It is not just the opposite of daytime but rather a setting for the continuities and discontinuities of atmospheres, stories, and lives. In contrast to daytime, nights are often seen as realms of darkness, sinister secrets with hints of violence and evil. Ironically, images about nightlife also conjure the modernist montage of technological rationality, bright lights, and cosmopolitan urbanity. Stereotypically, denizens or creatures of the night are often portrayed as always already deviant and ghostlike. They often include figures like sex workers, perverts, and other dark creatures. Such figures are also portrayed to be nonserious, pleasure-seekers who search for comfort under the cover of nightly anonymity in recreational palaces that sequester them from the demands of various normativities of "real life." Nightlife, then, becomes a queer setting for the playing out of fantasies and is typically (though wrongly) construed as unreal. Set within this popular and facile frame, "real life" is something that happens in the cruel glare of daylight, while nightlife is an exodus from the drudgery of the daily grind, a period of rest, slumber, leisure, and unbounded pleasures.

Going beyond these narrow understandings of nightlife, I turn to the "other dimensions" that consider nightlife as an ambiance, a process, and a set of stories. As the epigraph from Joachim Schlör elegantly suggests, nightlife is more than space and time but rather is a site for the generation and proliferation of narratives, images, sounds, haptics, tastes, and aromas. As such, nightlife is the messy, immeasurable layering of multiple, often contradictory, and intersecting stories. Fairy tales can be construed as fabulations of the impossible and the improbable, the depictions of adventures and misadventures of extraordinary characters or allegorical figures lifted from the fray and tumult of the ordinary. Fairy tales (together with the vernacular camp meanings of fairy) are about aspirations, make-believe, hopes, and the comforts and pleasures of the unreal. Tragedy, on the other hand, is often seen as a descent into the banality of routine and habits, disaster and catastrophe. In this essay, I go beyond the seeming contradictions between fairy tales and tragedies within the nightlives of queer immigrants in Jackson Heights. Tragedies and fairy tales are coextensive and coproductive narratological forces of queer migrancy and queer nightlife. They are not so much discreet moments but rather a messy clutter of intersecting emotional ecologies, moods, and affective atmospheres. Both genres are seamless, porous, and unbounded.

Consisting of contradictory dimensions and layers, the nocturnal awaits and demands critical exfoliation. What follows is an excavation, an archeological exploration of the cultural strata, textures, and moods of a particular set of nightlives, and a sensorial mapping of the "other dimensions" of the queer urban nocturnal, specifically those of queer migrants. Already set off as strangers to the nation, queer migrants are also deemed as alien to the bright lights of gay modernity. Shifting from a nonmainstream gay bar to the streets, stores, and other scenes of an immigrant neighborhood in Queens, this work is at various turns an ethnographic record, a reverie, and a listing of atmospheres. Unruly at best, this work relies on particular times and places, and on a sense of my own self as author, observer, and participant reassessing and renarrating attachments and events of that period. Clearly, this essay tries to pave a path to a "fleshy" engagement with nightlife stories suffused with pathos and longing as well as provide a critical mapping of moments that contain potentials for exuberance, joy, and hope. To begin, I provisionally start with a sort of "fairy" tale that then winds its ways through various scenes of tragedies, mishaps, and pathos interspersed with spectacles, fabulousness, and exuberance. Following the fairy-tale form, I create and conjure the atmosphere, the fleeting and flimsy aura of Jackson Heights noir with a tinge of campy irony.

TALES OF JACKSON HEIGHTS

Once upon a time, in an island far, far away, there existed an enchanted place. The island was the island of queens; I mean Queens, New York. And the enchanted place was called Magic Touch, a gay bar. While I might be seen as waxing poetic and spewing out nostalgic dust in the last few seconds, I would temper this initial perception by pointing out that my nocturnal excursions in the queer space of Jackson Heights consist of a critical consideration of competing yet mutually constitutive forces of affect and action, make-believe and realness, the material and the imaginary. In the following stories, I will demonstrate how exuberance, leisure, and restless abandon comingle with gritty struggle and suffering in the shifting affective geographies of a neoliberal urban neighborhood. In the throes of rapid gentrification today, Jackson Heights was historically a Jewish and Italian neighborhood. It has transformed into what is now a predominantly Latin American and Asian residential and business space, one that includes Colombian, South Asian, Korean, Middle Eastern, Puerto Rican, and many other immigrant and racialized working-class communities (Manalansan 2005).

The portrait that I will present of Jackson Heights noir is primarily an embodied one, produced out of more than twenty-five years of ethnographic fieldwork and from my residence in the adjacent Woodside neighborhood in the eighties and nineties. My methodological approach is ethnographic, which is essentially about a focused atmospheric attunement (Anderson 2009). To paraphrase anthropologist Kathleen Stewart (2011, 445), attunement is a "tuning up to something," an "intimate compositional process of dwelling in spaces that bears, gestures, gestates," or indeed "worlds." Following Stewart, I am attentive to the accretion of ordinary scenes in everyday life such as "attachments and detachments, difference and indifferences, losses and proliferating possibilities" (448). Such ordinary bundles of scenes suggest the "plasticity and density" (446) of lives and living that, in turn, point to possibilities, dead ends, and messy intersections of queer day- and nightlife.

These orienting processes constitute the stuff of what I know as ethnography. Ethnographic attunement then is about wading through the incommensurable, the uncomfortable, and the counterintuitiveness of the everyday. An ethnography is not about clinically observing and recording spaces and lives but rather about being bodily immersed in the thick morass of things. The impulse to ethnographically record is due to an acute self-awareness of being both inside and outside the social schemes. Thus, my ethnographic approach to fairy tales is not in terms of a children's literary genre but rather in that of a sensorial "openness" to persistent aspirational hopefulness, rhythmic refrains of stories about pathos and the fabulous, the shape and density of the "air," and the fervent attempts at survival and aliveness by the queer migrant subjects with whom I have been in dialogue during this period.

TALES OF THE TRAGIC AND THE MAGIC

This essay thinks through ethnographic moments, small vignettes, or cases "selected out of countless potentially describable moments and scenes in which the sense of something happening becomes tactile" (Stewart 2011, 445). In other words, my ethnographic forays are affective and material examinations of the sensibilities and ecologies of queer Jackson Heights. The tactile or haptic dimension in my presentation begins with that enchanted but unfortunately now-defunct gay bar called Magic Touch.

Magic Touch—or, more officially, the Magic Touch Tavern—was one of the older bars in the area and was located on Thirty-Seventh Road, which was a cruising strip infamously known by some gay residents as Vaseline Alley. Magic Touch was located next to the Earle Theater, which showed porn movies but was eventually transformed into a cinema showing South Asian films, and, at the time of writing this essay, functioned as a food court. Formerly known as the Betsy Ross, Magic Touch was also the most diverse gay bar in the area. The other ones, like Duque and Friends, mostly catered to Spanish-speaking clientele; others were operated like private clubs where one needed a password and a local resident in the know in order to enter these nondescript places. Magic Touch met its demise in the late nineties, a casualty of the increasing commercialization and gentrification of the area.

The queer theorist José Esteban Muñoz (2009, 56–59) wrote about Magic Touch Tavern. In fact, I am the anthropologist mentioned in *Cruising Utopia* who introduced him to the place. He was captivated by the moniker given by jaded yet witty queers who deviously called it the Tragic Touch. But Muñoz was even more taken by the traffic of multiracial and interethnic bodies, sounds, feelings, and images. Unlike most of its Manhattan cousins, the Magic/Tragic Touch was a neighborhood bar, and was governed by a kind of informal anachronism and almost chaotic mix of musical tastes, clientele, and auras. There were hustlers, lesbians, drag queens, working-class folks, and professionally attired customers. "Don't Rock the Boat Baby," a seventies disco tune, was blaring the last time I entered the bar's portals in the early nineties. Despite the bar's reputation of being trapped in a time warp, a space drowning in pathos, Muñoz saw it as a contact zone, a fertile cultural junction, and an alternative queer space to the chic bright lights of the "city." The "city" is what Queens old-timers call Manhattan, that other island over the bridges and tunnels. In popular parlance, Manhattan stands in for the Big Apple's cosmopolitan veneer, while everyone who lives beyond this borough's precincts are seen as less sophisticated, more working-class and therefore less exciting. This is why snobby Manhattanites and self-deprecating outer-borough inhabitants call non-Manhattan people including those from Queens the "bridge and tunnel" crowd.

The Magic/Tragic Touch is the scene of a rhythmic performance of the multivalent and conflicting nature of queer migrant nocturnal culture. It is precisely a contact zone that lends itself to the unwitting intimacies of class, race, gender, and sexuality. One encounter at the bar left an indelible mark on my memories and feelings about the place. It was summer 1989, the AIDS pandemic was raging, the city was in the throes of chaos, and people were trying to come to terms with an increasingly neoliberalized country under President Reagan. I was with a couple of Latino friends who lived in the neighborhood. We were sitting at the bar looking at the people and listening almost distractedly to Madonna or whoever it was who was belting some love dirge blaring from the sound system. It was almost time for "last call," when this lithe Latino man in an apple green faux-silk shirt and denim pants came waltzing into the bar. He waved to my two friends and started dancing alone in a quiet corner. My friends called him over, and he was introduced to me as Mikie or Miguel. We asked whether he was there to grab a drink and spend the last few minutes before the bar closed. Mikie said he just woke up from his midnight nap after spending the day busing tables at a nearby restaurant. We asked whether he wanted a drink, and he shyly thanked us and said that he came in to dance to the music and enjoy the "air." One of my friends snickered, "Honey, you came to the wrong place, this place smells of cigarette, cum, piss, and beer." Mikie replied, "Yes, that is what I like. I don't need the fresh air of the countryside. I am a city girl." We all laughed. He admitted he only came in right before he went to work at 4 a.m. at a bakery in the neighborhood. He didn't have the money to buy drinks, but he also did not want to go to work drunk. He just wanted to dance and "enjoy the air." When I asked him whether his outfit was a bit too colorful for the bakery, he said, "All you see in that hot stuffy kitchen is grey dough and the smell of yeast. I bring a lot of color to that place." To that, one of my friends replied, "Miss Thing, you do bring a LOT of color, a LOT of color—a rainbow!!!" And we all laughed as a group. He then said that he would just dance to one more song—this time to Chaka Khan's "Life Is a Dance." And he twirled and he skipped, and after the music was over he waved to us and went out the door. One of my friends snidely commented, "Pathetic queen—he can't even buy a real silk shirt."

The bar was replete with the uneven rhythms and affective morass of the tragic and the magical. Mikie saw an escape from his burden but was still acutely aware of its limits. I take Magic/Tragic Touch Tavern not merely as a site of historical and cultural performance but rather as a sensorial touchstone or an affective springboard to other encounters and scenes of Jackson Heights noir.

OUT OF TIME, OUT OF SYNCH: FABULOUSNESS BETWEEN NIGHT VERSUS DAY

In the nineties, I was employed at the Asian & Pacific Islander Coalition on HIV/AIDS (APICHA), a nonprofit organization that was aimed at providing HIV services to API communities in New York City and that had an office in the Jackson Heights neighborhood. As part of my work, I met a South Asian man named Ajit who wanted to become one of our peer educators. When we spoke, Ajit told me to meet him for lunch at the Jackson Heights Diner, which is not a typical American diner but rather is famous for its relatively tame and tourist-friendly rendition of Indian cuisine. It was located on Seventy-Fourth Street, which was a veritable "Little India" with its sari stores, jewelry shops, and other businesses owned and operated by South Asians. I sat for a few minutes at a table waiting, when all of a sudden, a well-dressed Indian woman sat at my table. I did not recognize Ajit immediately as he was made up in a gray pantsuit with a glittery sequined blouse. He had a bindi on his forehead and a dainty shimmering purse in his hand.

While I have been accustomed to meeting drag queens as well as transgender women in my line of work, I was surprised to see Ajit in full fabulous splendor at one o'clock in the afternoon. I told him (I am using male pronouns here because he identified as a man and as a drag queen) that I was not shocked at seeing him dressed as a woman but rather was taken aback at how he was dressed like he was set for an evening out in a chic nightclub. He raised his forefinger and waved it dramatically, saying, "Dahling, being fabulous knows no schedule. Day, night, morning, afternoon whatever." We talked for a long while about his work—he worked several part-time jobs in hairdressing, office, and service occupations—and the difficulty of being an undocumented immigrant. By the time we finished chatting, it was already dusk—really, dark—one of those winter afternoons when the days are short. We walked out into Seventy-Fourth Street, and he said he was walking home a few blocks away. As we ambled down the street, he stopped to dramatically touch some green vegetables, bok choy I believe. Examining the produce closely with his freshly manicured fingers, he held a bunch in his hands as if they were a bouquet. Ajit paid for them and said he was using them for dinner that night. We parted ways at the end of the block, and I watched him sashay down Thirty-Seventh Road. In the middle of the early-evening traffic of cars and Brown people and in the soft glow of winter lights, he was a glittering figure to behold.

Ajit's spectacular diva performance gives way to other messy, sometimes violent, and oftentimes furtive performances of desire on avenues, streets, and alleys of Jackson Heights at night. His performance suggests that the city streets, particularly at night, are a virtual stage for different forms of performances, particularly that of walking. Walking in the city for some queers may be likened to Ajit's performance of "walking the runway," like a model to an imagined appreciative audience. Walking in the city can be transformed, especially at night, into cruising for a quick sexual fix and momentary physical fulfillments. Jackson Heights is known for being a gay oasis outside Manhattan and is considered to be a virtual theater of nightly traipsing and sexual hunting. But the very nature of the neighborhood, with its predominantly working-class immigrant inhabitants (at least in the late nineties and early 2000s), means that its story of nightlife is less about the actual persons and their individual exploits and more about the social imaginings and dreaming up of a space called Vaseline Alley.

SEARCHING FOR VASELINE ALLEY: PLEASURES LOST AND FOUND

> Some will say that all we have are the pleasures of this moment, but we must never settle for minimal transport; we must dream and enact new and better pleasures, other ways of being in the world, and ultimately, new worlds.
>
> —José Esteban Muñoz, *Cruising Utopia*

Unlike Manhattan and the other chic gayborhoods of that era, Jackson Heights at night bleeds into Jackson Heights at daytime. While we would want to separate the nocturnal from the diurnal, I would suggest that in a predominantly working-class and immigrant neighborhood such as Jackson

Heights, nights and days are intimately and messily enmeshed with each other. Joachim Schlör (1998) in his book *Nights in the Big City* has noted that nightlife has traditionally been conceived as an escape from the humdrum of an urban workday, a segment of time devoted to the pleasures of rest, sleep, and intimacy, and to moments of anonymity afforded by the darkness. But as he aptly notes, insecurity, fear, awkwardness, possible violence, sinister signs, and ambivalence mark the night streets of the modern city. This is especially true in Jackson Heights.

In the case of Vaseline Alley, notions of time and space are truly topsy-turvy. There seemed to be conflicting ideas about where it was actually located. This vernacular moniker, though often connected with Thirty-Seventh Road, home to the Magic Touch, is not part of the official map of Jackson Heights and has led to various idiosyncratic cartographies. During my years of fieldwork, I have heard people point to other streets and sections of Jackson Heights as the "real" Vaseline Alley. Despite these shifting, contradictory mappings, this site was considered to be a mystical, erotically charged, sinister yet fun place where lascivious desires are sated and fulfilled. And yet, this idealization, that attribution of a magical touch to the space, was often matched with a forlorn banality.

One of my informants in a household of queer immigrants of color told me,

> When I first arrived in Jackson Heights, my gay friends took me to a street where a bar was located. I thought we were going to the bar instead they told me to stay on the sidewalk and watch people. When I didn't react, they were surprised. They asked me if I saw anything interesting or exciting. I said no, they all laughed saying that I need to sharpen my vision as sexy things were happening under my nose. I said I did not know what the big deal was. Everyone was just walking or talking. Nothing extraordinary. Then, they then told me that I was in Vaseline Alley. One even called it the "street of dreams."

The slippery, dreamy, and sexy idealized notion of Vaseline Alley was more of an urban myth than an actual place. Several people (most of whom were working-class immigrants) I have interviewed through the years have conceded that despite the proliferating lore of this place and its idealization as a haven for lusty modern gay desires, their lives were filled with material concerns such as exorbitant rents, multiple part-time jobs, and the other travails of being poor immigrants. I realized that even the dreary reality, the very ground of Jackson Heights, is better left to the dreams and imaginative musings of its queer residents. This is not to say that no cruising or public sex actually happens on Thirty-Seventh Road or on other streets of the neighborhood, but what fascinated me about the stories from my informants is not so much the actual sexual feats and deeds, but rather the way that myth circulates as a compelling motivation to be up and about conducting the business of survival. As a Latino informant told me, "Any street can be Vaseline Alley—you never know. But then again, who has the time and the energy?" He went on to say that he was so dead tired after his graveyard shift cleaning offices in Manhattan that he could barely make it back to his apartment. He added that it would take another man to get naked and slap him on the face with his penis to even arouse him and entice him to have sex on the street corner or in some corner of an abandoned house. He admitted with a bit of sadness and emotional surrender that cruising takes too much time and energy, and he added that it was dangerous.

After 9/11, several of my informants became wary of standing around on the streets at night. During the day, Mexican and other Latino men would stand or sit in the corners looking for work. At night, it was a different matter, as they told me that standing around could be interpreted not just as gay cruising but as a sinister prelude to crime. Many informants were undocumented, and with the increased surveillance of immigrant neighborhoods after 9/11, they could be rounded up as suspected terrorists or just plain "illegals." Someone told me that the lure and erotic charge of cruising at night is doubly complicated by the fact that a backward glance can be a way to scrutinize a potential sexual conquest or a possible immigration agent. Indeed, many informants acknowledged the risks and danger involved in cruising, but they emphasized that being in an immigrant neighborhood at night—ambling or lazily walking around—can be cause for an arrest, a mugging, or a beating.

When I countered that these events can happen anywhere and to almost any queer, many would say that being Brown or yellow makes it doubly difficult. One of my informants, a middle-aged Korean gay man, said, "Sometimes existence of the gay bars in the neighborhood can be deceiving. Things here are not that simple." He argued that working-class immigrant queer men know that despite the existence of gay bars and other LGBT institutions in Jackson Heights, homophobic and racist bashing still persist, and violent forms of state policing on immigration have been ramped up in recent years. Many informants have said they would rather work and keep to themselves. In that way, they are able to survive. At the same time, they revel in the clandestine potentials and possibilities of what may happen in Vaseline Alley.

In the end, there are still erotic charges in the unknown and in the sinister. The feared policing and surveillance meld into the sexual energies that erupt at any time, especially at night. Yet, as many queer Jackson Heights natives have told me, a deep feeling of insecurity stains, distorts, and disrupts the circuits of desire. I am not saying that there are no sexual forays and adventures around the fabled Vaseline Alley or in other parts of the neighborhood, just that they don't always happen in physical terms. As one informant very elegantly said, "It is not that I have all the time to join in the nightly merriment, but the excitement of the brightly lit signs and booming music from the bars keeps me energized, wanting to be out in the world, despite the fact that I have to be at work six to seven days a week." The promise, the anticipation, and the imagined possibilities provide fuel and sustenance to people who inhabit Jackson Heights amid the trials and tribulations of being poor immigrants of color. There might be a lot of confusion as to where Vaseline Alley actually is located, but a search for it need not be in the various streets, roads, and lanes. For many queer immigrants from the neighborhood, Vaseline Alley is in the mind. In other words, the place exists in the imagination, desires, and aspirations of the people who oftentimes do without and who nevertheless imagine themselves as part of the magic and the fairy tale.

"YOU MAKE ME FEEL MIGHTY REAL": JACKSON HEIGHTS NOIR IN THE STARK LIGHT OF NIGHT

The three atmospheric vignettes I have presented unsettle our notions of queer nightlife. The cadences and rhythms of Jackson Heights noir can be felt through the tempo of the outdated disco songs at the bar, the scampering of Brown people walking about the busy streets, the crashing sounds of the number 7 train on its raised tracks every few minutes, and the smells of vegetables and fruits in the market stalls and curries in the famed South Asian restaurants. Queer nightlife in Jackson Heights is not a total temporal disjuncture from daytime, nor is it a distinctive breed of people and institutions that reproduce different species, habits, and pleasures. There are no specialized creatures of the night but, rather, inhabitants who are "alive" twenty-four hours a day in a city that never sleeps. Escape is never complete, always provisional, and always messy. Jackson Heights nightlife is part of a persistent and continuous concatenation of activities where labor, work, and survival are part and parcel of the imaginings of and longings for escape, pleasure, and fabulousness. Ajit's traipsing with a bouquet of bok choy and Mikie's dancing to the world in his faux-silk shirt may seem to be just momentary pathetic glosses in the nocturnal landscape. But I would argue that their lives uncomfortably yet productively blend the real with the make-believe in a manner that anthropologist Yael Navarro-Yashin (2012) has highlighted in her study of Turkish Cypriots living in an illegitimate, unstable territory. Navarro-Yashin notes that people in contingent and highly precarious states of existence produce practices and narratives that are amalgams of strivings and aspirations. They create affective geographies that are marked by borders, transgressions, losses, and dreams of home. In the end, they are alloyed discourses that engage with the mixed-up lure of the fairy tale and the tragedy.

Jackson Heights's nightlife produces affective landscapes that intersperse and fuse disparate times and spaces. These landscapes are suffused with energies, images, sounds, and aromas that touch and envelope bodies that in turn propel and shape the exigencies and challenges of endless days and nights. Some people may categorize these energies and efforts as banal resilience. But if we go back to Ajit's regal composure as he sashayed through a busy sidewalk at dusk, and Mikie's exuberant gyrations before settling into the humdrum of work, we can marvel at the stunning production and effects of queer trajectories and performances. The wayward dalliances of the material and the affective, the "real" groundedness of working-class undocumented migrant labor, and the flights of fancy around glamour and beauty—all of these move and touch people socially and physically. The cadences and impulses of such imaginings and material strivings enable a worlding, a worldmaking, a narrative of "real" strife and longing that speaks to cruel optimisms, cautious hopefulness, and messy persistence.

Jackson Heights's nightlife can be gritty, and it can be utopic, but at the end of the day it is real—a realness that is felt and that bleeds into the creative possibilities of intimate encounters, the forlorn misery of social abandonment, and of unfulfilled dreams. The aura and mood of this essay clearly evoke the smoky yet vibrant tunes of the late pop singer Sylvester, particularly the song "Mighty Real." In the song, "real" and "realness" are not so much objective visual and empirical nodes but rather a feeling and an attunement to the counterintuitive attractions and magnetic pull of discrepant routes of desires and intimacies, much like the tempo and air of a Jackson Heights night. I end with this song not as a conclusion but as a segue to looking forward in anticipation for the far horizon and the excitement of possibilities. I end with this song to conjure an atmosphere of languid tunes and fervent emotions. Finally, I end with this song to look excitedly to a future that is not here, while also casting a melancholic backward glance to a lingering past and the legacy on which the ideas in this essay are indebted, particularly to José Esteban Muñoz. He enabled the capacious yet critical attunement inherent this essay in order to narrate a world and worldmaking process that is palpable, magical, and, yes, mighty real.

Jockstraps and Crop Tops

Fat Queer Femmes Dressing for the Night

Caleb Luna

"I'm proud of myself," I reflected to a friend named Jules, another fat femme. "I went to this party alone, and I was wearing my high-waisted shorts and a crop top. It was daytime, and I even took an Uber there and back." The party in question was a new day party centering queer and trans people of color; a space where we gathered to dance, drink, mingle, cruise, and, most importantly, serve looks. They laughed, congratulated me, and shared their own thought process when leaving for a party: "I think about the Uber ride more than anything else when I'm getting dressed."

This exchange reveals some anxieties dressing for nightlife brings up for us as fat femmes: the questions we ask, and the decisions that go into dressing and adorning our bodies for nightlife as fat and queer femme people. *Where are we going—a queer bar, or a queer-friendly party in a straight bar? Are we going to the White Horse, a dive bar, or Club 21, the high-end queer Latinx club? Are we staying in Oakland, or going to San Francisco? If we're going to San Francisco, are we going to the queer bar staple the Stud, or are we going to the Castro?*[1] *Am I going to know people there? How likely is it to be full of mostly thin and nondisabled people? Am I going with my fat friends (strength in numbers), or thin accomplices? How are we getting there? If I drive, I can't drink. And depending on how far from the venue we park, or if we take public transportation, there's a higher chance of interacting with potentially straight strangers who might harass, harm, or even kill us.*[2] Truly, many of these questions are not exclusive to fat queers, and queers of many sizes might ask themselves the same or similar questions before leaving their home. These are not unreasonable fears; we live in a social and political climate that is increasingly hostile to both fat and queer bodies.

Fig. 1. The author, Caleb Luna, dressed for the function. (Photograph by Daniela Dusak, daddyqueen.com.)

SITUATING FAT EMBODIMENT

Eve Kosofky Sedgwick surfaces the stakes of these resonances in a 1990 conversation with Michael Moon. Sedgwick opens the conversation by detailing a dream she had about her experience with clothes shopping as a fat woman in a store that was "nominally Bloomingdale's":

> The labor of concentrating and representing "a general sense of the body's offensiveness" is not a form of employment that will seem archaic or exotic to large women in modern American society. It permeates the mise-en-scène of my dream, the store where "I was dubious about whether they would have any

> clothes that would be big enough for me," whose implicit tension and dread must be resonant for almost any fat woman in this culture. The confrontation of the complex labor of representing offense with the female homosocial marketplace of gendered visibility—the materialization of a fat woman in a clothing store—lights up the works of a pinball machine of economic, gender, and racial meanings . . . the primal denial to anyone of a stake in the symbolic order: "There's nothing here for you to spend your money on." . . . Who and what you are means that there's nothing here for you; your money is not negotiable in this place . . . this is instead the precipitation of one's very body as a kind of cul-de-sac blockage or clot in the circulation of economic value. (Moon and Sedgwick 2001, 292, 294)

Here, Sedgwick gestures to the "economic, gender, and racial meanings" that fat bodies carry (particularly in class- (and, by extension, racially-) exclusionary spaces such as Bloomingdale's), extrapolating the multitude of ways the queerness of fat bodies speaks *for* us, always carrying historical meaning that informs their contemporary possibilities: valueless (see Butler 1990b). But the socioeconomic order that determines bodily value is not produced in an ahistorical, deracialized vacuum.

Frances Hatherly (2015, 67) extends Pierre Bourdieu's theorization of *taste* to synthesize the classed role that fat bodies are scripted into, "as a visual shorthand to signify the working-classes' supposed bad spending, bad eating habits, and—in short—'bad taste.'" The economic value deficiency of the specifically fat woman's body described by Sedgwick carries with it historical valuations of which social classes, quite literally, have the financial capital to expend on fashioning their bodies. This economic valuation and social exclusion is informed by its own racial histories under Western empire. Sabrina Strings (2019, 7) clarifies that the classed *taste* that Hatherly outlines via Bourdieu has always been racialized: "racial discourse was deployed by elite Europeans and white Americans to create social distinctions between themselves and so-called greedy and fat racial Others." These "greedy and fat racial Others" are Black and Indigenous populations, conflated with a perceived distasteful reliance on sensual pleasures and, by extension, fat embodiment in the cultural imaginary of Europeans as they carried out their colonial projects.

Scholars of queer theory and colonialism might consider how the social privileges of thin embodiment—particularly for white, upper-class and cis heterosexual women—were introduced and enforced alongside and as *part of* "'settler sexuality,' or the heteropatriarchal sexual modernity exemplary of white settler civilization" (Morgensen 2011, 23.) This racialized and classed fat stigma becomes folded into the project of settler sexuality, most evident in the tasteful production of the wealthy white woman's body: "by the early twentieth century, slenderness was increasingly promoted in the popular media as the correct embodiment for white Anglo-Saxon Protestant women. . . . The phobia about fatness and the preference for thinness have not, principally or historically, been about health. Instead, they have been one way the body has been used to craft and legitimate race, sex, and class hierarchies" (Strings 2019, 6). The phenomena that both Strings and Scott Lauria Morgensen detail extend into the contemporary, and their urgency is reduced in the apoliticized experience of shopping and adornment, a staging ground to legitimate social hierarchies before our bodies ever enter the space of queer nightlife.

Settler sexuality marginalizes both fat and queer bodies, and Sedgwick seems self-aware of the affinities between her own embodiments and related identities. Kathleen LeBesco (2001, 85) brings necessary suspicion to the discursive comparisons made between fatness and queerness: "We've heard about genes, hormones, fear of being sexually attractive, and dozens of other causes for fatness and homosexuality, each one advanced with the understanding that finding a remedy would be a financially rewarding proposition." The material exclusion and *lack* of material to adorn and stylize fat bodies function in a manner similar to the historical legal and institutional exclusion of queer life from the dominant social order: as disciplining mechanisms to punish deviant bodies for our failure to adhere to heteronorms of settler sexuality, always raced and classed vestiges of settler colonization.

Beside the legislative gains that have decriminalized sodomy and made marriage, adoption, employment, and housing discrimination legally impermissible in some pockets of the nation, fat fashion and plus-sized clothing have gained a wider, almost legitimate, circulation in the fashion world. But what clothing options exist for some fat people usually remain limited in style in attempts to discipline our bodies into normative presentations. As LeBesco (2004, 70) figures it, "with the influx of fat-accepting commodities, fat folk are embraced as consuming subjects but not as social subjects." This is even more deeply true when we consider that stylish clothing that comes in extended sizes tends to be sold at prices much higher than—if not inflated to two or three times the cost of—fashionable straight-size (the ironic colloquialism for non-plus-sized) clothing. In this way, clothing for fat people continues to be economically inaccessible for most of us—especially under the economic barriers that fat stigma produces through wage reduction for fat workers, oftentimes leaving us with less disposable income to spend on luxuries like clothing that makes us feel good in our bodies (see Ernsberger 2009). This trend mirrors the gains of the mainstream gay rights movement, which continue to benefit and, in many cases, impact primarily the most privileged factions of the community across lines of race, class, and romantic partnership.

Thus, clothing has political stakes for bodies of all sizes; it is equally meaningful to walk into a store that has a plethora of clothing available for one's body as it is to be excluded by the restrictive sizing standards. The true goal of facilitating social belonging vis-à-vis clothing options for fat bodies is to both normalize and valorize thinness through the intentional erasure of fat bodies from the public space of these stores. While decisions about which bodies to clothe are frequently obscured behind fragile justifications for materials, size limits are not about overhead or profit: they are intended to produce and maintain the social and cultural capital of thin bodies through exclusion. The aesthetic exclusion of fat bodies is informed by, mirrors, and bolsters the social exclusion we experience, which is then weaponized against us, as if we can achieve these body sizes by simply *trying hard enough.* In its location outside these dominant social hierarchies, fat embodiment carries with it its own queerness, especially when it dares to express desire (LeBesco 2004, 89).

Fat stigma is produced and maintained by "the logical and very real threat of ostracism in a society that manipulates [people] by provoking terror of their own bodies: fear of fat is really a fear of stigmatization" (Hatherly 2015, 75). While social tides are changing, particularly in urban enclaves, fear of social stigma continues to be the driving force in many queers' lives as well: if not prolonging the claiming of a public queer identity, it continues to shape *how* our queer identities are performed publicly, when and where—and especially for gender nonconforming (including butch women and effeminate men, frequently signaled through *style*) and transgender queers, who face higher levels of violence for a visibly queer aesthetic. Beyond this, the question of *when* and *how* to disclose our queerness—and especially our queer partnerships, particularly through public displays of affection—continues to structure many queer lives. Sedgwick again reflects on the parallels between coming out as queer and coming out as fat through her own racialized and gendered experience: "there *is* such a process as *coming out as a fat woman*. . . . It is a way of staking one's claim to insist on, and participate actively in, a recognition of *the representational contract* between one's body and one's world" (Moon and Sedgwick 2001, 306). It is through the "representational contract between one's body and one's world" that we can see how the diet culture rhetoric of compulsory weight loss mimics a homophobic rhetoric of conversion therapy weaponized against noncompliant queers, especially already vulnerable queer youth. Youth of all sexualities are nonconsensually placed on diets by their caregivers.

COMPULSORY THINNESS AND FAT QUEER EXISTENCE

While I have been attempting to build on equivalences made in claiming a public fat or public queer identity, this approach is limited by the presence of fat stigma in queer spaces, including queer nightlife. As LeBesco (2004, 89) identifies, "queer circles generally provide little refuge from the sizism that permeates mainstream culture, and in fact foster anti-fat bias to a great extent, especially among gay men." Both historically and presently, divergent queer communities, which are commonly organized around a gendered politic, surface different meanings of fat embodiment, specifically across lines of gender and sexuality.

Much scholarship in fat studies focuses on the impact of fat stigma for heterosexual white women, for good reason. As detailed by Hatherly, Strings, and Morgensen, the production of fat stigma has been a concentrated project of settler sexuality under Western empire in an effort to discipline white women into a white supremacist, capitalist, patriarchal, and colonial social order. The contemporary fat liberation movement can be traced to the fat feminists and lesbians in the 1970s who, as veterans of and inspired by the Civil Rights movement, founded the first fat activist group in the United States, the Fat Underground.[3] The influences and overlaps between fat liberation and other liberation movements—Black, gay, and women's—seems most apparent in the third point of the seven-point "Fat Liberation Manifesto," published by Judy Freespirit and Aldebaran in November 1973, which reads: "WE see our struggle as allied with the struggles of other oppressed groups against classism, racism, sexism, ageism, financial exploitation, imperialism and the like." While not explicit, an awareness of the intersecting and overlapping nature of fat oppression across lines of race, class, gender, age, and nation is evident. Feminists and lesbians have always been best positioned to elucidate fat oppression as a byproduct of patriarchy, heterosexism, capitalism, colonialism, and white supremacy, aligning their primary goals with larger political projects.

Because the fat liberation movement focuses on fat embodiment as a corollary to gendered oppression, the right to self-fashioning has long been a rallying call for fat women, who historically and structurally face specific pressures to appeal to men's sensibilities. This pressure reappears in queer communities, when participants find themselves wanting to attract gay, bi, and queer men. The gendered differences of fat embodiment in queer communities is most rigorously explored in Jason Whitesel's 2014 ethnography *Fat Gay Men*: "for gay men, being fat as it affects one's sex appeal is most frequently judged by *men*—long recognized by feminists to be an oppressive arrangement" (43). Whitesel writes, "in heteronormative society, big men are at least recognized as 'gay,' whereas in gay circles, they are seen only as 'fat'" (36). As a gender nonconforming fat person who was assigned male at birth, I find some of my own experiences reflected in Whitesel's study and configuration of the experiences of fat gay men.[4]

While some lesbian communities (*The L Word* universe notwithstanding) such as the Fat Underground politicize fat embodiment, "gay men's media simplify and fetishize this [fat] sexual difference"—primarily through the creation of bear cultures and subcultures (LeBesco 2004, 90). Whitesel explores annual convenings of fat gay men and their admirers in what they term Big Men's Clubs. Originating in 1980s San Francisco as a response to size exclusion that continues contemporarily, these clubs do important reparative work in queer nightlife contexts, where fat embodiment continues to be feminized, ignored, or subjected to fatphobic violence. Whitesel's study details how fat gay men carve out alternative spaces where they can, essentially, enjoy the promised pleasures they are excluded from in traditional queer nightlife spaces—an ironic and oxymoronic designation, but apt nonetheless. He focuses primarily on annual convenings organized by these Big Men's Clubs, which occur much like any other circuit parties: they take place across North American cities, are hosted by various organizations and individuals, and are financially exclusionary to working-class and poor queers, who cannot afford travel, hotels, or the monetary burdens of vacationing generally. Circuit parties are also spaces of heightened cruising, partying, sex, and other queer performances organized around a broad theme or goal. While some such parties might market themselves as open to queers of all body types, they typically replicate the phobic and exclusionary atmosphere of the local gay bar, functionally welcoming the fit, wealthy, and predominantly white. Big Men's Clubs tend to differ from this *only* in their explicit catering to fat queers and their admirers. Whitesel reads these spaces as somewhat utopian—what José Esteban Muñoz (2009, 7) describes as the "not quite here"—places where fat queers can perform their bodies in safe and welcoming ways that our local gay bars, communities, and parties frequently disallow.

Specifically, Whitesel (2014, 81) tends to the politics of dressing for fat gay men in the space of these parties, especially in differentiation to the world at large as well as mainstream gay spaces: "Because it is unsanctioned for fat bodies to show skin and wear seductive clothing, and because big men are not allowed to flaunt their bodies, they don various outfits as their weapon for 'freedom fighting' to combat desexualization and to achieve 'temporary liberation' from the sizist politics of fashion. In picking out their wardrobe for the weekend, the big men engage in reinventing themselves as objects of desire and reclaiming their right to self-definition." While this reading is undoubtedly true, and the performance of embodied fat sexuality is certainly heightened if not ubiquitous in the space of the convening, the politics of dress and desire for fat queers extend beyond the spaces that Whitesel describes. Some of us perform our fat queer bodies in these resistive ways year-round, regardless of the otherwise exclusionary affective environment of the queer nightlife party.

PERFORMING DIVINITY

Fall 2016. I am out with friends: hair drenched with sweat, face flushed, a drink in one hand and the other in the air, with my flesh-full body behind me dancing, vibrating, and jiggling to the music. We are at a monthly queer dance party in downtown Oakland called Hella Gay, which is hosted at a bar that normally caters to the general heteropublic. One night a month, it becomes flooded with queer bodies, the dance floor packed so tightly at times that we are no longer individual bodies dancing; rather, we become one intertwined mass, moving in motion. It can become one of those spaces (you know the ones I'm talking about) that feels as if we have finally answered Emma Goldman's call, wherein *dance* and *revolution* become the same, or perhaps the rally before final transcendental action. Surely, at last call we will take the streets, and tomorrow the world will wake up anew.

This particular night, there was a concert at a venue across the street, and the dance floor was consequentially peppered with the surplus: concertgoers who mistook our rebellion for their after party. Although this party, like most queer spaces I have been in, was dominated by thin bodies, there were a handful of other fat partygoers. Despite the very real and pertinent risks of entering the gay bar space as a fat person, fat queers continue to disrupt the homogenous body of the queer party space by insisting on our presence and inclusion as rightful members of the community. But as I looked around, I was struck by what felt like a clear distinction between the fat partygoers who had come for Hella Gay and those who had merely wandered over from the concert across the street—that is, between those who were queer-identified (or at least in queer community) and those who were not.

It was at this moment that I truly began to appreciate how my queerness had informed my fat identity. LeBesco (2001, 83, 81) considers the strategies that fat and queer activism share, and the lessons that fat activism can learn from queer activism, reminiscing on the appropriation of negative imagery toward activist ends by groups like the Lesbian Avengers. Theorizing about how queer activists have utilized identity politics, LeBesco argues that "identities are never merely descriptive; rather, they are strategically performed," and she encourages fat subjects to engage in this performance with what she terms "playful subjectivity." Moon and Sedgwick (2001, 295) ruminate on the convergence of fat and queer identarian activism in the playful subjectivity of perhaps the most iconic fat queer historical figure: the late drag queen Divine, most notable as a star in John Waters's films from the late 1960s through the late 1980s. Moon notes, "As a huge [*sic*] man who repeatedly created the role of 'the most beautiful woman in the world,' Divine seems to offer a powerful condensation of some emotional and identity linkages—historically dense ones—between fat women and gay men. . . . This combination of abjection and defiance often produces a divinity-effect in the subject, a compelling belief that one is a god or vehicle of divinity." As implied here, Moon and Sedgwick's conversation rests on the seemingly disparate embodiments of fat women [of any sexuality] and gay men [presumably exclusively thin, in their formation]. Nonetheless, the transgressive potential of a simultaneously fat, queer embodiment is well articulated as the "combination of abjection and defiance."

This divinity was communicated in fat queers I witnessed around me, in their cut-off short shorts, fishnets, crop tops, brightly colored and patterned clothes, dyed hair and elaborate haircuts, purses and bags in the shape of donuts and other fatty foods, clothing that showed off stretch marks, fatty upper arms, luscious cellulite-adorned thighs, rolls of beautiful and tender fatness on our bellies, sides, and backs—all performances of bodies fat people are shamed into shying away from, in an effort to not draw *even more* attention to our fatness—dancing freely and feeling confident in their bodies, dancing with their thin and fat dates. In other words, the fat queers around me were enacting LeBesco's (2001, 82) analysis that "queer theory encourages us to play with our selves and to make a joyful noise in the doing." The embracement of not just our bodies, but also the foods imagined to have produced them, as joyful and pleasurable is a divine intervention.

Our divinity felt juxtaposed against the bodies of fat partygoers who had come from the concert, adorned in clothing that fat folks in heteronormative communities have historically been more effectively disciplined into. Long and loose garments that hid their fat bodies, hair pulled back or styled blandly, shirts that have a three-quarter sleeve so as not to show the fat upper arms, shapeless and oversized ensembles in modest colors and busy patterns meant to *minimize* and *distract*, zipped-up hoodies even inside the hot club. Nothing mesh, or sheer, or shiny, or ripped, or cut, or torn, or accessorized boldly, or bright, or tight, or anything else that heteronormativity disallows and queer fatness cultivates. It felt clear who among us was performing divinity, this combination of abjection and defiance, and who was not, their embodied performances stagnating at the abjection that has been thrust on them by white supremacist heteropatriarchy.

It is this divinity that I have come to understand my aesthetic of sleeveless and cropped tops, shirts so tight that sometimes my belly hangs out below, short shorts and tight pants, big hair, visible tattoos, and facial piercings to hold: a divinity made possible by a queer relationship to my own fat embodiment. That allowed me to transcend the possibilities fat bodies have been offered, and encouraged me to incorporate my body and its intimidating and uncomfortable size into a queer aesthetic that challenges dominant notions of normativity, shame, modesty, and respectability. And this divinity, underscored by a queer politic that resists oppressive norms, is much, much more than merely aesthetics. Our clothing expression is not merely about covering our bodies for the night; it is about how we strategically respond to fatphobia and what we have the mental and emotional capacity to respond to. LeBesco (2004, 73) argues that when fat people "disdain 'blending in' in favor of cobbling together a look from the scattered resources available and becoming more brave about appearing in ways that defy the 'tasteful' inventions of the commodifiers of corpulence, fashion *is* revolutionary; its newfound ability stymies fat oppression." Challenging these norms can open our bodies up to violence. Clothing that makes a fat body fatter (or simply unashamed), that breaks gendered and sexual norms, that signals queerness, and so on, comes with its own risks. And sometimes we risk it. Sometimes we make our own possibilities.

Emboldened by our divinities, fat queers have the freedom to play, resist, and fuck with colonial, raced, classed, and gendered norms that tell us to shrink, to be small, to be quiet, to not draw attention to ourselves. Each time our bodies spill out of rips and tears, under crop tops, tight clothing stretched desperately across the expanses of our bellies or thighs, caught in between our rolls, or we style our cellulite as accessory, we perform ruptures to the heteronormative, fatphobic conceptions of what we can and should be and do. Queerness calls us to brandish our boldness on our bodies. It hails us to an embodied resistance to beauty standards that rely on whiteness, light skin, thinness, muscularity, masculinity, able-bodiedness, an absence of scars and blemishes, the *right* amount of body hair, and so on. Queerness says *fuck that, and while we're at it fuck you.* Fatness reminds us that *we don't exist for you, and neither do these bodies.* Fat queerness says *we're disturbing to you because you need to be disturbed.* Queerness resists heteronormative structures, producing alternative potentialities that extend to bodies and to aesthetics. Fat queers perform a playful subjectivity, a divinity, within and against non-fat-positive queer nightlife spaces, as part of and an extension of our queer politic.

After the party that opened this essay, I ordered McDonald's. I came home and took off my high-waisted shorts, under which I was wearing a jockstrap (you know, *just in case*) and ate my burger in nothing but a crop top—but not before sending an outfit pic to my besties, adding the text, "I have reached my final form." The divine, indeed.

Notes

1. Both Club 21 and the Stud have sadly succumbed to gentrification and closed or relocated while I was writing this chapter.

2. In her performance *My First Denim Vest,* Mark Aguhar (2011) recounts a story of being harassed by youth for her outfit as a fat femme.

3. See "Charlotte Cooper and Judy Freespirit in conversation, June 2010". http://obesitytimebomb.blogspot.com/2010/09/charlotte-cooper-and-judy-freespirit-in.html

4. I write more in depth about how my gender is affected and constituted by my fatness in an essay for the online magazine *The Body Is Not an Apology*; see Luna (2018). This essay is also featured in the forthcoming anthology *Fat & Queer: An Anthology of Queer and Trans Bodies and Lives* (Jessica Kingsley Publishers 2021).

. . . waiting . . .

Emily R. Bock

> If I were asked for a definition of myself, I would say that I am the one who waits.
> —Franz Fanon, *Black Skin, White Masks*

It was a hot night. Made hotter still by the expanse of concrete emanating leftover heat from the long summer's day sun. Humid air clung to clothing, making clothes cling to the thighs and chests that moved slowly along the sidewalk. The car drove quickly west down the wide boulevard, passing a seemingly endless series of empty lots, dollar stores, and gas stations. *Are you going home?* the driver asked. *No, I'm going to a party*, I said looking out the window, trying to avoid the conversation that felt imminent. *What kind of party? This isn't a good neighborhood for a party*. I looked at his face in the rearview mirror then over at the meter increasing with every passing block, counting the distance in dollars from where I began to where I was going. *When I drop you off I'm turning off my cab light so I don't have to pick anyone up from 'round here*. His statement wasn't a question so I didn't answer, turned away so I didn't have to catch his eye, and didn't bother asking him to explain—we both knew what he meant. This part of Chicago, so far from the lake and all the beautification efforts that it seems to mandate, always tends to feel forgotten, probably because it has been for a long time now. Much like the South Side, there was a time when it was possible to imagine a good life in sections of the predominantly Black neighborhood of West Garfield Park. And much like the South Side, the city has systematically disinvested in maintaining good schools, clean streets, or any semblance of care for the communities that live there (Seligman 2005; Biles 2001). While crime in this neighborhood has steadily increased since its abandonment, unlike the South Side, there seems to be little citywide investment in seeing West Garfield Park's transformation.

Stopped at a red light a block away from the party, I could see the STD/

HIV testing vans parked outside the old community center and a couple of people standing close by. Unwilling or unable to wait through the tension-filled silence of the never-ending light, I said *I'll just get out here*, and I opened the door, clutching the headphones and makeup bag that hadn't quite made their final descent into the dark abyss of my oversized tote. The streets were empty save for the people at the gas station on the corner and the small group standing in front of the makeshift ballroom ahead.

Most balls happen at night—that special time when ordinary rules don't apply or at least don't apply in the same way. Advertised through flyers, on Facebook, and by word of mouth, this ball was scheduled to start around nine o'clock in the evening and go until around three in the morning, but by the time I pulled up at midnight, not a lot was going on. *See, balls run on ball time*, Tommy Avant Garde once told me with a side-eyed giggle.[1] The very first ball I ever attended in Chicago started three hours late, or at least three hours later than when I arrived. I remember thinking that I must have had the time wrong. There were only a couple of people walking around, setting up, and I awkwardly asked whether I was in the right place. They laughed at me and asked whether it was my first time. It was. But my second time didn't feel much different. Neither did my third or fourth. Over the course of my research, it became clearer that waiting for a ball to begin was not an accident brought on by poor party planning. Instead, waiting should be thought of as the first part of the event, the part where all the other parts come together to make a temporary and episodic whole. Waiting is the time where butch queens, femme queens, transgender people, gender nonconforming folks, and others slowly gather to create a very particular collectivity whose power and coherence extends beyond its momentary formation at the ball.[2] That hot, humid night would be no different, thus beginning the inevitable scene of waiting.

There are some people out back if you wanna hang, said Solomon Infiniti as he walked through the door and into the special VIP section holding a box of shiny decorations. I followed him to find a couple of people eating snacks and drinking Hennessey. *The DJ isn't here yet and lord am I gonna read his ass. That motherfucker better not come at me tonight.* I made my way through the large hall to the backyard and texted Terreance, *Where are you?* A handful of people were playing Double Dutch, laughing at the ropes nearly missing the heads and feet they circled. *Are you gonna get in?* Travis asked. *No, I haven't done that in years and I don't feel like making myself look a fool*, I said. He laughed, and we watched as the young folks played their game. *Girl, I'm on my way. I had to run home to pick up some shit but I'm on my way*. This was the first ball Terreance was throwing by himself, and he was incredibly nervous that no one would show up. Music burst through the back door, momentarily suspending the game. I poked my head inside to check on the evening's progress, but there were only a handful of people walking around the space. *Someone was messing with the sound system, I think,* I said to Travis, who, with a look of longing anticipation, was searching my expression for a sign that our waiting might be coming to an end. I stepped into the air-conditioned space for a moment to cool down, and though a couple of people trickled in after me, the space still seemed ominously empty.

Yo, there's that DJ. Motherfucker, I can't. I told Terreance that he was an ungrateful lazy ass, said Solomon, who was still darting around with tape in one hand and a vodka soda in the other. The DJ walked briskly to the corner on the right of the stage and immediately started setting up his equipment. I walked back outside to tell Travis about the DJ's arrival. *Well, maybe this thing will start after all,* someone said to the group still gathered around the game that was starting to lose players to the now-heightened sense of anticipation that the ball would begin. Tables scattered in the back of the space started collecting purses, bags, and phones. It was already pushing 1:00 a.m., and the space was only available for another two hours. The DJ started spinning a smattering of old and new Top 40 hits, and people began walking around the space with more energy. The affective shift from passive to active waiting can be such a subtle thing that you might miss it, only to realize you've been in this new state for some time. Even as the music filled the room, making it feel more alive and full, most people present were walkers and were crowded in the bathroom, putting the finishing touches on outfits while looking in the two rectangular mirrors hanging over the only two working sinks. Some leaned over the sink to get a better look as others helped zip up, pin up, and squeeze them into outfits. *Is it close to starting?* someone asked as they struggled with a zipper that wouldn't make its way up a back. *Maybe? I think we have to wait for the commentator to get here and then things can take off.* I stood behind the group and fixed my mascara, which was starting to show signs of exhaustion, before going back into the main hall. More people had arrived. Music muffled the growing sounds of excitement as people hugged and said hello. Laughter pierced through the beat of the driving house rhythm that lingers through the episode. Terreance arrived moments later with a group of about five people wearing all white. *We should start in the next few minutes or else we'll get kicked outta here before Legends, Statements, and Stars,* he said over his shoulder as he walked quickly to the stage. It was 2:00 a.m., and we finally did.

• • •

What questions are raised when we explore the force of what Tommy called *ball time*, when we ask what the temporal mode of waiting, in particular, tells us about how we are clued into a different way of being present and attentive? And how might waiting help us understand something about how ball members restructure attachments from the world out there toward ones invested in building a world together? We know that in everyday life, waiting operates as a temporal tether that maintains attachments to something, someone, or somewhere. However mundanely present waiting can feel, it is a future orientation toward an elsewhere. We wait because we are invested in accessing something that's not quite within our reach. What interests me here is not that waiting happens at the beginning of a ball; rather, following Ghassan Hage (2009, 1), I am interested in asking what the style and register of *this* waiting is and how it might change our understanding of the ballroom as an episode and this group of people as a collective. Starting at the beginning of a ball (which is of course always in the midst of things in the everyday), where we arrive only to wait, we begin to get the sense that waiting is doing something. When we wait, we slow down and recalibrate our expectations toward a present that is informed but not determined by our future dreams of the good life.[3]

In his insightful ethnography of the ballroom scene in Detroit, Marlon Bailey (2013, 2) makes passing mention of waiting when he writes, "balls never start on time, at least not by the time indicated on the flyer." It is true that though no two balls are the same, the one constant is that they always start late. But while the space between the "time indicated on the flyer" and the "beginning" of the ball might look like the same form of waiting we're accustomed to, I argue that it is in fact an active moment of reframing and attunement. During the ball, waiting is not the attachment to an expectation/object but the expectation/object itself. Of course, waiting can be difficult, mundane, exhausting, or boring, but here, waiting becomes the grounds on which this world is built. Waiting might look like catching up with people we haven't seen in a while or playing a game of Double Dutch, but in each of these instances, something is being prepared—which is to say that waiting is a time dedicated to gathering (up, together, around) all the differences between individuals to create a community. When we take a moment to pay attention to waiting, we start to notice how anticipation of the now works to structure the environment and architecture of the ballroom community, such that we recognize a collective where there was once a loosely felt coalition.

Throughout history, minoritarian subjects have been marked by their seemingly out-of-timeness to the throws and development of social life. For instance, in the United States, scholars have traced the violent ways in which Black life has been linked to a kind of slowness of thought and movement, historically binding Black people to "racist imaginings . . . used to justify their domination and subjugation" (Adeyemi 2019, 550; see also Brown 2008; Wynter 2003). This coupling is perhaps why time itself, and slowness in particular, has been used as an everyday form of resistance to discriminatory laws and dangerous and unjust working conditions (Kelley 1993). Indeed, how one operates in time has the potential to be used as a technique for survival. This literature is helpful when we consider how waiting gets taken up in the ballroom. Waiting, which is often used as a temporal mode of holding people suspended in time, used to dislocate individuals from community, gets reframed such that suspension becomes an opportunity for animation and individuals have the chance to form community.

• • •

Is it almost ready? Kitty asked through the grate that separates the kitchen from the community room. *Give us like . . . ten more minutes,* I hollered back as Jahday and I rushed to put the pasta we had made in the serving tins for lunch. I had been volunteering at the New York–based LGBTQ+ community organization for some time in various capacities, and on Mondays (pasta day) I worked in the kitchen. In order to serve as many people as possible, we always made two kinds of pasta, one vegetarian and one with meat. It was important for the community center to serve at least two balanced and filling hot meals per day. Or at least that was the goal; funding is always a problem when donations eerily coincide with the news of this or that major threat to queer life. We served lunch from noon to one every day, but the community room opened early to give the clients a chance to sit down, see friends, check Facebook, and cool down or warm up depending on the weather.

Today was an anomaly. I had dropped the first pot of pasta all over the floor, which, beyond the frustration of wasting food, cleaning up my mess, and making a whole new batch, meant that I was also delaying what would be for some, their first meal of the day. *Do you need help?* Preston asked, popping his head through the sliver of space we left open to keep the kitchen at a reasonable temperature. *Not unless you can make water boil faster!* Jahday laughed back. The quickened pace of our hurried choreography around the cramped kitchen kept time with the shouts and laughs of the clients pulling up tables and chairs and settling into the comfort of being among friends. We were officially late. I pulled up the grate so people could see us working quickly, to make sure they knew we were not putzing around. Chanel walked over to see what was holding up lunch. *It's my fault. I don't even know what happened,* I said as I stirred the sauce and cheese into the fresh pasta, steam billowing out into the room. *It looks strange but I'm gonna try it 'cause you made it. I only eat the lunch when y'all are here.* I laughed. Her subtle shade was not directed at us. We were two of only a handful of Black people who worked at the community center, and it was not the first time someone had mentioned that they didn't eat the meals unless "we" had cooked them. Chanel's presence at the counter began to draw a crowd, and clients started lining up behind her. I told them we weren't ready, but they knew it was better to be in line and get the meat pasta than wait and be stuck with the vegetarian option.

Normally, after we had served everyone in line, we would wait for any latecomers before giving people more, but because we hadn't started on time and lunch can't go past one o'clock, we quickly called for seconds. People hurried back over to the line. *Is there no more meat? No only the veggie,* I said. *Yeah, I'll take that and a little more salad.* As I got to the end of the line and had served the last of the pasta, someone came up to the counter and asked for lunch. *I'm all out of pasta but I have sandwiches and snacks,* I said as I walked over to the fridge to make sure I wasn't lying. *Man,* they started, *that really fucking sucks. I got stuck waiting for my case manager who never showed up for our meeting and now there is no lunch. I came all the way uptown from work and I have to go back down and like, why does this place always fucking play me like this?* I hated when this happened. I hated being in a position where I represented yet another institution that had made them wait for something they needed only to disappoint them in the end. It might seem so trivial but every time someone wasn't fed, couldn't eat the food, or didn't like the food I wanted to cry. It is such a privilege to only eat what you prefer. It is so hard to always be one step behind, be forced to take whatever scraps are left, because you were caught up in a waiting game.

• • •

Within a world governed by a normative timescape, one's capacity to move through time seamlessly, without interruptions, is a signifier of one's social location. Waiting is gendered and racialized and has the ability to interrupt progress and upset continuity by slowing tempo and delaying desired outcomes. And continuity matters—we often understand ourselves in terms of coherent and ordered narratives of the self. When those narratives are put on hold for some reason, we feel the lag as diversion or obstruction to the flow of everyday life. But interruption does not break an attachment to a future but rather alters its form. We can recover from being interrupted, but we are never quite the same as we were before. We understand interruption as an occasion when the flow of the ordinary is halted, and we are prevented from business as usual. What does it mean to be pulled out of the "usual" operation of things, to be prevented from comfortably moving in and among an ordinary whose affective landscape is loosely tangled with particular notions of being in time?

If time is money, then time wasted becomes yet another occasion around which one must find ways of negotiating socioeconomic impoverishment. And indeed, when the thing that you are waiting for is necessary for your basic survival, anticipation is overloaded. For Black and Brown queer people, to be interrupted by a scene/occasion of waiting is such an ordinary occurrence that our conceptions of Blackness and queerness have been shaped in part through such starts and stops. And with each start and stop, waiting changes our relationship to the future. This is perhaps why queer theory has found it so productive to think through the (im)possibility of a queer futurity (Edelman 1998; Halberstam 2005; Muñoz 2009) and why Black feminist scholars are similarly invested in working through various grammars as a way to understand the complex space-time of Black and Brown life (Campt 2017; Hartman 2008, 2016; Keeling 2003, 2009; Spillers 1987). But when the future is condensed in such a way that the "then and there" isn't always a given or is felt as a compression rather than an opening onto a horizon, when desires accumulate not to an endpoint but to episodes, the temporal structure of waiting and its relationship to the future must be reimagined. Waiting, as a capacity of the subjunctive, may very well look forward to an accumulated outcome, but it just as often defines the presence and practice of enduring (and surviving) the present.

In the space of the ball, endurance is not merely what we do to survive; rather, endurance itself is recast as a playful and pleasurable scene, one that we revel in and dress up for. Waiting as a technique of enduring the present creates the space in which those hours before the ball begins is less of a waiting for or on something to come and more of a state of waiting with. Where the grammar of waiting in the everyday is entangled with the hopes and desires of a future otherwise, the waiting of ball time is the extended moment when we shift our orientation toward building a world here and now. Waiting is an elongated activation that doesn't rely on a future desired end, but rather generates a temporary collectivity.

• • •

I once asked Linda LaBeija why people always show up so late to balls. Linda is the sort of friend that lets you ask the dumb question because she can tell that underneath, you are asking a question about how the world works. She is a stunning transgender activist and artist who has a witty sense of humor, a sharp intelligence, a limitless creativity, a radical sense of justice, and an overwhelming energy in life whose depths seem to know no bounds. Her youth only makes her wisdom and thoughtfulness more arresting. She looked at me and laughed, throwing her head back with delight. *I know when I'm late it's cause I'm at home making sure I have everything I need,* she said, getting more serious. *And it's crazy because you're literally at home making sure you have everything you need for two seconds of glory, for the chance for the commentator to say "Keep walking! Keep going!"* She sat quietly for a moment, then added, *I think part of what makes people late is similar to the way that ballroom escape[s] other concepts of gender or dance or what have you. It escapes time.*

Linda took another sip of her tea. We were sitting outside the library in Bryant Park, and the weather had gone from slightly chilled to brisk overnight. *It makes me wonder about what it means to be Black in America. And it makes me think of James Baldwin and constantly being in this state of anger or frustration and it's especially common among Black LGBTQ folks. You know, we're constantly dealing with a lot of stress and a lot of triggers. Like, there's a reason why there is such a thing as CP time, you know?* Listening back on the recording of our conversation, I can hear myself agreeing. She went on: *I think the reality is that not only do we want to come in our best, but we wanna come in our best to see people we haven't seen in a long time; we wanna come in our best to leave a good impression on the judges; we wanna come in our best so when we see the pictures we can say "Yes! We look good!"* A man walked over and asked for change. Linda kindly told him we didn't have anything and without missing a beat, returned to her thought: *And it makes me think of excellence, you know? It's the difference between excellence and Black excellence, and Black excellence will make you late!*

• • •

As the opening vignette suggests and Linda confirms, balls don't begin on time because people are "running late." Indeed, lateness necessitates the waiting we experience; or we could say that lateness creates the conditions of possibility for this particular form of waiting. But if being "on time" is a pressure point around which people experience the heavy weight of being out of sync from normative time, being late to arrive at a ball is a gift the collective affords to its members. When Linda describes why she's late, she's describing the relationship between time and the collective, a restructuring of the burden felt when we are required to abide by the temporal logics of the world, toward an investment in taking time to figure out how to be present together. And when she describes the desire to "come in our best," she is describing a commitment to a collective life centered on Black excellence that stands in defiance of all that seeks to limit the conditions for Black life in general, and Black excellence in particular.

The ballroom community time and time again finds ways of using the (collected, created, borrowed, stolen, and purchased) materials at hand, transforming them into radiant and extraordinary things.[4] And this collective work of bricolage includes the ephemeral materiality of time, where time itself becomes an opportunity to mess with what is available to create something in the meanwhile of the everyday. For Black and Brown members of the scene, for whom the ball is a necessary pause from days spent working and living in an anti-Black and anti-queer world, and for whom waiting in the everyday most often operates as a sign of powerlessness, waiting for the ball refocuses attachments to the unfolding now by insisting that enduring can be exciting, spontaneous, creative, and exhilarating, even if it is only for "two seconds of glory." Waiting reminds us that being together is, in and of itself, a moment of Black excellence.

Look at the people gathered around the runway and judges' tables—the people sitting at tables and others pressing their bodies closer to the platform in order to get a better look or chant a little louder. When we are brought into the fold of these moments of collective effervescence, when we've given ourselves over to these ritualized moments of togetherness, we sense what it feels like to escape time, even if only for a moment. As this community coheres around a shared physical space or activity, there are moments when the people gathered around the stage act as an audience (captivated by "a look" or voguer) and moments when they act as a crowd (hollering and chanting for a family member or against a rival house). In so doing, this collection of individuals gives up something of themselves for the creation of the whole, and a world comes into view through this loosening of the self. Another way of saying this is the transition from being in attendance to being a member of the ballroom community is one deeply tied to being willing to wait for it. These moments of "public subjectivity" are the moments when "we imagine, if imperfectly, indifference to those particularities" of the self and become a part of a collective (Warner 1992, 377). This is not to argue that we lose ourselves as a condition of membership to the ballroom community, but that our relationship to others and ourselves takes on a new form when we come into contact with this collective, in part through the act of waiting.

When we wait in the world, we are often waiting for something or someone. We can be passively and powerlessly held captive by the temporal modes we enter and remain there until we reach a fulfillment of some kind. Our attachment to the future event/person/place is what keeps us in the anticipatory space of waiting. But when we wait before and during a ball, normative time is suspended and we lose a sense of the ground. We float above the ordinary, escaping the pressures and obligations it brings to bear on Black queer life. The urgency that routinely structures the everyday slowly begins to ease its anticipatory grasp, and we sink into the state of being here, together, still. Because we know the ball will begin but never really know when or how, and we know that people are coming but are unsure from where or how they will get here, and we know that the beat will drop but are often surprised when it does, waiting invites us to experience the now. Waiting for the ball to start signals a sort of elongation of the present in order to call attention to one's place within the community. Waiting is a necessary in-between that rejuvenates and restores, shifting our attachments that are always wrapped up in futures back to the present in order to make the demand that we stay suspended there together.

Notes

1. Minus the clients at the community center, the majority of the names in this essay have not been changed.

2. This essay explores a very small aspect of life in the ballroom community. For a more complete history and study of this vibrant community, see Marlon Bailey's wonderful investigation of ballroom culture in Detroit, *Butch Queens Up in Pumps* (2013).

3. Following Lauren Berlant (2011, 2), I understand the "good life" to be a fantasy object constituted in part through the interplay of moral, economic, and intimate imaginaries. Good life fantasies are created within distinct contexts and work to structure the way people organize their lives as they struggle to attain some sense or measure of success. In the United States, the language of "the good life" is often framed within conversations of the American dream, the optimistic goal of gaining material success through hard work and perseverance.

4. Like many collectives, the ballroom scene comprises individuals whose diverse experiences, histories, fears, and dreams of the good life might make it difficult to recognize them as a coherent community. And while the predominantly Black and

queer members of this community share certain characteristics, and are collected together into houses, they share equally in their differences: some people are Icons and Legends while others are virgins to the scene; some are "bunny rabbits" (young people) and some are elders; some people have wealth while others live in poverty; some people are sober and others struggle with addictions; some people have made their ballroom success their personal gain, while others are still just trying to figure out how to play the game. But when one arrives at a ball, categories that matter in the everyday—the criteria by which we often measure ourselves—become malleable.

The Police and the Policed

Queer Crossings in a Mumbai Bathroom

Brian A. Horton

Armed with nothing but a few handwritten posters, a handful of outreach workers, several boxes of condoms, and a plastic dildo, Vinod frequently enters police stations with a mission of teaching police officers about safe sex. An outreach worker with almost two decades of experience, Vinod daily crosses the thresholds between the worlds of men cruising for sex in public and the police responsible for safeguarding public morality by catching men engaged in public sex. Under the auspices of HIV prevention, he organizes regular sessions with rows of police officers lined in formation and standing at attention. These meetings are framed as being relatively straightforward. And yet, as I witnessed while shadowing Vinod during fieldwork in Mumbai in 2016, these interactions between Vinod, his team, and the police disorient and upend the austere space of a police station. Bawdy jokes are made, cops turn bashful during condom demonstrations, and the affective charge of these spaces turns from seriousness to play. The culprit for this shift in the energy is Vinod's dildo. Sometimes an orange, silicone sculpture, and other times a solid wooden carving of a penis, the prosthetic cock almost always produces similar responses of bashfulness, laughter, and even confusion when it is introduced.

While these visits to police stations occurred under the auspices of HIV prevention, they were also "an excuse, an opportunity [*mauqa*] to talk about LGBTQ issues." By "opportunity," Vinod imagines these meetings as ways to bring the queer community and law enforcement together in the same space for meaningful conversation, through condom demonstrations. In short, the dildo created an opportunity to hijack the smiles and playful energy of the space to direct conversation from HIV toward sexuality. This optimism indexes Vinod's belief that "change does not happen magically and that outreach workers must take steps to affect change." His words also evince a certain kind of faithfulness and attachment to the police: a belief that by attempting to play *with* police he might be able to engineer a change in law enforcement's attitudes toward queers in public. Though a playful and at times sexual undercurrent marks the interactions between Vinod and the police officers, these moments stand in stark contrast to the experiences of queers who are policed in "sex publics" (Berlant and Warner 1998, 550). In countless interviews and in numerous instances from my work with Vinod as well as NGO staff that handle crisis cases, queers narrated negative and often troubling interactions with police. Several also recounted how cops participate in the very sex that they subsequently police.

Drawing on these contrasts, this essay engages interviews and ethnographic data from ongoing fieldwork with queer-identified people in Mumbai to suggest that to encounter power queerly is to experience not only the subjecting aspects of law but also its connections to pleasure, to the erotic, to the very sexuality that it refuses. By turning to the moments of erotic play at work even in the context of policing, I point to the queer crossings between the law, its enforcement, and the policing of "illegal" sex.

I argue that these crossings paint a more capacious picture of India's battle against the anti-sodomy law, Section 377.[1] Rather than seeing queers as fully subjected by the law or even hailed by its language of criminality, this essay points to particular moments of queer emergence (as dildo play, as cruising, as entrapment) that occur *because* of the law's insistence on policing and banning consensual same-sex behavior. Thus, not only must the law name and produce the thing it sanctions, but at times it must also traffic in the very behavior it deems illegal. What does it mean for police to engage in erotic forms of play (jokes, cruising, entrapment, and sex) as modes of policing the very sexualities that are banned by law? And what kinds of queer nightlife are enacted in these moments of play and policing?

By *play*, I reference a particular kind of joking, unserious, or ephemeral disposition that can temporarily suspend and confuse hierarchy, relations of power, and perhaps even the law itself.[2] Anthropological treatments of play have emphasized mostly gaming or ritualized aspects of competition between groups or individuals. But rather than cordon off play as wholly "separable from everyday life," I view play as "related to a particular mode of experience, a dispositional stance toward the indeterminate" that is revealed in everyday traces and gestures that are open to be read, interpreted, and debated (Malaby 2007, 96; 2009, 208).

This essay reads the encounters between queers and police in police stations and in bathroom stalls across Mumbai as forms of play that ought to be interpreted as queer nightlife. From Vinod's dildo workshops to the dimly lit urinals of the public restroom, these spaces tell an alternative to the well-established narratives of queer nightlife.[3] Much like play is a disposition marked by indeterminacy, this essay suggests that queer nightlife is equally indeterminate in its spatial and temporal boundaries. Whether it is the riotous laughter of cops holding dildos in a police station or the wandering hands of men underneath shimmers of light in bathroom stalls, this essay locates forms of queer nightlife that are, like play, vulnerable to being read, interpreted, and debated. In thinking with the concept of play, I argue that queer nightlife is further pushed out of parties, bars, clubs, and other cordoned-off spaces and brought into a larger public milieu. This essay extends queer nightlife in a direction that imagines the porousness of urban publics and privates, and in doing so signals the capacity of queer subjects to play with the world as well as encounter the risks and vulnerability of that play becoming weaponized.

The rest of the essay is divided into two sections, one on police and the other on policing. Following Vinod and his team's sensitization work in police stations, I explore what futures are imagined through safe-sex campaigns. I argue that play makes demands of power, asking that queers be allowed to live and let live in public spaces. Thus, for outreach workers like Vinod, dildo play is invested with optimism, a promise of goodwill, exchange, and commitment to mutual respect. And yet, these commitments are often reneged in the everyday encounters between queer subjects and the law. In the second section I draw on the experiences of people who have been policed while cruising to suggest that play is also a technique used to entrap and criminalize. Police use sting operations to literally and metaphorically play with people cruising for sex in public spaces. Such moves are often justified through the language of securitizing and sanitizing public space from sexual immorality. The contradictory scenes—the hand of a cop wrapped around the shaft of a dildo, and the tumescence of an erection in a public loo—offer glimpses of the queer passages between sexuality and state power, pleasure and policing, play and violence that nightlife engenders.

DILDO OPTIMISM

I reached the police station around seven in the evening. Although our meeting with the police was not scheduled until 7:30 p.m., Vinod wanted us to arrive early "just in case there were any issues." Armed with white paper charts with scribblings in Marathi, a small group of outreach workers greeted me before moving closer to the station. The blistering hot summer sun sank into the sky; the other outreach workers—Raj, Ankit, and Meet—milled about as we waited. Although several of them had done these sensitizations before, we all felt a little anxious, pacing back and forth in the lane right in front of the station. We did not want to go inside without Vinod, since this whole thing was his idea, his contacts, and his plan. The station itself seemed quite out of place. A massive, brightly lit structure, bureaucratic beige. It sat at the base of a large hill that was dotted with slums, apartments, and tightly cramped alleyways. It was one of the last buildings on a main road before the paved streets ended and winding paths of stairs and slope stretched up into a sea of closely knit living quarters.

After we had waited for what seemed like hours, Vinod emerged and beckoned us to come inside. We walked down a long corridor of offices, passing lines of people filing reports and making complaints, and came to a large open room at the very back of the station. The room was empty except for a policewoman sitting at a desk covered in ledgers and notebooks. Vinod told us to wait there, as he had to go talk with one of the officers before we started. The inspector had changed between when Vinod fixed the session and now, and the new inspector was a bit confused as to why we were there. Before exiting the room, Vinod opened up his backpack and pulled out a large box of Nirodh-brand condoms and a brown phallus made out of wood, placing these items on the desk where the policewoman was working. As Raj, Ankit, and Meet began unpacking and looking for a place to tape up the NGO banner as well as other small signs and posters, the policewoman looked up and began asking questions. "He Amcha NGO Ahe," it's our NGO, one of the workers said, briefly explaining the sign.

Vinod soon reentered, followed by a couple of officers. He was concerned that they would not be allowed to take pictures of the session because of the new inspector. One officer came to the desk and dismissed the policewoman, escorting her out. As she got up from the desk, she finally noticed the dildo, which had been placed upright so that the erection was in plain sight. She gestured toward it with her hands as if to ask what it was, before the other police officer gently pulled on her arm, talking to her in a low voice. Both of them exited the room, smiling and laughing at the penis. Before long, more and more police entered the room, some in uniform and others in plain clothes. We had reached the station right as shifts were changing, so there was a limited amount of time to make the presentation before people either needed to start working or race against traffic to head home.

Each new entry into the room took turns casually glancing at the dildo.

The looks on people's faces ranged from shock, to curiosity, to smiles. Vinod perhaps left the dildo on the desk intentionally. He was intensely aware that if he enters a police station just wanting to talk about LGBTQ+ issues, "they won't listen and will not be ready to hear what you have to say. If I talk to them about HIV/AIDS and show them how to put on a condom, their minds will be a bit fresher. Maybe there will even be a smile on their faces. And after catching that smile I can present on LGBTQ community issues." For Vinod, these smiles function as part of a bodily exchange of signs that connote mutuality, a willingness to hear and be heard on issues of sexual diversity. He got that and much more once the room filled up. The comments from the participants became bolder, bawdier, and much more direct. A group of officers, not in uniform, picked up the dildo and began playing with it. One asked how much it costs; another asked about the material ("shouldn't it be plastic and not wooden?"); a third suggested that it was quite small and that if he were to get one he would get one much larger. "Are you giving these away?" another asked. With each curious glance, people laughed, smiled, and of course made sexual jokes and puns about the dildo on the table.

Once the inspector was ready to begin, the police made two neat lines and stood in formation. With their arms behind their backs and chests puffed up, the officers listened as Vinod and the outreach workers began asking them about how HIV is transmitted. Shortly into the lecture, Vinod lifted the brown, wooden dildo to murmurs and smiles. He asked a senior officer to come demonstrate the proper way to put on a condom. A large, heavy-set officer came toward the front. While the officer unwrapped the rubber from the Nirodh box, Vinod balanced the wooden cock on his hand so that it was perfectly straight. As the officer slid the condom on properly,[4] the other police started to cheer. One whipped out his mobile phone and began filming. While this was happening, the other outreach workers began passing out boxes of condoms to the officers, who sheepishly accepted them. Vinod casually began mentioning that if the police see LGBTQ people, they should protect them and "not misunderstand" them. After a couple rounds of applause, some thank-yous, and many group photos, the group dispersed, the laughter and smiles died down, and the office quickly returned to business as usual. I watched as several officers slid the Nirodh boxes into their pockets. But quite a few thanked the outreach workers that had handed them out and politely returned the condoms, gracefully sliding them back into the hands of the outreach workers. The politeness of the return, the attempts to avoid offending the outreach workers, point to the intimacies forged—however fleeting—in the spaces of Vinod's workshop.

In the technical language of an NGO these meetings are referred to as "sensitizations"—encounters aimed at introducing various stakeholders to safer-sex practices and to the language of gender and sexual difference. Far beyond being some sort of queer petting zoo, these meetings are part of a broader strategy of producing new sensibilities, affective encounters between the law and its criminal other. Scenes such as this sensitization are striking because they disrupt the script of activist organizing and politicking as "serious" work or work that must perform itself through trauma, violence, or "the image of the wounded homosexual" (Suresh 2011, 469). Questions about queer life and death are recast through play, jokes, and undisciplined interaction. The dildo indexes how play evinces optimistic attachments to safe space for queers. It is also not a coincidence that the stations chosen for these sessions are located in areas known for cruising, where outreach workers hand out condoms and encourage those cruising to get tested. These demonstrations pivot on what Lauren Berlant (2011, 23) might call a "cluster of promises"—safety, respect, noninterference—that these NGO workers hope will be made possible through increased interaction with police.

This work is volatile and dangerous. In 2001 several members of Lucknow's Bharosa Trust were arrested for passing out condoms and performing similar demonstrations. The police raided their offices and confiscated their materials (including a dildo used for condom demonstrations), alleging that the organization was a front for gay sex (Cohen 2005, 269). Similarly, as Vinod revealed, when members of his group first approached the government about getting access to dildos for condom demonstrations, government officials accused them of just wanting the dildos for sexual play. Moreover, outreach workers are sometimes harassed while distributing condoms. Or the police will collect and throw away condoms left in bathrooms and other public sites. Given the difficulty of performing the kinds of work that outreach workers do, Vinod's visits to the police station both stage encounters between queer outreach workers and law enforcement and attempt to engineer solidarity and perhaps even compassion between the two.

What is the promise of a dildo? What kind of optimistic attachments are invested in the play that these interactions engender? Play in these moments rehearses an erotic relation that touches the limits of acceptable male homosociality but cannot fully cross it. These moments of play operate on promises to protect and serve the LGBTQ+ community that can never fully be realized. In his work on the barebacking subculture and seroconversion, Tim Dean (2009, 84) suggests that every gift is erotic in that it binds bodies to one another. Thus, to refuse a gift is also to refuse the erotic relations and even kinship that such presentations seek to make possible. Is the refusal of these latex gifts a refusal to share kinship between law enforcement and the criminal other? These refusals of condoms may perhaps mark a limit or threshold that cannot be traversed. As Lawrence Cohen (1995, 417) has suggested, penetrative sex crosses a threshold that turns *masti* and play from idioms into boundaries.[5] In all the police sensitizations that I observed with Vinod and his team, this refusal of the condoms among some police was a common occurrence. The denouement of these sessions, marked by this act of refusal, is striking perhaps because it signals the end of play, the return to mundane, serious order. I would not immediately read these moments as refusals of connection. To some extent the connection had already happened, the moment Vinod could catch their smiles. Rather, I would argue that these refusals of condoms were efforts to diffuse the erotics of the moment, opportunities for the police to signal their moral fortitude and not their possible promiscuity. But what stood out in these encounters was that they could also be opportunities for physical contact. In several instances, I noticed cops making small talk with outreach workers assisting Vinod or sometimes sliding the box back into the hands of the outreach worker in a handshake that held a little long.

Ultimately, these interactions between Vinod and police raise a litany of questions: How do the queer people who cruise, who go for nights out, who have sex in abandoned bathrooms, at the edges of train platforms, and behind bushes in parks experience the police and policing? When an officer in a sting operation runs his hands over their bodies does he smile like he does while holding Vinod's dildo? Does he laugh and make jokes as he accuses people cruising or engaging in transactional sex of ruining the nation? What happens to that very playfulness in Vinod's sessions when cops encounter queers cruising in trains, in loos, and in parks?

HONEY TRAPS

In August 2013, Ganesh Deshmukh, a local reporter from the Marathi-language newspaper *Lokmat*, created a furor when he organized sting operations of cruising sites in Amravati, a small city located in the state of Maharashtra.[6] Headlines like "Samlingi Purush Sambandhacha Amravatith Deshpatlivaril Adda" (Amravati Becoming a National-Level Den for Homosexual Activities) were plastered across the pages of the *Lokmat*, which has a wide readership. Deshmukh denounced cruising and hailed it as a ruination of India and its future:

> The situation is horrible. You will feel the foundations crumbling under your feet. Amravati, the cultural centre of Vidarbha, has seven commercial gay cruising sites active. One of these Gay "sites" is famous among Gay people nationwide. For many days the *Lokmat* team has roved through the gay crowd and through a sting operation has exposed it with proof. That the city of Gods also known as Indrapuri—Ambanagari has this gay commercial sex racket on such a big scale is a worrying aspect for youths. It is also fearsome and dangerous. (Deshmukh 2013)

Posing as gay men, Deshmukh and police officers led a sting operation, observing the patterns and behaviors of men meeting one another for legal, consensual, and (mostly) free sex. His article went on, "After the shocking news of a gay sex racket in Amravati, the police administration woke up and swung into action. On Sunday, in plain clothes, policemen of the crime branch spread their net. But the alerted gays did not get entrapped in the police net." For Deshmukh, public sex represented the decaying of India's moral, social, and cultural fabric. As his article continued, "India, with its culture and tradition, is now rapidly been eroded by Western culture of men trying to fulfill their unnatural desires. This has resulted in the city having around 3,750 to 4,250 men falling for Gay culture." Ideas of the nation and society as being in ruin, collapse, and decay figure as powerful ways for Hindu fundamentalists, the political right, and those opposed to queers to articulate their anxieties over the inclusion of sexual minorities within state institutions of law, rights, and citizenship.[7]

But in addition to the socially ruinous imaginings of cruising, queer public sex marks the crossing of two specific thresholds in terms of India's antisodomy law: sex in public places, and sex "against the order of nature." The policing of cruising is justified as necessary to maintain a clean and respectable public. And yet, the policing of this practice is neither respectable nor wholly distant from the erotic play that constitutes cruising. From their glances, to physical exposure, to sexual acts, those who police cruising spaces often cross the same boundaries that they aspire to regulate. The law crosses into the erotic zones of play and pleasure that it outlaws; the police produce the very acts and categories that they seek to control. What I am suggesting here is that play—even under the auspices of doing one's job—makes a temporary mess of the neat distinctions between queer criminal and law enforcement as well as between sexual desire and labor.

This particular technique of entrapping men who are cruising for sex is sometimes referred to as "honey trapping," where plainclothes cops or male decoys are used to apprehend people suspected of having sex (or intending to have sex) in public places, typically restrooms. In cases such as Deshmukh's sting, police use this technique to catch subjects and punish them criminally. In other cases, police, sometimes in plain clothes, use honey traps to extort men for money by threatening them with legal action or, worse, outing them to their family members. The policing of cruising spaces creates scenarios of confusion where the law and its criminal other—duty and sex, violence and play—temporarily lose certain categorical distinctions because the police do not necessarily catch men per se but rather lure, entice, and out them, succumbing to their own sexual advances in the process of naming and shaming sexual dissidents.

Shashank, a thirty-year-old, bisexual, married man, frequently visited many of the major cruising sites in and around train stations and so had developed somewhat of a rapport with outreach workers. Because he lived quite far from his workplace in town, he commuted upward of two hours every day. In the evenings, Shashank would get down at specific stations on the way home to cruise and fool around in the bathrooms. One night, during a routine stop at a station loo, he met a man who showed all the signs of being interested in sex. As Shashank retold it to me, they stood next to each other at the urinals and made eye contact. He said that the man "exposed his erection and began jerking off." He understood this to be an invitation and replaced the man's hand with his own and began stroking. Suddenly Shashank felt someone come at him from behind, and the man whom he was stroking also grabbed him. "We are from the police," the men said to Shashank, before hauling him to a police station nearby. There they searched his bag, threatened to tell his family what he was doing in the bathroom, and demanded a fine of 15,000 rupees.[8] In a similar case, which Shashank experienced years after this incident, the cops used a decoy. This was akin to a larger racket reported in 2015, when the wife of a struggling actor filed a complaint against eight policemen who were using her husband as bait to blackmail men cruising in bathrooms (Vaktania 2015).

Shashank's experiences indicate that the officer's participation in same-sex sexual behavior—even if for the purposes of stopping it—blurs the distinction between policing and the queerness being policed. These moments also demonstrate that the inviting glances of a stranger occupy the threshold of a range of potential effects from pleasure to punishment; this threshold constitutes the unpredictability that is looking for sex in public. Shashank's experiences exemplify what Brian Sutton-Smith (2006, 297) has termed the ambiguity of play, that we can describe the feeling of play but have an incredibly difficult time naming it. To put this in different terms: we can understand the sensations that play organizes, but it disorganizes our abilities to name and demarcate what it might actually be, and perhaps when it has transgressed into something else. In this case, erotic play is a matter of life and death for both the police officer and the queer. For the police, play—pretending to cruise and entrapping men through mild sexual advance—is a necessary tactic to securitize and reclaim public spaces from sexual deviants and derelicts. In other words, the sexual play of a honey trap becomes a way of making heterosexuality live and let die its deviant other.[9] Conversely, queers find life precisely through the risks attached to cruising and through stranger contact, which can (at least temporarily) upend social hierarchy (Delany 1999). The condom prevention work in police stations also foregrounds a playful request for the state's respect and noninterference, a wish that often remains unfulfilled. These passing moments signal a context in which public spaces are sites of escape and flight from the heterosexuality of domestic space. Thus, cruising becomes integral to the flourishing of queer nightlife.[10] Yet, such play in loos and on trains risks death, blackmail, and arrest (Gupta 2011).

During a moment of intense legal precarity, police-led sting operations, legally sanctioned exploitation and blackmail, and the erosion of civil liberties for sexual and gender minorities across India, it is perhaps counterintuitive to turn to play as a queer mode of inhabiting the world. But as this essay has argued, play gestures to moments of social indeterminacy and interruption that offer ethnographic traces of the contingencies of everyday life. Despite the precarious and dangerous times that queer subjects across India find themselves in, play signals a disposition toward the world that renders the world far more open than legal foreclosures might indicate. To reiterate, play indexes neither the transcendent resistance of the queer subject, nor the all-encompassing power of the biopolitical state, but rather modes of living, of ordinary life, that transgress the neat boundaries and narratives of subjecthood. In my broader research, I argue that, in lieu of taking for granted the fixity of subjects as defined through sexual object choice, we must ask how subjects move between multiple social positions and how movement frustrates the easily reproduced narratives of queer victims, perpetrators, law enforcers, and criminals. From queer to criminal to victim, the subjects that I have described here offer alternatives to the now ubiquitous tropes of the Global South sexual minority in need of saving via legal reform or Western aid. I emphasize this point here not to dismiss the work that transnational activism and international funding have done to spotlight issues of queer violence and erasure. Rather, I challenge victim narratives in order to draw attention to the multiple subjectivities, and perhaps even temporalities, that are elided by narratives of Global South queer suffering. Turning to moments of play as betraying the stability of the law and its enforcement, I suggest that there are openings for thinking about the queer subjects and anti-queer laws beyond the West as living and working in unconventional ways that exceed the narrative of universal queer suffering or homophobia. These momentary lapses, twisted confusions of work and pleasure, also point to the indeterminate nature of queer nightlife (as well as the law), helping us locate nightlife's potency and possibilities beyond the bars, clubs, and dance floors. The bathrooms and police stations become their own kind of dance, with a different soundtrack. And it is the stickiness of these tense, messy encounters, be it in a police station or a restroom, that gesture to crucial points of convergence, the play, between criminal and legal worlds in Mumbai queer nightlife.

Notes

1. Section 377 of the Indian Penal Code (IPC 377) prohibits carnal intercourse or sex against the order of nature. The New Delhi High Court read down (functionally decriminalized) IPC 377 in 2009, and the Supreme Court of India reinstated it in 2013.

2. Anthropological studies of play have detailed how play is a form of competition, kinship, and even ritualized eroticism; see Radcliffe-Brown (1940), Geertz (1973), and Huizinga (1949). For critical approaches on play and the erotic within studies of South Asia, see Singh (2015) on the erotics of play, Lal (2013) on female playfulness, and Katyal (2013) on idioms of sexual and erotic play.

3. Studies of queer nightlife have heavily centered on spaces like bars, gayborhoods, parties, and other social spaces as well as concerns over gentrification of gayborhoods (see Mattson 2015). More recent work (e.g., Ghaziani 2015) has suggested that increased queer acceptance has pushed queer life beyond the gayborhood. But much of the work in queer urban studies exists in spaces in which queer nightlife is cordoned off to specific sections of the city and located within traditional nightlife scenes like bars, pubs, and clubs.

4. It was not uncommon for people to put the condoms on upside down (inside out). In fact Vinod often used the frequency of incorrect condom placement to justify these sessions to the police.

5. In queer scholarship on South Asia, the terms *khel* (play) and *masti* (fun) are commonly used placeholders for erotic interactions that happen clandestinely or beyond the boundaries of social sanction. Often, *masti* names erotic relations that disrupt the lines between homosexual and homosocial.

6. In this particular context, the author expressed outrage because one of the loos

happened to be near schools and a park, thus coming dangerously close to innocent children.

7. Paola Bacchetta (1999) has written extensively about this phenomenon in the Indian context, where queers inhabit an oppositional figuration to ideas of Hindu nationalism and supremacy. Similarly, Kath Weston (1991, 25) has suggested that queers figure as a powerful image for right-wing politicians to evoke a "threat to the family" and perhaps heterosexuality itself.

8. This amount equates to approximately $230.

9. See Michel Foucault (2005) for a larger discussion of the state's right to make live and let die. I suggest here that his framing of the techniques of biopolitics might be useful for unpacking how heterosexuality is made to have a particular social life, while queerness, its ostensible other, is allowed to "let die" through manifold forms of policing and sanitization.

10. Though cruising is crucial to queer nightlife, it is also limited, given that queer women are not easily able to move through public spaces or lay claim to places beyond the space of home.

Relational Generativity in South African Queer Nightlife

AB Brown

It is February in Cape Town, and the city's infamously long summer holds strong. It is Cape Town Pride, and I am walking slowly down Main Road in the Greenpoint neighborhood, a gay enclave of the city. I am here with a group of LGBTIQ asylum seekers whom I have been interviewing, volunteering with, and running performance workshops with for many years. As part of our organizing efforts, we have decided to participate in this year's pride parade to help publicize our message about the erasure of LGBTIQ migrants in South Africa's LGBTIQ political landscape. After weeks of anticipation, thrifty costume design, and fine tuning the political slogans that we would smear across our poster boards, we arrived at the march. Located behind a luxury vehicle throwing Red Bull into the audience and before an elaborate float of shirtless white men advertising a local gay burger joint (which coincidentally repeatedly refused to hire any LGBTIQ refugee applicants), we chanted our slogans, we danced, the asylum seekers posed for every possible photograph and talked to every possible reporter—fulfilling both a fantasy of celebrity and an activist commitment to raise awareness of their presence in the country and the continent more broadly. The end of the parade culminates in a festival party across a couple of small streets dotted with gay and lesbian bars. I peel off to pack up some of our signs and arrange our transportation home, leaving my group of friends and colleagues to party and enjoy the festive atmosphere. When I return, I cannot find them anywhere. I search all the bars, push myself through each of the outdoor dance floors set up for the festival, until finally I find them, sitting together on a curb by one of the entrance/exit gates of the party. I notice their sour, downturned faces and ask why they aren't enjoying the party. "It's not for us," Marc responds. "Sure we can dance, but everyone is drunk and we can't afford the alcohol. And the people all around the party [the vendors] just keep trying to get us to buy their T-shirts, their toys. And we just have to keep saying 'no,' 'no,' 'no,' 'no thank you.'" We quickly regrouped and headed back to our organization's offices, turned on some music, and threw together some makeshift snacks from leftovers in the fridge. Our own kind of pride.

It is against this exclusionary backdrop that a number of queer nightlife parties are attempting to make more broadly inclusive spaces. Since 2018, South Africa's urban centers have seen a proliferation of nightlife parties that are specifically intended for cis, trans, and nonbinary femmes of color: from Anything Goes in Cape Town to Stay Low Keep Firing in Grahamstown, from Same Sex Saturdays in Durban to Cunty Power and Pussy Party in Johannesburg. These parties and their identity politics can be read as responding to the late capitalist developments of South African economic and social politics that were seeded in the neoliberal economic policies and liberal democratic inclusionary constitution negotiated at the time of the country's transition from apartheid. The post-apartheid transition staged South Africa's political struggles on the premises of identity politics, hoping to maintain a peaceful political transfer and displacing the more radical political and economic discrepancies between the fascist National Party, which established apartheid, and the socialist- and communist-leaning political parties—the African National Congress, the Pan-Africanist Congress, and the South African Communist Party—that resisted the apartheid regime.

This transition resulted in an articulation of constitutional rights based on identity categories alongside the maintenance of fundamental economic inaccessibility such that Black, rural, femme and nonconforming, and disabled communities are told they have rights, but remain unable to access affordable, secure housing, jobs, food, or transportation. Concurrently, South Africa's metropoles have become sites of international investment with the maturation of the country's democracy and its attendant capitalist economic structure. Together, these factors result in South Africa's major cities, especially Cape Town and Johannesburg, maintaining, if not exacerbating, segregation along lines of race and class established under apartheid. As these neoliberal policies mature and manifest in social spaces and everyday life, the "born free" generation (those born after apartheid) is becoming adults and more heavily influencing politics and popular culture. Shaped by this context, the political landscape they engage and imagine has largely shifted from a legal terrain to a cultural one, from access to land, work, and fundamental resources, to issues of representation, desire, and identity politics.[1]

The nightlife parties that are emerging across the country, and that I explore here, perform their politics in response to these conditions. In the face of the many failed promises of the post-apartheid era, they present a critique of access to class mobility, space, and promised resources and rights, asserting their own rights to fabulous, queer, pleasurable practices of comportment, consumption, and a coming together along the lines of identity inclusion. They simultaneously carve out space for queer of color communities in urban spaces that are quickly becoming unaffordable, often literally developing along the same spatial histories of racial segregation, replicating the very built environments of apartheid. In this essay, I explore how the neoliberal shift of post-apartheid politics gets mirrored in the political claims and enactments of queer nightlife and how an attention to intergenerational exchange might offer a connection across these political struggles for a more historically and locally situated queer politics in South African nightlife.

I draw on Dustin Bradley Goltz's (2014, 1523) notion of *relational generativity* to explore what a more multidirectional exchange across generations might offer to the way we imagine and do queer nightlife and therefore what we make possible through these vital interventions. In his theorization of intergenerational exchange, Goltz calls for a "queering of how we think about age, knowledge, and passing of tradition . . . challenging the logic of linear temporal progression of information with age." He draws on Elizabeth Freeman's (2007b) notion of how alternative forms of kinship can help us reframe belonging temporally to think of to belong as to *be long*, with an attendant political commitment to duration and sustainability that is not necessarily rooted in biological reproduction or self-preservation. Goltz's invocation of Freeman helps us use a queer intergenerational lens to think about age and aging in queer nightlife not only in terms of belonging to a specific space, event, or practice, but in terms of belonging to a genealogy of resistance, community, and support that helps reframe the often-stigmatized presence of older people in nightlife spaces. Intergenerationality calls attention to how, through the literal consideration of elders, queer nightlife could be a practice of longevity. Not only in terms of our physical survival—no matter our age—but in terms of longing by facilitating desire for and intimacy with long-term political work, placemaking, and community building. In a similar vein, Andrew J. Hostetler (2009) asks us to think of generativity as a collaborative, creative project across generations that can help us complicate the overdetermined binary of assimilate or accommodate, which we can see in the current developments in South African queer nightlife as well as in the LGBTIQ refugees' struggle to participate in community, politics, and pleasure across lines of nationality and class. These queer, creative reworkings of generativity, Goltz (2014, 1525) concludes, are "personal and communal, exploratory of the future yet historicized within our pasts, and . . . disruptive to social norms that try to determine whose life matters, how life matters, to whom we matter, and who shall be remembered." Relational generativity then begins to suggest specific tactics that we might draw into configurations of queer nightlife, for instance historicizing our practices, thinking about queer nightlife as a kind of remembrance, and paying attention to how these practices might shift how and where we place value.

By looking at age and intergenerationality in queer nightlife, I draw attention to the potential risks of producing dehistoricized or short-term memory notions of the community, politics, and worldmaking made possible by queer nightlife. For instance, each of these parties establishes its intention to be a safer space outside of heteropatriarchal objectification, often within a general rhetoric of safety, freedom, and empowerment of an identity group. The organizer of Stay Low Keep Firing started the party as a desperate attempt to create a safe space for, "WOMXN + NONBINARY because of how fed up she was with never feeling safe when out + just never feeling safe in general. . . . There will be NO men at Oldies [the party's venue] on Friday. The bartenders will be WOMXN. The dance floor will be filled with WOMXN. The DJs will be WOMXN. We will have a man outside of OLDIES just to make sure no one bothers us on the night" (Facebook event page, March 2017). In Johannesburg, the now internationally famous models and musicians FAKA started Cunty Power, stating, "Cunty Power aims to be a safe and empowering space for queer, trans and non-binary bbz. We believe that there is power in us existing in one space, dancing and sweating the night away without any fuckboys to police or shame us" (Facebook event page, July 1, 2017). Facebook conversations, Instagram posts, and interviews published in various articles reviewing the parties make clear that these events create supportive spaces for young people to explore their relationship to gender and to articulate a critical stance toward racist and misogynist attitudes within existing nightlife spaces that cater to white, cisgender, wealthy gay men. Beyond the scope of this essay, these parties also exemplify the ways in which queer nightlife aesthetics and politics circulate globally and offer an opportunity to better understand how these aesthetics and politics are located and reworked in relation to, but outside of, Western paradigms.

Each party I've attended or read about envisions queer nightlife as a space to take pleasure in gender presentation beyond the binary, to dance with like-minded people, drink, get sweaty, and feel good about oneself. They each have a cover charge, occasionally waived for students, they each host emerging DJs whose sounds range from pop and hip-hop to house and experimental sound, and they each take place in urban settings. For instance, Anything Goes takes place at Zero21 Social Club, which was historically an inclusive refuge amid Cape Town's affluent, polished, and often racist gayborhood in De Waterkant. The club recently relocated to the southern edge of the central business district, the Zonnebloem neighborhood, which was once home to freed enslaved people, merchants, and immigrants and is recently being rapidly redeveloped despite disputes over claims to land ownership by former residents who were forcibly displaced during apartheid. This move could at once be read as a spatial critique of the city's whitewashed gay scene as well as a direct correlation to the role LGBT consumerism plays in gentrification. Likewise, Pussy Party is held at Kitchener's Carvery Bar in Johannesburg's Braamfontein neighborhood, which was once home to the city's illegal gay nightlife scene as well as one of the city's most diverse immigrant populations, and which now hosts upscale clothing boutiques and artisanal coffee shops.

The few articles reviewing these parties within a South African context offer brief reviews of the parties and their organizers and then focus primarily on extended photoshoots of the fashionable attendees, indicating the ways that value within the spaces, their forward-thinking politics, and their good feelings emphasize the importance of fashion and an interest in and ability to access a particular sartorial aesthetic. This phenomenon was perhaps epitomized when FAKA, the organizers of Cunty Power, were chosen to provide the runway music for Versace's Spring/Summer 2019 show. The urban, fashionable, pulsing queerness of these nightlife contexts is vastly different from the contexts in which I've spent most of my fieldwork with LGBTIQ asylum seekers since 2010. And, while these parties may have better race and gender politics at heart, in many ways they replicate the asylum seekers' experience during Cape Town Pride. While primarily younger in age (under thirty), the asylum seekers who come from across sub-Saharan Africa practically never attend queer nightlife events because they can't afford the expensive, complicated, and long transportation from their homes in the townships to the urban centers in which many of these parties take place. Nor can they approximate the appropriate comportment or consumption practices of those who attend, at least as portrayed on social media and in popular press coverage. As the anecdote I share below details, the ways that they have carved out spaces of pleasure, communal gathering, and consumption with regard to nightlife are far less rigidly aestheticized or commodified, which opens up space to imagine and realize alternative possibilities for how queerness might be done in queer nightlife.

It is 9:30 p.m. when I reach the end of the directions Pukkie handwrote for me on a napkin. I am in the thick of Delft, a township or informal settlement about twenty miles outside of Cape Town. Delft is one of the most diverse townships in the Western Cape and has a reputation for being one of the most violent. At the same time, a number of the refugees I have come to know live in this area, describing it as one of the more accepting areas of both their foreigner status and their gender/sexuality. As one interlocutor once said, "You know, is [*sic*] like where people have the least, that's where they come together. And they see you have nothing too, so you are one of them." I've rambled down multiple wrong turns, executing very cool eight-point turns in the narrow, unpaved, potholed streets, before finally arriving at what I think is the right spot. But, I've thought that before.

With no formal house numbers, sidewalks, or driveways, I park as far off the road as possible and peel myself out of the car between the abutting corrugated iron wall and patches of weeds. I brush myself off and try to look like I know what I'm doing as I casually review the directions and look around for the right building. I see a group of people gathered by one unassuming gray concrete block structure and hear thumping music. I've found it; I assume. But how to get in? There is no apparent entrance in the front, so I start down a less-than-reassuring alley on the side of the building.

"Hey," a stocky woman with short cropped hair calls to me, waving me over.

I've never met Beauty before, but not a breath after she asks whether I'm there for Pukkie and I confirm, she squeezes me tight to her and says, "this way," in my ear.

Beauty enthusiastically ushers me over to a rusted gray metal garage door and lifts it just enough for us to walk under, closing it behind us, revealing a dimly lit concrete box of maybe three hundred square feet. Rows of picnic tables covered in bright, torn yellow-and-orange plastic tablecloths that advertise different beers and condiments line the left and right walls. One of these holds an array of ice buckets with beer and pitchers of punch and unlabeled alcohol. There is a pool table at the far end of the room and a small back room where food is being prepared. Pukkie exits the small back room, serving plates of food, spots me, and gives a high-pitched, "eh!" He delivers the food and then sashays leisurely to me with his arms akimbo in the air, wrists limp, eyes scanning the room to make sure everyone catches his catwalk. And he looks the part in a pink silk button-up shirt and pink glitter accenting his cheekbones. There is no question whose party we are at. He embraces me, offers me a drink, quickly situates me with a plate of food, and introduces me to his boyfriend.

Abraham and I chat while Pukkie serves a few more plates of food. Abraham is also not South African, though he is not actively seeking asylum. "I'm just trying to work," he says. They've been together for three months, and he can't exactly say how they met, "you know . . . you need a place to stay." Then Abraham turns to the room to welcome everyone there. He makes a few remarks in Xhosa, and everyone cheers. "I speak all languages," he comments, "in case anyone talks about me." Everyone laughs and nods familiarly to one another. And with that, Whitney Houston fills the room from an old-fashioned jukebox in the corner, and everyone is mingling. Many of the refugees I've been working with are here, as well as local South Africans across a significant spectrum of age and gender expression. People play pool; a few dance closely in a corner of the room. I sit on the edge of the room next to Raj, who wears a silk black-and-gold zebra-print button-up and is the Xhosa grandpa of the area. He introduces me to everyone down the line, explaining what each does and where each stays and adds, "You have to interview every one of us. But you'll have to come on a Tuesday when we're all sober." We laugh and talk more about his experiences growing up gay in the township.

Pukkie has made food for everyone and continues to serve. The grandpas observe the crowd, tell stories, and keep everyone in line—all while flirting—and it strikes me that this is one of the first times in over a decade of fieldwork that I have witnessed the refugees feel integrated into a South African context. No one comments on phenotypes that betray South African ethnicity, no one mentions papers, no one even really talks about belonging or not . . . they just are. And, everyone seems to know one another.

I am almost fully romantically wooed by this utopian moment, when Flavi, a trans woman from Burundi, comes running in the door to me and says, "I need you outside right now." Before we even get to the door, a police officer in a bulletproof vest is pushing through the crowd, making his way to the back room. Flavi wants me to talk to him, strategically positioning my white, US, English-speaking privilege to explain that we're just having an informal party, but he disregards me and wants to talk to the owner of the building. Some partygoers move immediately to the door, but most of us wait, a little stunned and a little hesitant about what exactly the problem is. Eventually, the officer moves back to the door, stands there, and speaks in a barely elevated voice, "No one else move. I'm going to detain you all." Then he radios for backup. As soon as he steps out of the doorway, however, everyone is up and out in a measured, but clipped pace. Friendly, rushed good-byes are had as we move our separate ways, and I step into my car just as a large police van pulls up to join the officer.

The shebeen, an informal bar in the townships, had an expired permit, and Beauty, the owner, had not had a chance to renew because of a death in the family. The raid seemed fairly routine to all involved, and it wasn't long before plans were made for another gathering the following weekend. I'm not proposing this alternative example of queer nightlife as a foil to the club scenes described above. In fact, there are many similarities. There was, however, a far greater capacity to hold space for people with a range of gender expressions, economic statuses, ethnicities, citizenships, ages, and abilities. While many practical tactics for expanding the repertoire of queer nightlife are at play in this space, I will focus primarily on the role of intergenerational exchange as a particularly rich offering to consider across nightlife cultures transnationally.

Many scholars have analyzed and critiqued the worship of youth and fear/dismissal of aging, especially in mainstream gay male culture in the United States. As a result, Goltz (2014) argues, many aging gay men and lesbians coalesce to heteronormative and capitalistic models of aging in order to demonstrate their ability to age "successfully" and maintain some form of desirability as older individuals.[2] These values arguably get perpetuated and expanded beyond white, cisgender, middle-class, US-centric gay male culture when identity-based parties replicate the dominant structure of nightlife. This presents the double bind of identity-based inclusion, in which the formerly excluded seize access to particular kinds of pleasure and representation while also internalizing the value structures embedded in those forms of consumption and socialization.[3] Lisa Duggan (2002) helpfully calls our attention here to the neoliberal structuring of queer nightlife and the "normalizing" effect this might have on intergenerational and culturally specific queer politics and sociality, ultimately replicating the dominant logics and oppressions of capitalist economic structures and flattening localized specificity. Similarly, Juana María Rodríguez (2014, 67) points out how the respectability politics of much mainstream LGBT organizing, as well as the putative legislation of kinship and consent, has delimited intergenerational desire, fantasy, and intimacy—along with our "shared social and sexual futures." An attention to intergenerationality lets us focus not on age as an additive identity category, but on a relationality not only to people of different ages, different ways of moving, bodily abilities, desiring, and coming together, but to time and history themselves. What might it mean to direct the potent aspects of desire, fantasy, and intimacy fostered in queer nightlife not only toward the world we want to live in, but the world from which we've come?

Intergenerationality, then, proposes a new temporality to queer nightlife that can help situate contemporary configurations of queer sociality in relation to historical politics, practices of belonging to community and place, and embodied structures of value and desire. This temporality has local implications for bringing the contemporary neoliberal and identity-based politics of queer nightlife in South Africa into more critical conversation with historical political struggles and tactics of organizing and enacting resistance. And, on a broader scope, intergenerationality might offer locally and historically specific versions of nightlife that could emerge in conjunction with the reproduction of globalized trends.

Age traffics in economies of desire. In conventional nightlife spaces, desirability is based on a youthful, able body, consumption, and a demonstrated knowledge of and access to contemporary trends in music and fashion. In the presence of aging, desire gets confused, reconfigured, and redistributed. Sociologist Paul Simpson (2013) clearly details this phenomenon across the United States and Europe by paying attention to what he calls *aging capital*: how, despite stereotypes of the rejection of aging individuals, older gay men can mobilize financial, educational, and lived experience capital to navigate power in gay spaces in more nuanced, though not necessarily unproblematic, ways. Goltz (2014) likewise calls attention to the fact that youth desire the elderly—they want a vision of the future, a sense of stability, and a sense of history, and of course they may even find older bodies desirable—at the same time that they may fear becoming old themselves. Here, historicization can help us index how the past shapes who is desirable and what or how we desire for ourselves and our futures; it structures the very politics and worlds we want to see and live in even as the exclusion of specific categories of people based on age dismisses political struggles, strategies, place-based memories, and ways of being together. This historicization has particular resonance in a South African context where fascist, racist, colonial oppression was so recently entrenched through the spatial segregation of apartheid and has more general implications for the kind of spatial politics and extreme wealth gaps we see being enacted through the gentrification of cities across the world.

In many African contexts, a relationship to elders is drastically different than in the West, though we can see a trend toward the primacy of youth in emerging, globalized queer nightlife in more recent parties throughout South Africa. Queer cultural production, activism, and scholarship that call on more historical and traditional understandings of gender and sexuality to account for African-specific configurations of queerness that preexisted colonization make claims on and appeal to elders and ancestors as the site of *valuing* rather than *rejecting* queerness within African contexts.[4] Culturally specific practices in South Africa of respecting and structuring sociality around elders might propose new formations of the politics and economies of desire in queer nightlife at the same time that this potential can tend to be diminished by parties that adhere to more westernized notions of who is desirable. As the elders who led the anti-apartheid struggle, a history out of which LGBTIQ rights in South Africa emerge, are beginning to die out, a popular (if generalized) concern that the "born free" generation's activism is demonstrating a dehistoricized focus on contemporary political conditions is beginning to circulate widely.[5] Intergenerationality might help us make connections, for instance, between political struggles for Black lesbians in South Africa today and the forcibly displaced South Africans who once resided on the very block that now hosts a trendy party.

What stands out in analyses of queer aging by Goltz, Hostetler, and Freeman is how elders contribute a sort of connective tissue not only to a past, but to place and therefore to other people. They model a relational subjectivity that is heavily defined by connection to other times, places, events, and people—even when those connections are to something not materially present. I witnessed this when Raj and the other queer elders at the shebeen launched into stories about what it was like to be gay under apartheid in the very township where we were sitting. Or when they enumerated the other local queer elders, living and deceased, who weren't in the room with us that night. These stories located people in a sense of place and history, holding space, for instance, in heightened xenophobic atmospheres in South Africa, for people from varying ethnic and national backgrounds to build connection to this place. In these moments, value and desirability shifted from individual style, consumption, or physicality to an awareness of where, when, and with whom one was partying. We can simultaneously see the redistribution of value and desire in many more humorous and matter-of-fact ways in the shebeen. At times elders literally interjected, almost as parental figures, calling out flirtatious behavior, encouraging certain affections, curtailing overly sexual advances, quelling tensions between younger members of the party, and making space for their own desires. They could get up and dance because the range in music was broad enough to encompass their likes, and they used their authority in the space to often ask a younger partner to dance. At the same time, there was plenty of seating, food, and physically non-exerting entertainment to foster community and facilitate the circulation of desire between older partygoers themselves.

The example presented here offers some concrete practices that might help us expand our imagination of queer nightlife and its politics. I am not proposing that we reconfigure all queer nightlife to include yet another marginalized identity. I am, however, looking for redefinitions of what qualifies as nightlife and the way that value is established even in conventional nightlife spaces. But even more than specific reconfigurations, theories of queer aging, especially relational generativity, suggest that it might be more useful to create nightlife culture in more explicit, multidirectional, and historicized dialogue and debate, ever more contextual and constantly shifting revisions to the way we politicize our desire and pleasure together. Queer, relational generativity asks how we historicize queer nightlife in the very embodiment of it; how we might always locate our nightlife activities in relation to a past, a locally specific place, and people who may or may not be physically present; and how we might imagine and enact a concern for and guide to the future through nightlife in creative, nonlinear, collective ways.

Notes

1. This, of course, is an extremely brief summary of a general trend, and the "born free" generation, among others, practice a multitude of political strategies that exceed the purview of this essay.

2. Goltz (2014) and Hostetler (2009) have each focused on the ways that gay aging gets narrated and represented in static archetypes such as the desirable youthful Adonis, the dirty old man, or the asexual and lonely grandfather, which then reify generational divides around obstacles of language, desire, and politics.

3. This is not to say that many resistant and hybrid practices do not persist or emerge within these conditions. Assimilation and resistance do not exist in a binary; however, a full consideration of this topic is beyond the scope of this essay.

4. Here I am thinking of artist Athi Patra-Ruga's rehistoricization of queer belonging on the continent, the explicit connections that musician Umlilo makes between LGBTQ political struggles and broader anticolonial struggles in South Africa, Nkunzi Zandile Nkabinde's (2008) exploration of queerness within traditional healer practices, John McAllister's (2015) look at traditional values in LGBTQ activism in Botswana, and Ato Malinda's (2015) analysis of the effects of globalization on Kenyan queer identity, among many others.

5. This observation is primarily rooted in numerous conversations I've had over the years with South Africans, typically over the age of fifty, as well as a recent trend in youth theater focusing on incorporating more apartheid history into primary school curriculum.

"Dance with Me in the Disco Heat"

Nowhere Bar's Temporal Shifts

Karen Jaime

January 31, 2015, marked the tenth anniversary of a monthly party, Double Headed Disco, DHD for short, at Nowhere Bar, a dive bar located in the downtown New York City neighborhood of the East Village. Located between First and Second Avenues on East Fourteenth Street, Nowhere lies within walking distance of New York University and in proximity—one train stop away on the L train—to the hipster-populated neighborhood of Williamsburg, Brooklyn. Due to its geographic location and aesthetic, Nowhere attracts students, young hipsters, and a mixed crowd of gay men and gender fluid queers looking for a space that challenges the increasing gentrification of the East Village. A large black awning jutting out from the front door to the street with the word *nowhere* printed in white bubble-type letters across the side helps usher in weekly regulars and recent transplants. On weekdays, just down the three steps and past the front door with QUEER BAR painted in hot pink capital letters at the bottom, the bar remains dimly lit, its scuffed wood floors visible, while a hanging light over a worn felt pool table illuminates the area in front of the two bathrooms. The stale smell of urine mixed with chlorine wafting out from the closed restroom doors provides a particular olfactory experience.

On weeknights, Nowhere hosts rotating parties such as Macho Mondays (a party independently promoted with a cover charge and pay for gay go-go boys), the bear-themed Buddies on Tuesdays, Work It! on Wednesdays, Fire in the Hole (a party catering to ginger-haired folk and their admirers) on Thursdays, and Witch Camp (a party for those who enjoy satanic psychedelia and occult rock) on Fridays. But on the last Saturday of the month, DJs Jeff Jackson and Disco Connie (Noel Alicea) hold court during Double Headed Disco, an event that blurs the past and the present in order to imagine alternative queer life worlds and possible futurities.

I analyze the queer worldmaking potential of DHD from my position as

Fig. 1. Noel Alicea (a.k.a. Disco Connie) and Jeff Jackson. (Courtesy of Jeff Jackson.)

both participant and observer. In addition to attending the party as a customer, I also worked as a bouncer/security at Nowhere Bar for a number of years during graduate school. That I am a queer, butch, Latina lesbian who gained entrance into the predominantly cis male party has informed my experiences as both customer and employee. My gender identity and sexuality structure how I interact with the space and the attendees, especially since the hot pink sign on the bottom of the front door was only changed from GAY BAR to QUEER BAR *after* I began working there. Additionally, while the party was open to all and there were cis and trans folks present, I was one of the only butch women. Yet, alongside the textual reconfiguration of the space from gay to queer, my presence was further cemented through my inclusion in promotional materials for DHD. For example, when I worked there, Jeff Jackson (also known as Miss Jackson) and Noel Alicea spun the records—no CDs or downloaded tracks were played—and Mr. Karen (as they referred to me) was credited with adhering to a "discerning door" policy. This door policy was not rigid in terms of who was allowed entry. Customers were allowed entry if they presented identification verifying that they were twenty-one or over, demonstrated that they were not so intoxicated that they could no longer be served alcohol, and had not previously been banned from the bar for offenses including not paying their tab, initiating physical fights, or disrespecting any bar employees or other customers.

Being a Brown butch rarely made my job difficult while working DHD; the crowds were predominantly cis male and queer, and my masculine gender presentation alongside my race and ethnicity afforded me a particular cachet while working the door. DHD catered to a more diverse crowd than the other parties at Nowhere, with the notable exception of Macho Mondays, which included a number of cis male dancers of color, gyrating to a hip-hop beat. DHD, with its disco soundtrack and its focus on music and dancing, drew a crowd that diverged from the bar's regular clientele. I position my time at Nowhere Bar during DHD in conversation with the work of José Esteban Muñoz in *Cruising Utopia* (2009) in order to interrogate the temporal shifts that this party makes visible in catering to diverse ages, races, ethnicities, genders, and sexualities.

As the sole doorperson, I was responsible for greeting patrons, securing their safety, responding to angry noise complaints and visits from neighbors, and dealing with the subsequent visits by cops. Ultimately, I functioned as the intermediary between the space outside and inside the bar. My job centered on maintaining the "culture" of the bar, while simultaneously attempting to adhere to changing city regulations. This increase in policing the behavior of patrons in nightlife venues, particularly those located in formerly undesirable neighborhoods such as the East Village, owes much to the support of affluent gays. Muñoz (2009, 54–55) describes this pattern as "assimilationist homosexuality." He attributes the shift to the mayorships of Rudy Giuliani (1994–2001) and Michael Bloomberg (2002–2013), especially Giuliani's "quality of life campaign," which resulted in "an ongoing attack on cultures of sexual dissidence." "Quality of life" referred to a practice of heavily policing a number of normally noncriminal activities such as standing, congregating, sleeping, eating, and drinking in public spaces, as well as minor offenses such as leaving graffiti, urinating in public, panhandling, littering, and engaging in unlicensed street vending. "Quality of Life" legislation served as the justification for noise complaints that often resulted in an increased police presence at nightlife establishments. While these complaints ostensibly focused on noise, they pushed queer bodies and the performance of queer sexuality back into the private sphere, simultaneously silencing the "bad" citizen-subject and relegating her/him/them out of sight. The penalization of quotidian activities such as standing outside of a bar cruising, smoking a cigarette, and engaging in conversation conformed to and advanced protocols of homonormativity. Lisa Duggan (2002, 179) defines homonormativity as a "politics that does not contest dominant heteronormative assumptions and institutions but upholds and sustains them while promising the possibility of a privatized, depoliticized gay culture anchored in domesticity and consumption." In contrast, DHD—a party held at a dive bar that served cheap drinks and had homemade decorations adorning the walls—politicizes gay culture by refusing to relegate queerness to the abject past and by redefining the relationship between "home" and the domestic sphere. DHD functions as a queer home-space that blurs the line between the public and the private, the past and the present, through the culture produced in the bar sonically and visually.

Additionally, during DHD, I contributed to both creating and maintaining a specific "culture" within this "home" and negotiating its extension outside the bar. Outside of Nowhere, I was tasked with ensuring that patrons talked, smoked, and cruised one another by the sidewalk, away from the windows of the complaints. The relocation of patrons to the curb and away from the bar allows for passersby on the intervening sidewalk—which separates the curb from the bar—to function as an interjection, interrupting the music and culture being produced within the bar, and preventing it from extending to the public sphere of the city.

The culture produced by DHD in terms of argot, music, and overall aesthetic began with a onetime birthday celebration, promoted as "Disco Noel," for Noel Alicea, current DJ of DHD and one of the many queer Puerto Ricans animating queer nightlife in New York City. His DJ partner, Jeff Jackson, founded the party with DJ Pete Money, both of them white, queer culture makers invested in a racially mixed archive of music and social practice. As a friend of Jackson's, Alicea frequented DHD and earned the nickname Disco Connie, shorthand for Disco Connoisseur, due to his love of disco music, in particular rarely played tracks. Jackson's friend Brian Fitzpatrick renamed Disco Noel as Double Headed Disco for the second month's event. Fitzpatrick used the phrase *double-headed* as a tongue-in-cheek reference to the phalluses of the two cis males spinning records during the party. Fitzpatrick—nicknamed BJ, in reference to blow jobs—boasts a knowledge of vintage gay porn and provides video compilations of vintage skin flicks for the monthly function. Fitzpatrick's movies play on a loop throughout the party, from ten at night until four in the morning, on the TV screen located in the center of the bar. The grainy porn, often in black and white, calls on a 1970s and early 1980s gay male aesthetic: the mustaches, hairy chests, and lack of condoms all speak to a sexual practice that predates the AIDS crisis. These muted pornographic films, played for a crowded bar, urge viewers to congregate en masse in front of the screen, where they watch and discuss the films outside of the private domestic space, creating an alternative community within the larger disco dancing crowd. In addition, while the films on the screen predate the onset of the AIDS pandemic, many partygoers faced the loss of community members and dear friends during the 1980s and 1990s. Seeking a home, they come to DHD because it provides a refuge, a reminder of an era and of people gone too soon, while simultaneously celebrating queer of color life and survival.

The flyers for DHD similarly create a visual landscape while forecasting the sonic one for attendees. For example, "Say Grace"—for the Saturday following Thanksgiving—showcases two images of a nude Grace Jones facing each other. These flyers, placed throughout the bar, visually announce that her music will largely be played on rotation. Other posters include "The Boss," featuring a flawless Diana Ross directly facing the camera as she places her hands over her sleeked-back hair, and "A Kiss Before Pride," for a pre-pride party, which showcases two mustached, shirtless white men facing each other, one cupping the other's face as they both lean in for a kiss.

While the DHD party highlighting the music of disco icon Sylvester borrowed his song title "Over and Over" for the flyer, I focus here on his song "Dance (Disco Heat)," in particular the following lyrics: "Dancin's total freedom / Be yourself and choose your feelin' / Come on get up I want to see ya swingin' swayin' / Fancy slidin', glidin', rockin', reelin' / . . . Come on get up ev'rybody dance / Cookin' on my feet in the disco heat / Hustlin' through the night / Mornin' light shines on me again" (Sylvester 1978). These verses transport queers of a certain age through nostalgia into a different, seemingly bygone era of New York City. Disco musically shifts the temporality of the space from the present to the past using Sylvester's falsetto as a call for everyone to get up and dance. Dancing in this moment extends beyond the movement of gay men on a dance floor as an affirmation of their sexual identities. Gregory Bredbeck asserts that disco "was not just a space in which gay men expressed an already formed identity. It was also a key site for their interpellation as gay men" (quoted in Lawrence 2006, 147). In hosting a monthly disco function at Nowhere Bar, Jackson and Alicea hail queers into a new way of being that moves beyond the present-day homonormative politics. They create a space within Nowhere that is sonically racialized, playing soul- and gospel-charged disco tracks, drawing on Black and Brown aesthetic production through sound and accompanying gestures—the call-and-response, the clapping, the exclamation of "YES!!!" with finger snapping and waving—that signal how the sound of disco is the sound of queers of color resisting both racist state violence and homophobia. In turn, Sylvester's call to get up and dance results in the physical articulation of historically Black and Brown dance forms such as voguing. Alongside voguing, it is not uncommon for some party regulars, alongside Alicea, to place one extended arm upward, fingertips grazing the low ceiling of Nowhere, in order to runway walk through the dance floor, synchronizing their physical gestures with the music being played, visually forging a connection between DHD and old-school house/drag ball competitions frequented by communities of color. These moments make visible through practice how queer of color subjects use disco as the sonic backdrop in performing in, and creating, queer life worlds.

Moreover, in addition to challenging the antiquated cabaret laws in New York City that outlaw dancing in a majority of bars and clubs, dancing during DHD also serves as a site for multigenerational, cross-racial, class-diverse, and queer (with respect to sexualities and genders) contact to occur, challenging the networking focus outside of the bar's doors. Here, Samuel R. Delany's (2001, 123–29) disambiguation of contact and networking is helpful. In *Times Square Red, Times Square Blue*, he argues for the necessity of *contact*, or the chance encounters between people who might otherwise not meet, as a way to resist New York City's increasing focus on networking. Delany uses the term *networking* to refer to the professionally organized gatherings of similarly raced and classed peoples that obfuscate any possible interaction with people that might be "different." This distinction proves useful to understanding the relationship between Nowhere Bar, Double Headed Disco, and public sex. Similar to the pre–AIDS crisis sexual practices playing on the TV screen in the bar, the random public sex acts that occur in the dark back room of Nowhere Bar hark back to the bygone era of public sex theaters that Delany frequented and wrote about.

Disco, as a temporal marker of queer identity politics serving as the party soundtrack at Nowhere Bar, allows for a return to random public sex. In writing about disco as a queer, rather than gay, mode of performance, Tim Lawrence (2006, 147) states that "the venue [does] not simply affirm" but also hails gay men "into a new way of being." While, as Lawrence writes, disco "in the beginning, was gay," with gay dancers frequenting gay clubs in order to celebrate "their newly liberated status by dancing with other men, and discover[ing] a vicarious voice in the form of disco's soul and gospel-oriented divas" (144), DHD marks Nowhere Bar as queer. Nowhere, originally and still predominantly a gay bar, now defines itself as queer, gesturing toward the sexual practices and gender identities it celebrates and promotes.

While for the older generation, the party is a vehicle that transports them back into a gay time, for the younger queers, DHD provides a different experience and offers them a new way of being, beyond that which exists outside of the doorway. For them, the party's disco soundtrack arguably functions as a form of camp and kitsch that enables their access to a historical queerness always framed as in the past. Camp enables them to rehearse "enacting [the] self against the pressures of the dominant culture's identity-denying protocols" (Muñoz 1999, 120). Camp thus also enables DHD to serve as a site of minoritarian queer worldmaking—what Muñoz (2000, 74–75) terms *everynight life*—by highlighting the potential for nightlife to operate as a "zone where the affective dominance of white normativity is weakened." I find the name of the bar useful as it literally challenges the impetus of aspirational politics, where the subject must be working toward a there: at Nowhere, there is no over there; the there is right here. Nowhere becomes one way to translate the queer utopia that Muñoz theorizes. In turn, DHD provides a homespace for the dispossessed queers looking for "a utopian nightlife community" (Muñoz 2000, 75) of shared affect and structures of feeling: feelings of nonbelonging, of nostalgia for a rapidly disappearing New York City, where queerness continues to give way to LGBT normativity and politics of reproduction, consumption, and respectability.

My position as the person who contributed to maintaining the culture of Nowhere Bar during Double Headed Disco by securing the door provided me with a unique vantage point. As a queer, Latina, butch lesbian, I inhabited a space adhering to gay social logistics—the random public sex acts that often occurred in the dark, back room at Nowhere, and the sociality fostered by the vintage porn films playing on the small television set off to the side of the dance floor—that differed from my previous experiences working in lesbian bars and nightclubs. I functioned as both within and outside of the community on the dance floor, behind the bar, and in the DJ area. I am queer but not gay, and I came to understand the lived experiences of gay men of color from a particular temporal framework, while simultaneously witnessing the shift from a markedly gay aesthetic to a contemporary queer one. It is this shift from gay to queer, from past to present, from older to younger and back again, both through sound and movement, that allows for a queer, Brown butch like me to also find a home and heed Sylvester's call to get up and dance, at least for one Saturday night a month.

"people bring their histories to the club"

An Interview with DJ Rekha

Kareem Khubchandani

Rekha Malhotra, known as DJ Rekha, was born in 1971 and grew up in a middle/working-class Indian family on Long Island, New York. They started DJing in the early 1990s and are credited with making Bhangra music central to South Asian club culture in the United States. Bhangra is a Punjabi folk music and dance form that originates in northern regions of India and southwestern parts of Pakistan, and that saw important growth in the British diaspora beginning in the 1980s. Rekha's party, Basement Bhangra, which started in 1997 in New York City and ran for twenty years, made the diasporic and subcontinental Punjabi sound central to US club culture. We see the legacy of this cultural work in the sampling of bhangra in tracks from Britney Spears, Jay-Z, and Missy Elliott. But as Rekha makes clear in our interview, predating and surrounding their contribution to bhangra is their journey into DJing through antiracist, feminist, and queer organizing. Though Basement Bhangra became an incredibly popular and diverse destination, its success relied on the grassroots community that Rekha cultivated before its rise. In this 2014 interview, Rekha shares their path to DJing, the curatorial approach they take to queer nightlife, and the exhausting labor of being a nightlife entrepreneur who has to do it all. Our conversation evidences the labor that precedes the beginning of a night, from the flyer and decor design, to an imagining of who the audience will be in order to develop the right sound, to the migration histories, educational experiences, and radical activism that shape nightlife communities.

KAREEM: How did you get involved in the desi performance-music-activism scene in New York?

REKHA: I was doing activism before I was doing music. I got involved as a college student, when a couple of key things happened. One: in New York, we had a wave of violence against South Asians in '87, the Dotbusters [a white

Fig. 1. Portrait of DJ Rekha. (Photograph by Sangament Media.)

supremacist group targeting South Asians, people who "wear dots" on their heads]. The most famous case is Navroze Mody, who got killed. But there was a second really violent notable case, a doctor named Kaushal Saran, who was left for dead, beaten in front of a fire station around the same time. By the time his trial came up for civil court there was a movement aground to rally around him and AALDEF [Asian American Legal Defense and Education Fund] was organizing, and there was this batch of people that were about five years older than me that were in law school or young lawyers or in grad school that had done some organizing work around the Navroze Mody case. I also interned at Sakhi [a South Asian gender justice organization]. I didn't grow up with a lot of South Asian peers. I got to college. I went to a commuter school. There were a lot of South Asians. There were a lot of desis. I got very involved. A very important person was this professor, Dr. Madhulika Khandelwal, who's done a lot of early writing on communities of Indians in Flushing. She was really important. We all went to protests together and that was kind of my first taste of community and activism.

Independent of that, things were happening within our community. We sort of started seeing the emergence of South Asian DJs. My cousins were in high school and we connected on music, so we kinda just put our nickels together to buy tracks and equipment. The second DJ gig I ever did was as an intern at Sakhi. I volunteered our services, our DJ crew, and—

KAREEM: For a fundraiser, or—

REKHA: Yeah, it was one of their fundraisers. And, one thing led to another and a lot of my early gigs were community events.

KAREEM: So, prior to Basement Bhangra, were you doing—

REKHA: Basement Bhangra was in '97. I was in plenty of things before then.

KAREEM: When you started Basement Bhangra, was that, for lack of a better way of phrasing it, was there some queer intentionality there?

REKHA: There wasn't any conscious intentionality, but it was a very queer space.

KAREEM: 'Cause of you and your people you—

REKHA: I think because of me, because these were my social circles, Sakhi, and lawyers, and the desi community. And the drag queens used to come a lot. But that party just grew to a level where I don't even know what hit me, and I didn't know who was coming. And there were definitely some bumpy things to deal with. After Basement, I started Bollywood Disco, and I really wanted to make it a gay/straight space, and I think that was really tough because homophobic people didn't respect the space. And gay people were like, "We also don't wanna be in that kind of space." It's kind of hard. Dancing is really personal, you know?

KAREEM: Will you talk about that more? It sounds like you tried to have a mixed space. But people also get possessive over what's *their* space.

REKHA: I mean, people bring their histories to the club, they have their desires. It's the nature of consumer culture. As a DJ, you're always negotiating what people know and what they don't know and what you wanna tell them, always. And you're always trying to be tempered about how you present; at least, I am. An amateur DJ will play all the hits really fast the minute the party starts. You wanna build. You wanna create a moment. You wanna create an experience. People aren't going to dance to songs and music they don't connect with personally. I just think that there's a certain cultural baggage that South Asians of a certain class in the diaspora bring, this culturally specific expectation of service, a "Where's my tea?" culture. I was for hire, and sometimes I felt like the music *naukar* [servant]. As an artist, let me tell you, no DJ in the world wants a request. DJs can share stories for hours about stupid requests: "Do you have an iPhone plug?" and "Can I keep my bag here?" and "Can you play that song?" I'll be like, "I *just* played it." And they're like "Can you play it, again?" or "I'm leaving," or "I missed it." I mean . . . [shakes head].

KAREEM: You hosted Lipstick Optional, the first queer desi women's party in New York. What was it like?

REKHA: So the women's party was interesting. This woman used to own a club called Meow Mix. It was a lesbian bar, and she opened a place in Brooklyn called Caddy Shack. It was a really different space and crowd from my other parties. It wasn't Basement Bhangra. It wasn't Bollywood Disco. I got to play a lot of stuff. We had some really fun great nights there. But there were also racism and class tension. Just 'cause people are gay, it doesn't mean you're always gonna get along. It just doesn't mean there's not structural racism that enters a space or structural classism, down to the bartenders and the way they treat different people. Then I got complaints that my crowd is not drinking enough. I'm like, "You're not serving them right!"

I think that we create a space that's welcoming, but it's also no frills; it kind of has an energy that says, "Don't fuck with us." I'm not big on being very decorative, or wearing costumes. I want it to be a club night that happens to play South Asian music. Those are the signals I personally give out. And, I've been to other parties and I've DJed at other parties where they play a lot of Bollywood and they'll dress up, and I really hate that. I read that as culture on display unnecessarily, and then I feel like we're creating our own objects of fetish, you know? I just want it to be a club. It's not a wedding. You don't need to dress up. Journalists have written up about Basement Bhangra and they've talked about women in saris, and that doesn't even happen!

KAREEM: Next dream party that you wanna—

REKHA: I'm sick of . . . [sighs]. I just wanna play. I don't like being the one throwing parties. It's exhausting. I mean, I have bits and pieces of help.

It's not like I'm completely alone, but I don't have a staff. I have people who are freelancers, they come and go. And when it's just me I'm like, "Let me write another exciting e-mail about this party I've done seven hundred times. And what's new *this* time?" It's like, I like throwing events but I don't like the marketing and that stuff, and it keeps changing. It sometimes feels like you're reduced to some sort of high school popularity contest, and especially as I'm aging I'm like, "Am I still cool anymore? How come there's a few less people this month?" or, "Oh no, something else is happening that night. Is everyone gonna go *there*? Everyone *said* they were coming!" and it's just that. It's nerve racking.

KAREEM: Where do you see yourself fitting in the larger story of New York's nightlife?

REKHA: I don't know. Sometimes, I feel like I'm really part of that story and sometimes I feel like I'm invisible in that story. In New York City, when we started, we got a lot of acclaims and recognition in nightlife, but as we've become a stalwart, we're not the new kids on the block anymore. It's amazing to me that despite how long I've been doing this, it'll be someone's first time at Basement, or someone'll be like, "I've actually never made it." I'm like, "Really?" But, that's how New York is. You hear about things and grow up there your whole life and you've just never gone to the Statue of Liberty or whatever. Yeah, sometimes I feel a part of it. Sometimes I don't, you know?

Inside

Pedagogies of the Dark

Making Sense of Queer Nightlife

Eddie Gamboa

Prompt: Fill in the blanks with your favorite obscenity. If the blank is already filled, say it out loud, becoming more emphatic each time you see a filled-in blank, more boisterous, more . . . lusty.

[   ] is animated by the dark, whose opacity serves as an invitation to practice queer sexualities. Chain-linked fence braided with the rubber of discarded tires obfuscates a mass of undulating bodies, fumbling around as forces of nature compel orbits of attraction and repulsion, men coming toward and moving away from one another. Sweat saturates the air with a musk that sticks to the skin of the nose, until it vanishes by seeping into you. A grunt to the left that only makes me burrow my gaze deeper into my drink, adjusting my ears to the music being pumped into the room, and trying not laugh when I recognize Carly Rae Jepson's "Call Me Maybe" setting the rhythm for the sex happening throughout the room. My eyes are still adjusting to the clashing dim orange hues of the lamp that hovers too close to the surface of the bar, and the cool whites of the projection screen mounted to the wall. On it, pornographic scenes provide the backlight so that we all sit in a kind of darkness, the kind where the only things one can see are the shadows of textures—the craters of denim, the cracks in concrete, the folds and wrinkles of flesh. Of course, this loose collection of snapshots does not clarify [   ] as a site of queer nightlife so much as calibrate one to a style of queer nightlife. Which is to say that these moments serve as forms of ephemera that manifest in the dark, and thus rely on a preservation of the dark's opacity in order to get a *sense* of them (Muñoz 1996, 6).

For those who find themselves in this basement, the dark is not merely a comfort, but a constitutive element of their queer identities and sexual practice. Obviously, there is a storied history of queer subjects relying on the dark as a refuge, a space and time that provide a reprieve from violent surveillance networks and enable opportunities for self-expression, connection, and community formation. Stretching across literal dark alleyways and metaphorical closets, opportune moments seized in tearooms and the comforts of nighttime economies, the dark frequently provides the backdrop for the rehearsal of queer eroticism. However, the dark is more than a setting for possibility, the dark is also an orientation that develops a style of sexual pedagogy. On a practical level, being in the dark can be disorienting, disrupting the repetition that produces our compulsory movement as the body searches its repertoire to improvise new gestures that provide a *sense* of where, when, and who we are as light fades (Ahmed 2006, 158). For those meeting in this basement, a space designed to facilitate immediate, "impersonal" erotic contact, darkness functions as a rehearsal space where queer men practice forms of sexual relations, learning how to be together in the dark.

Night is not merely a time or place in which the opportunity to be queer arises, but rather a pedagogical method for imagining, practicing, and sustaining queerness itself (Palmer 2000, 290). In this chapter, I am interested in what constitutes a pedagogy of the dark, which I understand as a mode of cultural knowledge production. Performance provides an ideal framework for interrogating the sexual pedagogies of the night, given its focus on the body as a *sense*-making organism, attending to the information accumulated through the senses and put into practice vis-à-vis embodied experiences with self, space, and others. In the dark, senses are reoriented, and we learn to sense differently, meaning that we learn to make sense queerly. It is sense making, a necessary precondition to worldmaking, that I center within this work.

Yet to merely describe the pedagogy vital to practicing queerness in [ ] is a double-edged sword. On one side, it is impossible to interrogate the practices that make a queer erotic site like [ ] possible without rendering it susceptible to surveillance and regulation that too often target queer subjects (Heap 2003, 460–63). If the dark is imagined as a site of refuge, then scholarship, even in good faith, shines a light that banishes the precarious cover already extended to these outlaw intimacies. Laud Humphreys (1970, 188), whose infamous ethnographic examination of men engaging in scenes of improvisational sex in public restrooms featured a wide array of ethical questions, argued that the suspension of our consideration for the safety of shadows was crucial for the "pursuit of truth, the creation of countervailing knowledge, the *demystification of shadow areas of human experience*" (italics added). On the other side, description alone limits our ability as readers to develop our own sense of the dark. The opacity of queer sexual spaces demands imagination, even from those who are distant from them—to fill in the gaps of what we cannot see with a fantasy. Lee Edelman (1994) uses the scenario of the cop entering the tearoom to explain this concept. In it, a cop can walk into a bathroom to find a man pressing his hips into the partition of a bathroom stall and produce a narrative that concludes the man is having sex, and what kind of sex he must be having. If a crucial element of learning is participation, then we must extend the opportunities to make sense of the dark to the reader in ways informed by, but distinct from, what can be documented.

As a preliminary response to these dilemmas, I am interjecting a series of performance prompts throughout the text that I invite the reader to participate in, one of which served as the epigraph to this chapter. Moving through the darkened spaces of the gay club encourages a multisensorial engagement with the environment, others who occupy it, and our relation to both. The sensorial is a crucial mode of approaching a pedagogy of the dark and disrupting the voyeuristic comfort of the reader through an alternative form of engagement, a queer reading practice. I extend a queer tradition of incorporating the body into scholarship and memory, a tradition that is often found in appendices or scattered throughout texts and that always brings the queer(ed) to the sensational: the recipes found in E. Patrick Johnson's (2008) oral history *Sweet Tea: Black Gay Men of the South* and the Lady Chablis'(1996) autobiography *Hiding My Candy*; the choreographic and linguistic lessons showcased throughout Jennie Livingston's (1990) documentary *Paris Is Burning*; the illustrations and advertisements tucked away in the gay/lesbian section at Barnes & Noble that made palms sweat and opened possibilities.

I gesture toward these queer pedagogues for their interventions in the documentation of queer nightlife, which inspire, and are inspired by, a pedagogy of the dark—a sense-based method that seduces and indoctrinates as a means of survival. I use the prompts, which were written with men I interviewed in [ ], as a means of queerly orienting the reader to the aims of this chapter, which are twofold: first, to identify methods of cultural transmission crafted by individuals who participate in the gay sexual cultures that populate [ ]; second, and parallel to the first, to enact a pedagogy of the dark through the chapter, as a means of creating the conditions of readers to make sense of this work, as well as to maintain the darkness that makes [ ] each night.

Prompt: Spell out the name you like to be called in a moment of passion by circling letters on this page.

The streetlights bounce off the windows, amplifying its reflective quality and making it easier to see myself inside [ ]. It is 11:30 on a brisk October night as I stand at the door, trying to scrape my ID from my wallet as my stomach begins to drop. The door pulses to a beat, although the music on the other side is barely audible where I am standing, as if the building shivers to my approaching hand while masking how far I will actually travel once I pass through the sheer white curtains that greet each visitor. [ ] is a collective of queer-identified bars and businesses on Chicago's North Side. A set of posters line the wall featuring the usual cadre of nameless men, their manicured bodies, tanned skin, and name-brand underwear distinguishing them from the men who populate the bar itself. I breathe a chubby, balding sigh of relief at the sight of men who look more like me.

The air is sweet, but artificially so, almost saccharine with mixed colognes and mouths rinsed with alcohol. All I wear is Old Spice deodorant, my breath still heavy with a meal hastily eaten too soon before my arrival. Blue circles clash with green lines, as red and orange backdrops alternate frames on an empty dance floor. Cutting across the dance floor, I cannot help but feel masked by shadows. It is as if the lights were designed to move around my body—briefly touching every part of me before swerving in another direction. I make my way to a stool with unsteady limbs, although whether it is the seat's legs or my own does not matter. My drink of choice is a Shirley Temple. I dig into the glass with my fingers to remove the cherries, leaving them to stain the napkin on the bar.

I note this awkwardness as a means of acknowledging those at [ ] whom I did not notice, who did not stand out to me, while simultaneously making a space for you, the reader, to accept the awkwardness of the prompts as a condition of reading this chapter. Discomfort abounds within spaces such as these, particularly among those who do not know how to act, or whose performances defy refinement. It is easy to frame this discomfort as a failure of the space to formulate the pleasures it promises (Bersani 2010, 3). However, this is to escape the inherent discomfort that makes up queer socialities. Michel Foucault (2000, 447) remarked on the importance of vulnerability as a response to masculinity, which he framed as a "nakedness" among men. It is only in this discomfort that alternative possibilities arise, or as Foucault puts it, "It's a desire, an uneasiness, a desire-in-uneasiness that exists in a lot of people" that draws people toward one another.

By extension, discomfort is not merely a queer affect, but also a racialized one. Even if [ ] is not designed as a predominantly white space, it is located within a city designed to maintain segregated populations. Granted, there are invitations to events that cater to Black, Latinx, and trans patrons advertised all over [ ]. And the family-owned Mexican restaurant next door remains open as long as the bar does, amplifying the makeshift coalitions developed by proximity. That does not dispel my discomfort as a Brown femme with a wide-set nose, flesh that hangs forward instead of expanding into broad thickness, and hair that pokes through the fabric of my clothing as I sit at the bar. Bodies of color, which may disorient in additional ways, are forced to reconcile their sensory education of the space with the sense that they may not belong (Ahmed 2006, 160). The bar is dimly saturated in a red light by the lanterns fastened above it. The screens flash brightly with scenes of white men finding pleasure anywhere: a cock sliding into a mouth in a hotel room, a hand leaving red imprints on a plump ass in the woods, a man rolling on a condom in a butcher shop. The videos never stop, consistently drawing my eye as I stand against the wall stirring my Shirley Temple. My leg shakes uncontrollably, as my body never settles into [ ].

This restlessness, the sensations that compel my eyes and legs to move, is not merely discomfort. Or at least this discomfort is not a negation of my presence within the space. Instead, it is a compulsion to performance: my body wants to move because [ ] is designed to move bodies. In this way, discomfort is not an impediment to possibility, but rather the means through which we preserve it (Roach 2012, 53). The dark evades the regulation of the day by constantly shifting, placing pressure on the body that expands what constitutes contact. A body never settles into the night, but rather trains itself to react to the ebbs and flows of the dark. Like two people contorting themselves in a cramped space in an improvisational act of public sex, such a pedagogy is about finding pleasure in the displeasurable through performance.

Prompt: Using your fingernails, trace lines into the palm of your hand. Now rub your palms together. Harder.

I am debating whether I should make my way to the basement, which would require me to strip down and leave my clothes at the coat check. It is two in the morning, and [ ] is only getting fuller. An officially sanctioned after-hours club, [ ] greets a steady stream of all those not ready to go home, or who have yet to find a home to go to. The grated steps lead to another bar area, this one much darker than the one upstairs. Around the corner is a hallway, lit only by an exit sign, where a clump of bodies cling together. The musk that fills my lungs is tinged with the scent of alcohol that has lingered on the breath too long, and bile that may not have spilled but definitely rose up. The basement is designed for immediate sexual encounters among patrons, its architecture inspired by spaces historically used by gay men looking to engage in public sex (Bérubé 2003, 40).

Sitting at the bar with me, Logan expresses comfort about moving within

[ ]. "On the dance floor, you dance. In the basement, you fuck. When you are done, you go to the bar. You've got to hit up the whole place anyway, since the coat check is up at the bar." Logan lets out a yawn, stretching the upper half of his body by raising his arms and his flannel shirt just enough to reveal a protruding belly. Logan's reflection reminds me of performance scholar Ben Spatz's (2015, 10) axiom: "You are what you do." Developing a theory of technique, Spatz argues for an agential understanding of the body, which is compelled to move in ways that are sedimented into it through aesthetic and quotidian training. Within the confines of [ ], patrons enter into specific relations not only with one another, but with the space that induces identities that are intimately attached to the bodily movements that are both demanded by and attracted to those very spaces. In other words, [ ] operates as a microcosm of broader nighttime economies, often imagined as a carnivalesque suspension of prohibitions, but in actuality highly regulated, directing bodies and acts to specific locales and inviting specific modes of being for the right price (Lefebvre 1970, 320). [ ]'s areas are deliberately designed to invite performances of being, and being together, a classroom that enables experimentation and contains possibilities within a designated area.

Thus we have a site that compels performance, as it shapes how those performances manifest. And yet [ ] cannot stop the leakages throughout the space. The effects of intoxication carry scents and tastes from one area to the next, interrupting scenes and sparking new ones. Men meet at the coat check and initiate their sexual encounters as they move between spaces. Queer performance supersedes the confines of the markets that seek them out, or are established to corral them. A pedagogy of the dark is one that is highly structured, but never certain of its placement. As the patrons move about the space, it is easy to get lost in the shuffle and submit to the compulsion to perform—whether it is grabbing the body closest to you, feeling your drinks coming back up, or simply removing a coat and finding yourself feeling around in the dark. It is just that kind of night.

Prompt: Reach for a zone of your body you do not consider erogenous. Rub it until you make a sound. Or the skin breaks. Or both.

Four in the morning, nearly closing time, and the dance floor remains barren with the exception of a few couples that twirl across as they make their way toward the exit. The basement is closed for the night, meaning no one else is getting fucked tonight . . . at least not here. There is a frustration charging the room, although many patrons seem more concerned with winding down than animating the space with dance, with sex, with their bodies. That is, until one man takes to the dance floor, wearing nothing but a jockstrap. A lone being on the dance floor, whose performance serves as not only a reminder, but a rearticulation, a redeployment, a reperformance of the basement's sexual possibilities.

He leans against the bar, glass in hand, blending into the scene as just another man in [ ]. A prerecorded mix of Gina Star's "I Want It Now" blares from the speakers, and his hips begin to move from left to right ever so slightly. Behind him, the pornography playing seems to synch up to the beat as if it were planned, as if bodies were destined to move to this song. Men fuck as he begins to tap his foot, his eyes glued to the screen. Suddenly he throws back his drink. As he moves toward the dance floor, the lights begin to swirl around him.

It begins in his knees, which bounce up and down slightly off the beat of the music. His hips are swinging more forcefully, his pelvis thrusting slightly forward before pushing violently back, drawing attention to his ass framed by the jockstrap. Feet remain perfectly still as if he is glued to this spot, as if he is making room for other bodies on a crowded dance floor even though he stands alone. Hands roam his body, beginning at his slightly protruding belly, coming up his chest, his neck, his head, lifting higher and higher as he feels his arms, his hands twisting into each other. The music has hit one of many crescendos as he shuts his eyes, his body beginning to swivel without fully turning. A green light cuts across his body as he undulates, surrounded by invisible men pressing against his backside. I know those movements because I have done them before. He does them alone, crowded not by bodies but by spirits. The beat continues as the song fades into the next, and his body begins to slow.

Prompt: Place your shirt over your nose and inhale until you remember the person, place, or time that made you smell this way. Hold it in.

What compelled the Dancer remains a mystery—the music, or an arousal, or simply a body helpless to the call of queer performance. No matter the reason, the dance ended as jaggedly as it began, with a stumble toward the bar. He reaches for his empty glass and takes one of the ice cubes into his mouth. He resumes his stance from before, his eyes returning to the same pornographic scene, one leg crossed over the other. I look back to the empty dance floor.

Prompt: Come back up for air.

Improvisational dance in the club is the constellation composed of past performances, gestures etched into the body that enable it to imagine forms of movement to this beat, to this room, to this crowd. Kinesthetic awareness, or the awareness of one's body and the body's awareness of its environment, serves as a crucial experimental space in which queer people develop a shared sense of moving—and, more importantly, being—together (Buckland 2002, 93). This is true in a literal sense: negotiating the parameters of the space and the proximity to others with movement patterns that evoke, or provoke, different ways of relating to others is a necessity on the dance floor. In other words, the dance within the queer club is a moment of learning how to move, and who to move with, as a collective (97). At the same time, improvisational dance contains the possibility of a kinetic sociality, but a glimpse into queer worlds destroyed and worlds renewed. For example, queer people of color on the dance floor interrupt the presumed whiteness of many queer locales through an improvisational technique informed through racialized, embodied referents that manifest into style (Rivera-Servera 2012, 149–50). Dancing queers are radically present, building a world from the embodiment of the past to practice another world all together, one that will last the night. Or perhaps it will only last a moment, a moment that settles into the body, ready for the next opportunity, the next night.

Yet this Dancer is not invoking just any elsewhere. Rather he is wholly invested in summoning a particular elsewhere, the sexual spaces whose closure demands a different sort of performance. His dance is as much an act of translation as it is documentation, much like the ethnographic project we find ourselves in now. This is evidenced in multiple ways: First, his attire, which is starkly different from that of those present. Most are casually dressed, an abundance of jeans and flannel meant to accentuate a hipster masculinity as much as to shield from the Chicago January creeping outside. The jockstrap is emblematic of the basement's dress code, which requires men to strip down to their underwear. The Dancer holds no investment in the sartorial choices of the men who chose to come into the bar, and is more beholden to a policy meant to not only regulate but facilitate erotic contact. Second, his movements, which I understand as inspired not by the genre of music, but rather by how he was able to move to such movement in the past. While there are a variety of ways to dance, this dance functions as a translation, not quite a simulation, but rather a memory of the body that facilitates such movement. The pelvic thrusts, which move slightly forward before taking two steps back, so to speak, are the clearest reference. Bottom to bottom, femme to femme, I see him very clearly.

The dance is an ethnography in its own right, although like any lesson it is taken up in any number of ways—from the crowd members who dismiss it to those of us who watch and especially to the man who takes the Dancer out of the bar. It is a sensorial contact that extends toward multiple audiences, seducing them into a myriad of relationalities, beyond titillation through passive description. We are left with a carnal documentation, a knowing that emanates from the body or, as Amber Jamilla Musser (2014, 20) puts it, a shift away "from understanding the other as unified and transparently available to us and [an invitation] to experience affinities on a corporeal level with others through sensation. . . . [This] allows us to grapple with the position of the other while maintaining a sense of the impersonal flows that bind things together."

Prompt: Place the text underneath your thighs. Spread your legs wide enough to keep reading. Now keep reading.

And here is where the night should end. Here is where many nights do end, on the sidewalk crowded with taxi hails and drunken laughter. But an epilogue sears its way into the chapter, a violent interruption that forecloses the possibility of ending with a romanticized gesture toward queer memory. Because it is impossible to remember what we bring with us without acknowledging what we have lost along the way. On a Wednesday evening in June, this acknowledgment brought me back to [ ], where a group of Latinx queers happened to find one another on the anniversary of the Pulse nightclub shooting. I want to say it was unintentional, improvisational, but perhaps this meeting was preordained. Where else could we go to mourn?

It had only been a year since we met, gathering on a corner-turned-altar in honor of the forty-nine mostly Black and Brown queers killed in Orlando, Florida. Earlier that day, there was a vigil on a pier overlooking Lake Michigan as the sun set. The wind would not allow candles to remain lit; spattered raindrops refused to let tears flow alone. We each left alone, walking quietly back to our lives, only to find one another again at [ ]. That night, cumbia and merengue never stopped playing, and our bodies never stopped moving. Pan dulce some brought from home was shared as much as the liquor. Two women climbed onto a stage, each cupping the other's face while moving closer, grinding into each other, smiles never losing any ground on their faces. Because the only way we knew to mourn was to live, and this is how we had learned to live, in the dark like this, unapologetically swallowing one another.

Here, the practice of mourning is rehearsed in gestures of pleasure, reaching into the past to make moving into the future bearable. There is *something* to coming here, separately, and finding one another, finding comfort in the excessive repetition. We are not doing anything new, yet we are making something new and familiar, something akin to hope, something like utopia. On this particular night, in which the demographics are vastly different as mostly Black and Brown bodies congregate on the dance floor, and in the basement, and at the bar, and in the DJ booth, we find ourselves doing what we do best: living a queer future. Reflecting on that night, a friend I made reminisced that we were "fucking with depression." Not only were we physically connecting despite what we had lost, and what we will lose, a reality we cannot escape even by traveling to other queer worlds, we were also disrupting the negative's hold on our lives—fucking with how the depressive is expressed.

It is this experimentation that marks the kinds of documentation that pedagogies of the night invite, the ethnographies we write to teach others how to navigate the dark, the performances we embody that press into our bodies, make us move another way, and train our selves to want, or at least know, pressure (Musser 2014, 11). Two queer Latinas stood on a stage usually reserved for gay white men, and pressed their bodies into each other. We must learn how to do that. Because if "what we do transforms who we are," think of all the things we could be, all those we could find, if we trusted our selves enough to feel our way through the dark (Spatz 2015, 53).

Prompt: Reach for the person closest to you, but never make contact. Now reach a little farther. And a little farther, but never make contact.

Queering Dancehall in the Diaspora

Sabia McCoy-Torres

In a West Indian neighborhood–based Brooklyn dancehall party promoted to attract the community's most enthusiastic performers, I notice Paws Ambush, a local dancer. She consistently draws the attention of partygoers with her impassioned and skilled exhibitions of dancehall movement. Not only is Paws Ambush the only woman in her otherwise all-male dance crew, she is the only woman member of any dance crew in the party. Unlike the outfits of other women dancers in the club, there is nothing intentionally sexy about what Paws Ambush wears: a cropped zipped-up jacket, jeans, and sneakers. Rather notably, she also dances in a style that, within dancehall's heavily gendered vocabulary of movements, is more common to see men perform.

As the crowd of observers around her dance crew grows, Paws Ambush suddenly charges into the empty space formed between her crew and the spectators. She slides into the semicircle, zigzagging to claim space, with her face forming an intense grimace that captures her impending forceful and energetic execution of movements. Her body motions in polyrhythm, contracting and releasing. It mirrors the various overlapping percussive elements characteristic of dancehall: pounding and deep, to the point of distortion, bass overlaid by hi-hat cymbals that mark the down and up beats, while the snare alternates every few measures between accenting only the down beat and marking both the down and up.[1] Paws Ambush's body hits multiple beats at once. Her arms form diagonal shapes as she then swiftly cuts the air between them with sharp, sweeping motions. Her torso energetically pumps forward and back while she traverses the floor. Her face continues to illustrate the intensity of the music and her movement. It commands attention as she asserts her position within the crew and demonstrates her exceptional skill on the dance floor.

The others in Paws Ambush's crew stand back, avidly bouncing and waving their arms in support, as she occupies a multidimensional space with varying levels of verticality, her feet rhythmically marking intricate geometric designs on the dance floor. During a percussive and bass-heavy explosion in the music, Paws Ambush powerfully thrusts her body forward to mark the moment, seeming to expel all air in the space in front of her in a burst. She then slides back into formation in the semicircle as another crew member enters to take his turn impressing spectators and competing crews and drawing the attention of the party's videographer. His task is not easy as Paws Ambush's performance is a hard one to follow.

A perhaps ordinary dance moment in other settings, this one, captured in my fieldnotes from summer 2013, was quite significant for its nonconformity with prevailing gender presentation in Brooklyn-based West Indian dancehall performance spaces. A number of elements were nonconforming. Typically women are independent dancers, but Paws Ambush was a collaborative member of an otherwise all-male dance crew. Second, she performed movements that within dancehall's repertoire are typically considered masculine. Third, Paws Ambush's performance of these movements put her at odds with a conventional performance practice in dancehall—intentionally signifying gender and sexuality in accordance with its most heteronormative and gender conforming representations.

Dancers signify gender using binary modes of presentation that are widely recognized as masculine and feminine within dancehall performance, aligning these modes with their perceived gender (woman or man) within the space, which is always expected to align also with their presumed sex (female or male).[2] By rejecting feminized movements as her only available options, Paws Ambush rendered the gendering of movement irrelevant to her and demonstrated that her expression of gender would not be limited by dancehall's dominant binary constructs. The effect was to participate in a gender queer performance that, paradoxically, made the movements gender neutral if not a contestation of femininity and critique of its necessary alignment with sex.

These examples of nonconforming dance, self-presentation, and crew membership, combined with other moments in which women in New York City–based dancehall nightlife challenge prevailing representations of gender and sexuality, serve as lenses to interpret how spaces for sexually and gender queer subjectivity expression are emerging within the West Indian diaspora. Limitations on gender and sexual expressive terrain are constantly in place. Indeed, an expanding range of expression is most visible among ciswomen, which indicates a limitation affecting cismen performers in dancehall parties. Still, queer embodied performances and their value are worth examining.

Looking at women's performance in dancehall nightlife, I offer that through dancing that does not conform to gendered expectations, women manipulate the gender and sexual politics of dancehall. In effect they critique the basis of these politics and include expressions of queer Caribbean subjectivity. I use *queer* as a term to capture corporeal expression that within dancehall-style dance is considered to be hetero or gender nonconforming. I propose that through implicitly and explicitly rebellious embodied acts, women evidence the "trickster strategies" (Horton-Stallings 2007, 5) used to challenge heteronormative and heteropatriarchal performance modes, and they demonstrate ownership and self-direction of their sexualities, bodies, and corporeal narratives. Also, in transgressing gender binaries in dancehall, women disrupt reified gendered and sexual categories of expression and engagement, as well as the relationships of power on which they rest.

The dancehall nightlife venues (bars, lounges, and nightclubs) that I examined from 2011 to 2013 and intermittently into the present are considered to be heteronormative and encompassing of cisgender people. This is by far the constitution of the majority of West Indian dancehall parties in Brooklyn, where this research took place, and also Manhattan, where I conducted supplementary investigations. There are merits, however, to exploring queer locations within spaces defined by hetero- and gender normativity. The value lies precisely in the possibility of observing how queer subjectivity ruptures normativity within Caribbean social and cultural spheres. Examining these points of rupture unveils more sites of transformation than does observing isolated nightlife scenes already designated as queer. Given the ethnographic context, when I use the terms *women* and *men* I am referring specifically to ciswomen and cismen.

Exploring women's performance is fundamentally important. Women demonstrate their power, presence, and desires for embodied sexual and gender emancipation when they contest the heterosexuality, gender normativity, and male supremacy of dancehall. To observe how they manipulate patriarchy and normativity to play with relationships of power is to note the multivalent ways in which they find agency, engage in corporeal critique, and carve pathways for queer expression. Their successes change the shape of dancehall performance and nightlife. A closer look at women queering dancehall reveals the work that is done, often unintentionally, to reframe how gender, sexuality, pleasure, rebellion, autonomy, and self-determination are shaped within West Indian communities in the diaspora.

In this exploration, I begin first by offering a closer reading of Paws Ambush's skilled dance attack to interpret how it ruptures confining constructions of gender presentation in a performance that amounts to queering dancehall. I then move on to an examination of dance between women that can be read as a critique of heteronormativity and male supremacy, one that offers up room for expressing queer subjectivity.

WORKING AGAINST DANCEHALL'S GENDER BINARY MOVEMENT

Dancehall-style dance, around which a global culture is formed, is highly gendered. Some movements more typically constitute women's style of dance, and others define men's. Nothing about Paws Ambush's exhibition detailed above carried the flare of women's movement in dancehall, such as highly stylized wining waists; smiling, stoic, or "attitude gyal" facial expressions; pronounced chest and butt movements; circular movements of the head; or languid, liquid motions.[3] Her movements did not conform to gendered choreographies such as the "hot wuk" (hot walk) and "dutty wine" (dirty wine), or more recently the "bubble" and "bruk back" (broken back), that women typically perform. These dances are characterized by dramatized circular motions of the head, waist, and hips, sharp pelvic contractions, and energetic bouncing of the buttocks. These movements accent vibrations of butt cheeks, breasts, the whipping hair, and also the vagina to directly point to corporeal markers of femininity. The dichotomous attachments of motion to a gender binary tend to be widely maintained.

There is such a thing as gender-neutral movements, for example, transition steps like gliding from one space to another or slapping one's knee or thigh to mark a change between movements, and the dances that dancehall artists make popular by creating songs to match them. These include the "nuh linga" (don't linger), "Willie bounce," and "tek weh yuhself" (take away yourself). What makes these dances gender neutral is the absence of movements that signify corporeal distinctions that, in the dancehall aesthetic, are associated with the feminine or an imagined feminine aura: butts, breasts, hair, and fluid movements, for example. They also do not incorporate aesthetic references to the masculine, such as performances of violence like using imaginary assault rifles to spray invisible bullets into the air.

Contrary to gender binary dancehall movements, Paws Ambush's dancing revealed the hallmarks of the men's style of dance, including high-energy, aggressive, sharp movement attacks; angular motions; traversal of space, intricate geometric footwork; and experimentation with fast-tempo, up-and-down vertical motions. She demonstrated what Jonathan Bollen (2001, 304) refers to as *queer kinesthesia* or "a kinesthetic disruption of naturalized, gender appropriate action." Her moment of improvisation, along with her membership in the crew, connoted a form of queer kinesthesia in its distinction from broader expectations of women's gendered performance.

In addition to Paws Ambush's decidedly defeminized dancing, her name, a part of her self-presentation, is not in keeping with those that women dancers tend to choose for themselves to invoke constructions of femininity, such as Diamond, Foxy, Likkle [Little] Bit, or Slim. On the contrary, her name invokes masculinity in similarly gendered terms, capturing the aggressiveness of war in "Ambush" and a ruggedness tied to the animalesque in "Paws." Indeed, she is a force of ambush on the dance floor, and her exhibition of power and skill among the men alludes to a ruggedness. Furthermore, the gender neutrality of Paws Ambush's outfit demonstrated her desire to not be read as a gendered, or at the very least feminine, subject. This desire falls outside the conventional practices of gender representation in West Indian nightlife.

Paws Ambush's crew membership, self-stylization, and dancing evidence how the "cultural politics of movement" (Cvetkovich 2001, 320) can be manipulated to affect and corporeally critique gendered politics in dance spaces. Fashion and naming are further complements to practices that manipulate gender binaries in revolt against conformity. To choose to perform in ways that counter prevailing gender constructs in dancehall is to open up space for, and make visible, queer subjectivity. To do so within West Indian social and cultural places and nightlife is to unveil the myriad Caribbean subjectivities that are contained within them.

Nonnormative gender presentations in dancehall—like those of Paws Ambush—are becoming more expansively popular and observable as the years of my continuing research go by. This is especially the case as Brooklyn dance crews that notably decode the gendering of movement gain recognition. The choreography of Blacka Di Danca, an internationally revered, male, Brooklyn-born dancer of Trinidadian origin, and his collaborations with women stand as examples. His choreography, which he teaches internationally and which often goes viral within dancehall community digital spaces when he uploads his dance videos to platforms like YouTube and Instagram, invites women to join in the degendering of movements once deemed specifically masculine. As women around the world—from India, Sweden, Japan, and Croatia to Brooklyn and Miami—participate in the global dance challenges that Blacka initiates and upload videos of themselves performing his choreography, they join in challenging dancehall's gender constructs. In doing so, they collectively contribute to queering dancehall and make the counternormative normative. Such global actions are physical and digital illustrations of the agentive decoding taking place in the dancehall parties I analyze here, like Paws Ambush's exhilarating show. Effectively, what has been denoted as queer is becoming a new and more inclusive gender-freeing dance practice.

I see these deconstructions of gender and dance as evidence of the mobility accessed through migration that emancipates queer subjectivities and offers room for increasingly diverse representations of gender and sexuality in the West Indian diaspora (McCoy-Torres 2018). It must be noted and underscored, however, that what is specifically decoded and re-envisioned is women's performances of dancehall movements that participants deem to be masculine rather than men's execution of dance that participants interpret as feminine. Indeed this contrast is evidence of the firmer boundaries guarding the gendering of men's dance, which reflects deeper social dynamics informing the intimacies of West Indian social spaces both inside and outside of dancehall nightlife, dynamics that limit the extent of corporeal liberation. Next, I turn to a form of performance that comments on heterosexuality, (homo)eroticism, male supremacy, and their representation in dancehall nightlife. I suggest that it is a form of commentary that emancipates queer subjectivity.

PLEASURE, APPRECIATION, AND DESTABILIZATION OF GENDERED PERFORMANCE ROLES

On the Lower East Side of Manhattan at a weekly Caribbean Reggae Night party (which includes dancehall) that Afro-Caribbean people nearly exclusively populate, a pair of women dance closely together to dancehall music. One is bent in front of the other, wining her waist and bouncing her booty up and down all in the same motion. She is close enough to the woman with whom she dances that her skirt swishes from side to side as it brushes the most superficial surface of the groin of her partner's tight jeans. She has a smile on her face and presses the tip of her tongue between her teeth as if to illustrate the fun and pleasure she is experiencing, and to suggest that her performance can be considered a tease.

The partner behind her takes on the role that men typically assume in dancehall movement exchanges. She angles her pelvis slightly forward and follows the woman's slow wine and fast wine, moving around and around, and occasionally forward and back, shadowing the movements of the woman before her. They together mark the rhythmic and percussive changes in the music. The standing woman's face shows both focus and fun. She occasionally chants some sounds of encouragement: "oooooh!" or "eyyyyy!" The women around them, who are clearly friends of the two (who are also obviously friends), chant in support as they also wine up their waists while spectating.

Like Paws Ambush, these women move counter to prevailing conventions of women's dance. Indeed, they invert the accepted ways of presenting gender roles. These roles are best evidenced in what I call *performed eroticism*, partnered dancing in which a woman leads a man who is standing behind her and who is expected to keep up with her moving waist, hips, and butt as she wines before him (McCoy-Torres 2017). In these exchanges, the woman is positioned as, and performs the role of being, the center of pleasure. Of course, being the center of pleasure is not exclusive of receiving pleasure. To be a source of pleasure is also often to experience it. The roles of pleasure giver and receiver are both quite active. The standing partner—again, typically a man—must demonstrate his ability to keep up with the moves of the woman before him or lose his opportunity to indulge in the pleasures of dancing with her, making his effort all the more imperative.

Women are empowered actors in these corporeal narratives when they control the dialogue, which is often the case. They lead dance exchanges with their mastery and skillful execution of movement, from their position as the prize, and as gatekeepers of access to their bodies. Already, in its heteronormative execution, performed eroticism alludes to and destabilizes dichotomizing concepts of sex acts and their gendered spatial coordinates, which imagine pleasure giver as masculine (and top), and receiver as feminine (and bottom). Ultimately, performed eroticism reads as a form of play and challenge as opposed to an interaction intending to lead to sexual engagement. It is also a way of exhibiting sexuality.

In moments like the one detailed above, two women re-create performed eroticism's corporeal discourse, but without the heterosexuality, thereby confusing the gender binary. Still, the woman who is standing and the receiver in such reenactments usually gestures in ways that are observed of men in heteronormative performed eroticism—biting her lips, showing satisfaction in her ability to keep up with her partner, puffing out a boastful chest in her brief moment of attention. In other words, the standing woman performs, if not embodies, specific representations of masculinity that are common in dancehall. In turn, by engaging in performed eroticism together, women gesture toward certain gender roles in dance that allude to stereotypes of sex acts, biology, and their connection to spatial orientation. However, when women subvert these gendered sexual constructs, the corporeal discourse of performed eroticism enacts a relationship that does not depend on traditional gendered dance roles or the sex acts and biologized spatial orientations they allude to. Women effectively define and demonstrate alternative ways of being that exceed these roles.

The intentionality of the exchange and the proximity of women while dancing highlight their sexual independence, exhibiting other possibilities for embodying and expressing sexual and gender subjectivity and pressing normative gender and sexual constructs to their limits.[4] These expressions are decidedly queer within heteronormative and male-supremacist dancehall nightlife and its accepted forms of representation. In such moments of interaction, women are agents of unconcerned and liberating revelry, and offer embodied exhibitions of diverse gender and sexual subjectivities. The excitement visible among women queering performed eroticism seems to originate precisely in their indulgence in rebelliously subverting dancehall's gendered roles and, by extension, the biologized spatial orientations of sex roles the dance alludes to. In doing so, they also playfully displace male supremacy and heteronormativity. Beyond subversion, this type of dance exchange between women demonstrates a complex economy of pleasure that brings into question its very spatial coordinates and gendering.

When women engage in performed eroticism among themselves, I see it as having introspective erotic qualities that are reflective of the embodied pleasure and gratification that arise from celebrating and claiming ownership of one's physical being (McCoy-Torres 2017). In turn, women enact their self-appreciation by illustrating their indulgence and appreciation for other women as reflections of themselves. In other words, self-adoration is a reflexive process connected not only to self, but also to the mutual recognition, appreciation, and awe of other women. Indeed, that reflexive process is inextricably linked to love, both for oneself and for the other, who, when women dance together, is a reflection of self.

When performed eroticism is introspective and illustrates love for one's self through admiration of the other, it is aligned with framings of the erotic as a spiritual resource (Lorde 1993) that is crucial to autonomy and self-possession (Alexander 1997) and allows for a liberatory self-governed sexuality (Allen 2011). Through mutual recognition and rapture, women show love for themselves as seen in the reflection of the other, and also show love for the other. The introspective yet exchanged dimensions of performed eroticism are especially significant in light of the ways in which women are competitively pitted against one another in broader social spaces. They are also important to creating opportunities for the veneration of bodies that have been historically dehumanized, contemporarily delegitimized, and systemically left unprotected and undervalued. Such performance acts can, thereby, effectively be read as political and representative of gender and sexual emancipation.

The queering of performed eroticism offers a view of the micro-register embodied ways in which Caribbean people work in plain sight to contest the boundaries of hetero- and gender normativity in dancehall, and by extension in Caribbean sociocultural life. By reading the affective structures that the dance produces, we come away with more complex tools to understand the shifting subjectivities that are produced in dancehall scenes. These embodied performances further invite us to consider networks of feeling, reflection, reflexivity, and sensuous experience that are untethered from sexual desire, an optic that is foregrounded in queer studies. In turn, they open up avenues for interpreting the dynamism of queer subjectivity and its expression.

This is not to imply that the act of queering performed eroticism or the queer dimensions of its introspection are exclusive of sexual desire. Rather, while they can be indicative of sexual desire and orientation, they are not necessarily so. Indeed, many women who participate in these embodied exchanges do not identify as lesbian, gay, bi, queer, questioning, or anywhere in between. I put forth, however, that this does not mean performed eroticism among women—or its attachments to introspective eroticism and gender nonconforming dance—is not queer. On the contrary, these embodied acts exemplify West Indian women's refusal to be contained and defined by gender and sexual constructs, heteronormative *or* otherwise, and are thus reflective of queer subjectivities. Indeed, their emancipatory insistence on gender and sexual performance considered to be nonnormative in dancehall disrupts "the order of things" (Ahmed 2006, 161) in ways that emphasize the queer West Indian subjectivities mobilized in the diaspora.

The performed eroticism between women that I am describing and the acceptance of it gesture to some ways in which West Indian immigrants to the United States describe their increasingly tolerant attitudes toward LGBTQ communities (McCoy-Torres 2018). This is especially true for those who immigrated to the United States as teens or adults, particularly men. Increasing tolerance provides the platform on which West Indian women can engage in "trickster strategies" (Horton-Stallings 2007, 5), according to which hidden critiques take shape in plain sight. Women engage in such strategies by experimenting with dance that transgresses sexed and gendered norms of embodied expression. Effectively, if not necessarily intentionally, such actions demand that diverse representations of gender and sexuality be reckoned with in dancehall. The implicitly rebellious acts of dancehall tricksters demonstrate women's ownership and self-direction of their sexualities, their bodies, and their corporeal narratives.

Here, another aspect of desire comes into focus, the desire to declare, through exhibition, agency over one's body. This desire has a self-pleasing effect, connoting an important sensorial element of embodied practice. While indulging one another in self-possession (and what we might call by extension "reflexive-possession"), women show that expressions of gratification and sexuality can exist independently of men, as an explicitly agentive practice among women. Sexually subversive, woman-affirming trickster strategies come to the fore to manipulate the social politics of dancehall as they relate to gender and sexuality. Indeed, women dancing together, or dancing in gender nonconforming ways, unveil "the microagencies of dancerly acts" (Rivera-Servera 2016, 96).

CONCLUSION

Women queering performed eroticism, and the liberatory and subversive critique I suggest it offers, is vulnerable to the criticism that it is in service of the male gaze and not the politics of inverting tropes of gender, sex, and sexuality. To this critique I would respond that women's intimate dancing is not considered a male visual attraction or spectacle in dancehall nightlife as it might be in other popular performance spaces. If they are spectating, which they do not always do, men are generally unengaged observers of queer performed eroticism. They do not cheer on as women friends might. They also do not intervene through gestures of rejection or derisive language, instead holding rather passive positions. Their choice to observe in a disengaged manner, or not observe at all, signals indifference at least and ambivalence at most, rather than enjoyment or invested excitement. Queering performed eroticism presents a challenge to the heterosexuality of dancehall from which men extract their power. Rather than presenting men with the option to attempt to conquer the intimacy between women, as could be argued would be the case in other performance cultures, queering performed eroticism in dancehall pushes men outside of intimacy and the erotic.

An indifference to women engaging in performed eroticism with one another does not necessarily indicate that observers, including men, are not interpreting or reflecting on this practice's meaning, either consciously or unconsciously. Burt Ramsay (2001, 209) proposes that "it is not possible, in a patriarchal and homophobic society, to make disinterested aesthetic judgments about cultural products that challenge normative ideologies of gender and sexuality." With this I agree. Onlookers stand in relationship to unfolding discourses in dance.

The performances of West Indian women detailed here invite observers to deconstruct their perspectives on gender/sexuality, including its ties to heterosexuality and confining ways of expressing gender subjectivity. Their dancing, furthermore, asks observers to consider the possibility of intimacy and pleasure existing between women alone. Women challenging corporeal limitations also make clear that their gender subjectivity can encompass all the energetic, aggressive attacks, mimesis of violence, force, power, spatial dynamism, and omnipresence that in dancehall are specifically ascribed to bodies read as male. The "cumulative impact" (C. Cohen 2004, 27) of nonconforming gender and sexual performances is that they create room for more wide-ranging subjectivities to be incorporated into Caribbean social and cultural life and practice, emancipating queer subjectivity therein.

Notes

1. An example of these percussive elements can be heard in the "Dem Time Deh" riddim (rhythm).

2. Here I draw on the literature of Judith Butler (1990a, 1993) and Jack Halberstam (2003, 2005), among others, who acknowledge gender as an identity performance that within gender conforming contexts makes visible hegemonic and widely understood gender binary constructs of woman/feminine and man/masculine. Their scholarship further acknowledges gender as being distinct from sex, a biological determination of male or female that is made, usually by medical professionals, at birth. Within gender conforming social contexts, sex is an assumed determining factor in what one's gender performance will be. In the dancehall contexts observed here, sex and gender are expected to align, and gender is proudly performed.

3. Wining is a relatively gender-neutral motion characterized by circular pelvic, waist, and shoulder swirls. Women elaborate on these basic motions to give them heightened complexity. Women create the dynamic texture and stylization of wining by polyrhythmically moving their waists, torsos, shoulders, chests, bent knees, and feet in circular or forward-and-back motions. Body parts move all at once and sometimes in opposing directions, regularly changing tempo, rhythmic, and percussive accentuations.

4. The close dancing between women described here is quite different from women's close dancing to soca music at Carnival in Trinidad, which Daniel Miller (1991) examines, for example. The proximity of closeness distinguishes soca dancing among

women at Carnival (which might be physically close but not intimately touching) from performed eroticism between women. Additionally, women dancing in front or back facing close proximity is not as common in dancehall as it is in soca and thus is a more deviant practice in dancehall. What furthermore distinguishes the dancing of these New York City women is its intentional queer representation of gender normative roles.

"I Came Here to Work"

Transgender Latinas' Labors in the Club

Andrea Bolivar

The small dance floor is packed, and it is hot. Sweaty bodies rub up against one another as they dance voraciously to a Mexican cumbia. Two cisgender women are dancing together to my left. Earlier, one of the women shared with me that she grew up near La Hueca and always heard "bad things" about the club.[1] Her family and neighbors would often disparage it, but once she realized that she was bisexual, she overcame her fear of the place and decided to check it out. She now comes almost every weekend. Dancing there, she says, is "therapeutic." The rest of the crowd is composed of other same-gender couples, both men and women, and a few straight couples, all of whom are Latinx. I am somewhat surprised that there are no trans women dancing on the dance floor—La Hueca is known as a trans Mexican club, after all.

La Hueca is a space that is built by and for transgender Latinas. Located in a historically Mexican neighborhood on the Southwest Side of Chicago, La Hueca is one of the oldest LGBTQ clubs—and Latinx "drag" bars—in the nation. In the early 1970s, Conchita Papaya, alongside other trans Latina women, raised money to open it by selling *discos* and tamales in the streets. The women wanted it to be a place where trans Latina women could perform, and where queer Latinxs could belong in a time of extreme homophobia, transphobia, and gang violence. Conchita eventually returned to Mexico to take care of her parents, and since then the club has been owned by gay and straight Latino men. Its focus on trans women remains, and it is still viewed as instrumental in increasing acceptance of gay and trans people on the Southwest Side, and among Chicago's larger Latinx community.

While all the folks on the dance floor are cisgender, almost all the servers are trans women. They work their way through the tables set up in front of the dance floor, taking people's drink orders in skintight, short dresses. Other trans women are lounging against the walls of the club, watching and waiting for potential clients, while others are backstage getting ready to perform. The music cuts off, and everyone, as if on cue, immediately scatters off the dance floor to sit at the tables. Some are left standing because if you don't come soon after midnight, the seats are all taken. Regardless, everyone is patiently facing the dance floor, now the stage. They know what is about to happen. The show was supposed to start at 2:30 a.m., but it isn't until 3:00 a.m. that Spanish techno music starts to bump from the speakers, before, finally, a tall, curvy, middle-aged trans woman struts onto the stage, microphone in hand. She is wearing a tight, sequined, royal blue gown, and she slowly gyrates her hips as she looks out toward the crowd. The audience members cheer, and she rips the ballroom gown off. Underneath, small patches of the sequined blue fabric barely cover her nipples, and a short skirt made of frayed cloth exposes her G-string. She brings the microphone to her mouth, extends her other arm out toward the increasingly loud crowd, and belts out, "Bienvenidos al mejor show de Chicago!!!"

While predominantly white queer clubs have long been theorized as places of pleasure, utopia, and escape, centering trans Latinas and their space making and community building draws attention to the centrality of labor in their lives: the trans Latinas in La Hueca *work* the space. Though this observation is seemingly revelatory compared to how white queer and trans folks are understood in white queer clubs, the connection between trans Latinas and labor is not new, but part of a broader historical script. Latinxs, in general, are popularly envisioned as a ready supply of labor for the US nation and its capitalist needs, and they have been exploited as such throughout history. Trans Latinas, like their bodies more broadly, are stereotypically associated with labor. Trans women, especially trans women of color, are often all unequivocally imagined to be sex workers. My ethnographic examination of the lives of sex-working trans Latinas in La Hueca, however, takes account of not only the types of work that are imposed on them—both literally and discursively—but also the work they actively engage in to sustain themselves, create space, and nourish others.

Feminist scholars have shown a renewed interest in disentangling and expanding the forms of laboring that go into any particular kind of work (e.g., Elias, Gill, and Scharff 2017; Hesmondhalgh and Baker 2011; Warhurst and Nickson 2009). Scholars of queer of color critique have highlighted the various forms of work that queer people of color perform to create life and community that are otherwise denied to them by dominant society (e.g., Allen 2011; Bailey 2013; Rivera-Servera 2012; Ward 2010). Marlon Bailey (2013, 16) offers an important expansion of understandings of labor in his ethnographic examination of ballroom culture in Detroit, wherein he argues that scholars must define labor beyond purely market-based logics of formal or informal economic participation. Doing so is necessary to (re)conceptualize the multiple ways that queer people of color labor and the various economies in which they are active agents. Bailey writes, "In part this expansion of the concept of labor reflects how creating culture, family, language, gender, and community requires constant and strenuous work—labor." Building on Bailey's work to reconceptualize the connections between work and community, I expand notions of labor by focusing on the strenuous work performed by transgender Latina women, as they engage in queer Latinx worldmaking. I specifically focus on the role of sex, kinship, and spirituality—which are not commonly thought of as modalities of work—in the maintenance and production of La Hueca and the trans Latina community more broadly. I demonstrate how such work consists of multiple types of intersecting and overlapping domains of labors. Thus, in addition to expanding understandings of labor, this chapter expands understandings of processes of queer Latinx worldmaking, helping remedy the dearth of research on transgender Latinxs and their lives.

SEX WORKIN' IN THE CLUB

La Hueca is known as an important site for sex work in Chicago. Many trans Latinas participate in Chicago's sexual economy because they cannot secure employment elsewhere, a well-documented result of systematic transphobia (Broadus 2006; Irving 2012; Spade 2011; Whittle 2000). Yet, the women's seeming unemployability within the formal labor market is compounded by racism, xenophobia, and nationalism. In fact, one woman began doing sex work precisely because she was detained for being undocumented. When she was released from the detention center, she found herself in an unfamiliar rural city where she had no money and nowhere to go. In order to have food and eventually a place to sleep that wasn't in the streets, she turned to sex work in the city. Such examples illustrate how state-sanctioned and socially acceptable forms of racism, classism, and transphobia work against trans Latina women in the United States in ways that only reinforce their political, social, and economic marginalization. In response, women often engage in sexual economies of labor.

Chicago's robust sexual economy thrives on racialized and sexualized ideas about trans women and Latinas and, more importantly, the ways in which the two come together. Transgender folks are hypersexualized as they defy the gender binary—as well as related assumptions about appropriate sexual behavior—that undergirds dominant society. The sexual objectification of trans women comingles with racialized ideas that Latinas are naturally hypersexual. Many women expressed that they are fetishized by clients and society more broadly not only because they are transgender women, but because they are trans *Latina* women. For example, clients might request that they speak Spanish, dance, or dress up as maids. Yet, trans women use how they are seen as a capital-gaining aesthetic, giving a fantasy to acquire a fee, and making do with injurious imagining.

La Hueca facilitates sex work in a few ways. As the night progresses, more and more trans Latina women stand outside of the club, making themselves available to potential clients driving by. Sex workers also hang out inside the club and wait for potential clients, some of whom were first met online and invited to come to the club. Because of the sex work traffic within and around the club, some neighbors have long fought to shut down La Hueca. Doing so would have a number of negative consequences for sex-working trans Latinas and their livelihoods, safety, and well-being. Meeting potential clients in semipublic and populated spaces allows sex workers to get a feel for clients before being alone with them, especially clients they have found online and are meeting in person for the first time. By meeting clients in a space that was created for and by trans Latinas, they may feel less vulnerable. If they do decide to engage clients in nearby locales, having the support of the people who work in La Hueca—people who respect trans Latina women—can be immensely helpful in dangerous situations. Grounded in the framework of La Hueca, the power of clients, which can otherwise be unrestrained, is somewhat checked. In short, La Hueca can sometimes make sex work safer for trans Latina women.

TRANS MOTHERS, TRANS DAUGHTERS, AND KIN LABOR

The trans Latina space that is La Hueca, like the trans Latina sexual economy more broadly, also allows for the development of kinship connections via affective labor. The labor-intensive practices of sex work as well as the myriad of hormonal and physical processes of transitioning are often done with the help of "trans mothers" who provide emotional care and support, and oftentimes food and shelter, for their daughters. They teach their daughters how to be trans women and offer advice about makeup, hormones, silicon injections, and surgeries. They also teach women how to get started in the sex trade; if they have already begun doing sex work, these trans mothers encourage safer sex practices and share tips for getting more clients. Many interlocutors such as Brittni found their trans mothers in LGBTQ clubs.

Brittni was twenty years old and confused about her gender identity when she met her trans mother, Isabella, who was forty years old, at La Hueca. Isabella performed at the club, and before she offered to be Brittni's mother, Brittni spent many months helping her prepare for performances. She helped Isabella create costumes and choreograph dances, running around the city for last-minute, missing props, and staying up late into the night practicing routines. She also helped Isabella apply makeup before performances and made sure that Isabella stayed fed and hydrated throughout the night. Throughout this time, Isabella taught Brittni about transgender identity and helped her transition. In addition to teaching her about trans womanhood, Isabella taught Brittni how to be a successful sex worker. Isabella stayed on the phone with Brittni all night, sometimes, as she cried about the difficulties of her transition and her fear that her biological family would reject her. This is to say that Isabella and Brittni have engaged in multiple kinds of labor throughout their relationship, a substantial amount of which was affective. Labor was central to Brittni and Isabella's relationship, and La Hueca was the chief space in which this kin labor was exchanged.

A MIRACLE IN THE BATHROOM

An additional form of translabor exists, an ethics of feminist kinship on another plane. In La Hueca, some women met godmothers in Santería. These godmothers are also sex-working trans Latina women. Santería is an African diasporic religion that originated in the Caribbean and that, drawing from Yoruba and Catholic religious practices, revolves around santos or orishas, who are different manifestations of God. Brenda learned about both transgender identity and Santería—now the two most important aspects of herself and her life—at La Hueca. For her, as well as for many transgender Latinas, Santería is a spiritual *labor* as much as a spiritual practice: it requires strenuous physical, financial, and emotional work.[2] Santería, much like gender (Butler 1990a), is not something someone has, but rather something someone does. Moreover, spirituality—along with sexual labor and kinship connections—produces material outcomes for the trans Latina women that compose La Hueca.

Brenda went to La Hueca as an effeminate "gay boy" and saw the trans women performing onstage, knowing immediately that she wanted to be like them. One performer took Brenda under her wing and helped her transition. She went every night of every weekend for years, waiting impatiently for each week to pass so she could go to La Hueca and finally belong. She got close with all the "girls," especially Sadia, who was slightly older and would become her godmother via Santería. One night at the club, Sadia received the news that one of her closest friends, also a trans Latina woman, had been arrested for drug-related activities and could go to prison for a very long time. Sacrificing opportunities to service clients and perform onstage, she rushed into La Hueca's tiny women's bathroom and pulled Brenda with her, for Brenda also knew the friend. Sadia did an impromptu reading to find out about her friend's fate. In a reading, the *santera*, or person who is initiated in Santería, communicates with the santos via a complex ritual of rolling, throwing, and reading of *caracoles*, or cowrie shells. Elegguá, the owner of all crossroads, acts as an intermediary, communicating to the rest of the saints and then relaying their messages to the *santera* via the shells. Sadia argued with Elegguá, yelled at and pleaded with him in English, Spanish, and Yoruba. She got sweatier, and the small bathroom got hotter. Eventually, the saints told Sadia that their friend would be charged with a crime that carried a potential sentencing of forty years, but that she would serve less than one year. Sadia and Brenda were relieved. The friend would go on to serve six months in prison.

It was then that Brenda knew she wanted to be a *santera*. Sadia initiated her and thus became her godmother. Now, Brenda's main sources of income are sex work and readings. Notably, *santeras* charge a fee for readings, and they often have regular clients. While I do not mean to conflate sex work and Santería, both function as meaningful realms of labor in her life, realms that intersect and provide economic support, social networks, and sometimes even personal empowerment and fulfillment. Furthermore, Santería overlaps with and bolsters the other forms of labor—economic, sex, and kinship—in these women's lives. According to Brenda, she would have perhaps never found her gender, her faith, her two jobs—sex work and readings—or her freedom if she did not start going to La Hueca.

THE WORK(S) OF TRANS OF COLOR WORLDMAKING

It was just past midnight, and Brenda confidently walked through the door at La Hueca, in black stilettos, tight black leather pants, and a see-through white shirt. She turned to me and said, "Mi'ja, I came here to work." The women in the project, including Brenda, often lamented that trans Latinas are publicly associated with either death or sex work. Brenda's attention to the work she was committed to in the club could be viewed as an attempt to challenge such stereotypes about trans Latinas, their bodies, and their (non)lives. While she did indeed engage in sexual labor, the world of sex work converged with other spheres of labor that were ultimately life giving, such as kin labor and spiritual labor. The women's relationship to all three overlapping forms of labor was dialectical in nature—these realms demanded work from the women but also bestowed numerous benefits. Thus, while an ethnographic examination of La Hueca, a space created and maintained by the work of trans Latinas, expands understandings of queer clubs, labor in general, and sexual, kin, and spiritual labor more specifically, it also expands understandings of processes of queer of color worldmaking in the United States.

Notes

1. La Hueca, like all other names in this chapter, is a pseudonym meant to protect the identity and safety of attendees. I have also purposely not named the specific neighborhood in the Southwest Side where the club is located.

2. Anthropologists and other scholars (e.g., Beliso-De Jesús 2015; Vidal-Ortiz 2006) have written about Santería as an important spiritual practice.

La Gozadera

Lesbian Transfeminist Worldmaking in Mexico City

Jennifer Tyburczy

It was raining, hard, as it does in June, *la temporada de lluvias* (rainy season) in Mexico City. Still, and nearly always, the pair of twenty-foot-tall corrugated metal doors was wide open. Thin, red curtains tied like a *marica*'s midriff hung unmenacingly, coaxing the passerby to enter and stay awhile.[1] Nestled in this sanctuary and slightly high from the combination of sweat and smoke mingling in the air around me, I watched all the pretty people voguing to C. Tangana's hip-hop anthem "Mala Mujer" in their skintight black and fluorescent green leggings and four-inch stiletto boots. They worked the runway appropriating what have become signature hemispheric voguing moves (Bailey 2013) but with a rhythm, style, and tone that were *sumamente mexicano*. This is Punto Gozadera (known locally as La Gozadera), located in the Plaza San Juan in the *centro* of Mexico City.

La Gozadera—a play on the verb *gozar*, which means to take pleasure, sexual or otherwise—is not a queer space, nor even a *cuir* one, as queer is often spelled phonetically in Mexico City and other locations throughout Latin America (Domínguez Ruvalcaba 2016; Valencia Triana 2014; Viteri 2014). It is definitively, as Mirnix Roldán, one of La Gozadera's four principal employees, told me in an interview in 2017, a "lesbotransfeminista" space. However, queer/*cuir* is not a term that often circulates in these communities, as it is primarily viewed by Mexico City's emerging dissident generations as an apolitical style. Queer/*cuir* is something to be worn or bought, but not a term that politicizes the myriad concerns that dominate lesbian and transfeminist communities in Mexico today: *feminicidios* (femicides), self-defense, diverse Latin American feminisms, sexual pleasure, consent, nonviolence, polyamory, literature and music, and, as I will briefly discuss later, *posporno* (post-pornography). Most importantly, Roldán explains, La Gozadera is "a meeting space so that feminist causes from different intersections in different contexts that were taking place in Mexico City or in the Mexican Republic had a space to find one another, where feminist lesbians could get together with other feminists, with transfeminists, and coexist in a space of enjoyment, in a space to eat, to drink beer, to show up and go out on a date or to flirt."[2] This combination of sex and social justice intoxicates the people who frequent La Gozadera, and since I first came to know of and visit La Gozadera in 2015, I too, a US-born and US-based academic, have been invited to *gozar* and have fallen under its seductively inspiring spell.

Today in Mexico City, there are numerous queer/*cuir*, gay, and even *marica* spaces, but there are few (and I would wager to say no other) spaces expressly dedicated to either lesbians or trans women, and definitely none that serve a combination of the two. The point of the space, according to Roldán, is that "we want to preserve the political in nightlife, that is what happens when you open the possibility for a women's night where there are no stalkers, when you make sure that the girls leaving the party catch a taxi, to see where they're headed, make sure they're safe, be repeating [throughout the night on the microphone] that this is a space free of violence."[3] La Gozadera was born of a time in 2015 when lesbians and trans women in Mexico City were experiencing incredible backlash; this backlash arose from powerful homophobic and transphobic groups such as the Comité Nacional Provida, a civil association that would go on to hold massive nationwide protests in 2016 that promoted violence and contributed to the rise in the surveillance, discrimination, and murder of trans women. This space also emerged at the crucible of intra-LGBTTTI politics,[4] where largely gay male gatekeepers and sex-negative and/or transphobic feminists censored, demeaned, and sabotaged the cultural productions of lesbian transfeministas in a variety of locations that ranged from museums and avant-garde performance hubs to bars and nightlife culture.[5] Out of these contexts, a global phenomenon of noncorporate, artistic, and subcultural sexually explicit media characterized as *posporno* became a crucial genre for lesbian and transfeminist nightlife throughout Latin America.

In November 2015, nearly one year after scandal rocked the Universidad de Buenos Aires and the Argentinian popular press over a *posporno* event,[6] the Centro Cultural de España in Mexico City (CCEMx) pronounced that the sixth annual FEMSTIVAL would be canceled. FEMSTIVAL is an international sex-positive festival that promotes intimate links between diverse feminisms, explicit sex, and genderqueer performance. In the two years leading up to the 2015 FEMSTIVAL, CCEMx had actively supported the festival and provided space, funding, and resources for this event and many others that were billed under the banner of *posporno*. The order that *posporno* would no longer constitute a permissible form of performance at CCEMx threw FEMSTIVAL and its organizers, known locally as Las Cirujanas, into chaos. As they looked for another location, Las Cirujanas and the management of La Gozadera came together and decided to hold the 2015 festival in the Gozadera space. While the 2015 FEMSTIVAL was one of only a series of events that led to the establishment of La Gozadera as a site of sanctuary for sex-positive event planning and as a space for highly political and daringly erotic feminist cultural productions and conviviality, the 2015 FEMSTIVAL certainly put La Gozadera on the map as a potential location for sex-positive lesbian and transfeminist worldmaking. Today local, national, and international audiences are drawn to this now vibrant and active spot for women-centered nightlife in Mexico's capital city.

Like *posporno*, La Gozadera has become an indispensable site for the generation of diverse and nonnormative multisensual pleasure in Mexico City. On any given day or night, one can stop in for a delicious coffee, *agua del día* (drink of the day), or the signature vegan and vegetarian *tlayudas*, flatbreads prepared and served by lesbians and trans women, the only people that La Gozadera hires. Events ranging from book presentations to performances to the famous *lesbviernes* (lesbian Friday parties) engage the mind and body in activities that incorporate conversation and debate, dancing, undressing, kissing, or fucking in the *zona violeta* (violet zone/dark room). La Gozadera's social justice and lesbian transfeminist outlook suffuses all of this: when the dance floor pulses with sweating, desiring bodies, those in charge of the event that night repeatedly announce over the microphone that this is a space of nonviolence and that any sexual act must be consensual. Violators of these rules are asked to leave, and the police have only ever been called once (though they never showed), for reasons well known to locals. La Gozadera's spatial philosophy is deeply anti-police. The four principal employees know full well that the presence of these uniforms can cause *malestar* (deep discomfort) and trauma among the publics who gather there and who may have been abused by state forces that were never intended to protect them.

Indeed, La Gozadera actively defines itself as a space free of emotional, symbolic, economic, corporate (including pinkwashing), and state violence, a place where practices of pleasure that are frequently rejected or policed in other environments can and do circulate. The self-managing collective prioritizes and fosters events that have been cast off from the agendas of "cultural centers" and the institutional status of "art." Together, these events provide feminist artists, activists, and sometimes academics (I was honored to present my first book there in summer 2017) a site to foment discourse and expression that transcend the spoken and unspoken rules of decorum in hetero- and homonormative environments alike. The point is in the meeting, in the coming together, in the taking up of physical space—a welcome and sadly infrequent phenomenon in lesbian feminist communities in both the States and Mexico City in these neoliberal and digital times. More often than not, and especially in the United States, queer women's communities constantly bear witness to the closing of our nightlife (and daytime!) spaces, while gay men's spaces begrudgingly offer us a "night" where we may feel welcome (or not) but not comfortable in an environment that never was and never will be ours. At La Gozadera every night is our night. It is a space where we can, perhaps for the first time in some of our lives, sink into *comodidad* (comfort), where our "bodies extend into spaces, and spaces extend into bodies" (Ahmed 2004, 148).

In drawing from Sara Ahmed's term *comfort*, which she uses to describe how heteronorms thrive spatially, I do not mean to suggest that the publics that frequent La Gozadera are "so at ease with one's environment that it is hard to distinguish where one's body ends and the world begins" (Ahmed 2004, 148). La Gozadera is all too aware of the conflicts that can divide even those communities who call it home: in my conversations with patrons, most all of whom prefaced any critique with their love and admiration for the space, some had stories to share about the time when a DJ played a reggaeton song with misogynist lyrics, or an incident in which a *marica*-identified visitor drank in excess and had to be escorted out, or a time when a trans man started policing the dancing techniques of a cisgender patron they perceived to be sexist. In effect, a nonnormative form of comfort is engendered and circulated in a place where "one fits," but not permanently, or in the same ways as in hetero- and cisnormative environments. As lesbian transfeminist communities and their allies change, so too will the dynamic shift between bodies and performances in the space of La Gozadera. This shift sometimes happens explicitly, as when a former lesbian *cuata* (feminist appropriation of "buddy") transitions into trans masculinity (and is thus no longer eligible to attend, for example, the *lesbviernes* events), or when a curious passerby who is read as *buga* (straight) wanders in and takes up space to experience (and in many instances appreciate, I was happy to see) something captivating to them, such as those beautiful voguing vixens. At La Gozadera, these conflicts, just as much as the kissing, the fucking, and the dancing, constitute the work of what José Esteban Muñoz (2009) has called the collective and utopian project of "queer worldmaking." The intra-lesbian transfeminist debates I was privy to during my ongoing visits to La Gozadera also point to the need to expand the concept of queer worldmaking so as to be attentive to how the very term *queer* has shifted in the twenty-first century as it has become more accepted hemispherically. I would like to suggest that the everyday conversations and decisions that happen inside a lesbian transfeminist space such as La Gozadera put pressure on the definitions, adaptations, and rejections of queer and *cuir* that circulate throughout the Americas.

La Gozadera, Roldán explained to me, is "a space in which women are the protagonists, in which feminists are the protagonists. And it is a space not to give voice, but to allow others to find their voice. These are like the axes on which La Gozadera turns."[7] Numerous people I spoke to in 2017, after La Gozadera's initial two-year run and its financial and interpersonal struggle to keep those massive corrugated metal doors open, told me that the space had changed their lives, had saved their lives. And indeed as I sat there in the pouring rain, eating my vegan *tlayuda*, chatting with the waitress, and watching the voguing practice, I found myself saying aloud, "This place could change the world."[8]

The author wishes to thank Nad Ma, Las Cirujanas, and everyone at La Gozadera, especially Cynthia Chiang, Ingrid Colín, Mirnix Roldán, Wendolin Arenas Morales, and Libertad García Sanabria, for their warm welcome and their generosity in sharing their stories about everything La Gozadera.

Notes

1. In Mexico City, *marica* is an identificatory term that stands in contrast to the identity category *gay*, especially the latter's history with whiteness and certain social classes marked by privilege. When one self-identifies as *marica*, they mean to indicate a social experience that is less fixed or solid, in contrast to homonorms of ideal gayness, with the perception that some of these norms emerge from Anglo or gringo contexts that have little to do with sexuality as experienced in and around Mexico City.

2. This interview was conducted in Spanish and translated into English by the author. The original: "espacio de encuentro para que las luchas feministas de diferentes intersecciones en diferentes contextos que estaban dándose en la Ciudad de México o en la República tuvieran un espacio de encuentro y que se combinaran las lesbianas feministas con otras feministas, con transfeministas, y que convivieran en un espacio de goce, en un espacio de poder comer, poder beber la chela, poder llegar y hacer dates o ligar."

3. The original: "que queremos conservar a nivel político de la noche, decir qué pasa si posibilitas una noche de mujeres en el que no haya acosadores, se busca que

las chicas cuando salen de la fiesta tomen un taxi, ver a dónde se van, estar al cuidado, estar repitiendo [durante toda la noche en el micrófono] que es un espacio libre de violencia."

4. LGBTTTI stands for lesbian, gay, bisexual, transexual, transgender, travestí, and intersex.

5. A classic example of intra-LGBTTTI political infighting in Mexico City occurred after the 2015 opening of the exhibition *Archivos Desclosetados: Espectros y poderes-disidentes.* Leading gay men in Mexico City verbally attacked and denigrated curators Nina Höchtl and Naomi Rincón Gallardo for what they viewed as egregious errors and absences in the historical record, but which I view as a distinctly lesbian and intersectional approach to the archive as a hetero- and homonormative site of knowledge production. For more about the exhibition, see Höchtl (n.d.). For one of the more infamous critiques of the exhibition, see Feliciano (2015).

6. For quintessential coverage from the Argentinian mainstream press, see Clarin.com (2015).

7. The original: "un espacio en el que las mujeres son las protagonistas, en el que las feministas son las protagonistas. Y es un espacio no para dar la voz, sino para poner la voz. Son como los ejes que tiene La Gozadera."

8. Unfortunately, the transfeminist core of La Gozadera has been rocked since I first sat down to write this essay. This development speaks to the fragility of these projects just as it reflects and participates in the growing prevalence of trans-exclusionary radical feminist (TERF) activity that has swept Mexico City and often violently targets trans leaders. As of October 2020, and as a consequence of the COVID-19 pandemic in Mexico City, La Gozadera is in the process of closing its doors but with plans to open in another location, dependent on an ongoing fundraising campaign.

Ecstatic Resilience

Sable Elyse Smith

And so the party continues. Every night I dance to the triplet hi-hat trap boi fantasy. A slow syrup oration, deceptively similar to my code-swapped histories—punctuated by an 808.

Every night I dance to the sex-laced crescendo as bands make her dance, or the desire for another's body, as the heart decelerates and drugs slowly seep out of the system, I only want u when I'm coming down or fuck faces. There is a rhythm for everything.

The "party" is about a moment of suspension. Feeling a rigorous sensation in the body, a pulsating tip-to-tip. Like Paul B. Preciado's Testogel—the moment it seeps in is palpable. Like pins and needles all prickly across the skin's surface and a slow numb that calls attention to each beat of the heart, harder and harder. And the Sensation conjured by this dance is void of history, geographic location, and pain. It's a sensation that is without my scars or muscle memory. It is without his trauma of domestic violence. It is without the memory of crack or our eighties birth. It is without those small deposits of rage. It is without because even the sweat releases something from the body. Without—because we are giving everything and to splurge is an act of depletion.

I've listened to my peers recite remixed versions of the names of the recently fallen, lately. I've watched the faces in white spaces as the words leave lips. I moisten my lips to receive these names. I insert my own name, at times wondering the difference between me and them. I am so moved by this murmur propping up each individual's performance or nonperformance. Propping me up as the energy in the space constricts and begins to envelop me and certain "others" in the audience. And I think about the camouflage of mourning and how space shapes itself around each of our bodies, pushing in a little more each time.

This is a chance
This is a chance

The dance, however, is not an escape. It is a punctuation. It is about claiming an instant of time and something that can be mine completely. Though at times I share it with others, as we are all our own orbiting planets spinning in excess in proximity to one another. And sometimes our bodies touch. Sometimes I run my shoulders up against his. And there is a transfer. A silent affirmation. We are taking up space at the same time and spinning the most delicate webs out of the strongest material imaginable. This is the dance. This is the work of living between that distinct moment when we push past exhaustion to elation. Ecstatic resilience glittering down.

• • •

I want to dance. Slick with sweat and cum and saliva. I want to hold the body in a state of titillation—rushed to its peak by the simple act of being alive; by taking a breath, by breathing. The club is a sanctuary for queer liberation.

Audre Lorde writes:

For those of us who live at the shoreline
standing upon the constant edges of decision
crucial and alone
for those of us who cannot indulge
the passing dreams of choice
who love in doorways coming and going
in the hours between dawns.[1]

In the beginning they say gXX created the heavens and the earth. The earth was without form and void, and darkness was upon the face of the deep. And the fiction continues.

Being without form and void suggests a folding onto itself, so that it may always be both, negating the other. While the dance just holds us in, detaches our weight, and gives us a small respite. It is a portal. A tiny dressing room to construct and sharpen our outfits, our attitudes, our swag and presentation as we go out in the world and perform our positions, hoping to acquire or swap into other positions, permission to be amorphous.

A woman I dated once was really attracted to my ability to slip. She put language to a fluidity that she identified in me. For her my slippage to female was only visible when we fucked. Though in fucking I oscillate back and forth in a way she did not find present as I walked through the world not fucking.

And so I wonder about the rhythm of my walking. This walking through as opposed to being rested in. This pendulum sway from form to void.

• • •

Funk music does not occupy a space separate from the sex and drugs. It is about a visceral manifestation of pleasure—to negate the flaw is detrimental. It is about sitting in a Caprice on Slauson, slouched down in your seat real low, eyes low, blazed, two 10s in your trunk, listening to Bootsy, to Parliament, to E-40, to Tupac, to Curtis—to the vibration in the seat that leaves a plush velvet fabric and enters the spine, the forearms, the ass. It is about understanding the conditions that birth a fabric.

A form created in the sixties, resistance is embedded in its syncopation. Funk is about the journey. And sometimes just to be a body feeling is revolutionary.

I think of James Brown sliding across Ed Sullivan's stage in 1966, both exclaiming and singing "I Feel Good." I think of the rapidity of his steps—as an autonomous choreography that straddles a stark line between performance and refusal. An acknowledgment that at some point the ground will refuse to uphold.

I see the ground buckling myself, and so we shake it. Shake it as vigorously as the earth shakes itself loose in California, along certain fault lines.

In search of fluid space.

• • •

Eddie Hazel lifts the gravity in one's room. He jams it into the chest cavity with one long note in E-minor. A guitar solo played on top of itself echoes in the parts of us that have already been made hollow. Time stops. I imagine a callousness across the tips of his fingers—some hard shell of labor. Catharsis peaks with each wail of the guitar, and we float weightlessly deeper into the void, and maybe the body rattles like trunks when a deep bass vibrates through them. His guitar bleeds all the language out of the lament. It festers in the body. It sits against the spine applying pressure.

And I ponder that space between the moments where language falls away from sound; or the moment that sound becomes language dragging with it a weight that resides in the body, forcing us to confront it.

The music is both thick and empty. So that we may climb into it and be many selves at once planted on tabletops, hips rocking back and forth, smiles slick across faces, Black joy is an act of resistance.

Note

1. This extract is from Lorde's poem "A Litany for Survival" in her 1978 collection *The Black Unicorn.*

After Closing Time

Ambivalence in Remembering a Small-City Lesbian Bar

Clare Forstie

You're driving up Danforth Street, a short road that passes through a postindustrial neighborhood in the seaside tourist destination of Portland, Maine, and it is summertime. Portland is a small waterfront city with fewer than one hundred thousand people and is increasingly enmeshed in global, neoliberal politics (Manalansan 2005). Indeed, for a few moments while driving, you pass through a neighborhood in the process of gentrification, one of many on the Portland peninsula. If you blink, you may miss a small, beige, two-story boxlike building on your left. It's for rent—nothing new in this part of town. The lack of windows on the first floor and the door angled toward the corner of the street suggest "bar"; the new beige siding and windows suggest "formerly sketchy bar, now ripe for new use!" Perhaps you pause for a moment, thinking, "I wonder what this space used to be?" You're aware that this building once, more than a decade ago, housed the self-identified lesbian bar Sisters. You shake your head and mourn the loss of what you understand to be a vital Lesbian Institution in the state and, more generally, in the *region* of northern New England. You ask yourself where all the lesbians have gone. Simultaneously, you're relieved, thinking that such a space isn't really needed anymore in progressive, inclusive Portland, or you're reflecting about the trans-exclusionary boundaries of other cisgender-specific lesbian women's spaces, like the Michigan Womyn's Music Festival. You feel a range of emotions, and you remember the first time you entered the bar, nearly two decades ago.

When it first opened in 1995, the entryway was painted purple—somewhere between lavender and midnight—and a glaring neon light blazed through a first-floor window visible from the street. Nicki (a pseudonym, as are all names in this essay), who worked at Sisters as a barback, remembers offering directions to folks who called looking for the bar: "Danforth Street, 'look for the purple door,' that's what we told everybody that called, a really nondescript building. . . . You just, you looked for the purple door. Not much to look at on the outside, uh, not much for parking, kind of in the middle of nowhere, not a lot around it." Inside, despite the efforts of bar owner Ann to keep it "nice," patrons saw Sisters as a dark and "divey" space for finding—and, eventually, losing—community. Upon arrival, you stood in a short line at the door, then nervously handed your ID and three-dollar cover charge to a woman you read as butch before entering the bar proper. Immediately in front of you was the dance floor, already crowded with thirty or so women dancing in couples and small groups, as well as a smattering of men. You could see the DJ against the far wall, and you headed right to the bar, which took up the Danforth Street wall and which was crowned by a small television tuned to a silent baseball game. Beer was available in bottles only, and the bartender worked exclusively for tips, so you tipped as generously as you could. Perhaps you headed toward the pool table (or were there two?) in the back corner, or straight through to the door leading to the tiny patio at the far left. Perhaps you squeezed into the U-shaped table just in front of the bathrooms, along with your friends. You drank at least one beer—that's certain, given that you were anxiously visiting the bar for the first time, hoping to feel at home at last.

Sisters Dance Bar, or just Sisters, was located at Portland's outskirts, not far from the city's working waterfront. While Maine was sprinkled with a handful of gay and gay-friendly bars in the late 1990s and early 2000s, Sisters was known to my participants as the only lesbian bar north of Boston (in the United States), one in which patrons were primarily (although not exclusively) young, white, and middle- and working-class. Sisters is one example of small-city queer community, an instance of a type of remembered place where lesbian and gay community members could find one another, drink, dance, and feel some degree of safety, comfort, and ambivalent feelings of home within a hybrid public-private space. Portland is a small city located in the space between small towns and the larger, urban centers that refuse a linear narrative of progress (Browne 2009; Brown-Saracino 2018; Ghaziani 2014; C. Johnson 2013; Orne 2017; Weston 1995). Due to their size, location, and specific histories, small cities open possibilities for understanding community ambivalence through their queer nightlife spaces (Forstie 2020; Stone 2018). In Portland, information about Sisters was spread largely through word of mouth, as lesbian newcomers to Portland in the early 2000s were instructed to look for the purple door. Sisters opened in the mid-1990s and closed in 2005, leaving about a decade of queer nightlife behind it.

In this essay, I argue that the memory-making processes surrounding closed queer spaces reflect the kinds of ambivalence that persist in communities, ambivalences we should keep in mind as we analyze queer nightlives. Ambivalence in queer nightlife spaces means a desire for queer-specific spaces alongside a desire for their absence. Building on the work of scholars arguing for ambivalence's utility as a concept (Bondi 2004; Butler 2002; Merton 1976; Smelser 1998) and those who emphasize temporary queer community spaces (Gray 2009; Greene 2014) and the ambivalence of community (Joseph 2002; Love 2009; Muñoz 2009), I argue that ambivalence describes queer communities' experiences of their nightlife spaces and helps individuals make sense of community change. The ambivalence of Sisters patrons reflects conflicting desires about the boundaries of lesbian spaces and whether and how such spaces should be considered queer. In interviews that I conducted in 2009, patrons expressed ambivalence about Sisters in three ways: (1) in their embodied, remembered sense of home in community and queer spaces; (2) in their ambivalence about the loss of such spaces; and (3) in their cautious explorations of the queer spaces that might replace them. We benefit from an analysis of ambivalence in queer nightlife spaces because such work enables a richer understanding of queer nightlife spaces of the past, fosters a recognition of the inequalities re-created within these spaces, maintains a necessary sense of instability in ongoing community-making processes, and facilitates a framework for planning for queer nightlife spaces of the future (Halberstam 2005; Muñoz 2009).

SISTERS AS AMBIVALENT HOMESPACE

Sisters, bar owner Ann explained, was created to provide a safe space for women in Portland, a place where lesbians could meet, drink, and dance "without the fear of . . . being hit on or the fear of maybe being discriminated against." Participants described it as a kind of old-school lesbian space, one where patrons' gender expression tended toward the butch end of the spectrum with a notable absence of visibly femme-identified lesbians. These gender aesthetics affected whether patrons felt a sense of comfort and of home in the bar. This butch aesthetic was also explicitly connected to a "Maine woman" aesthetic for some patrons, particularly those who had previously lived away from Maine or moved to Maine "from away." The "Maine woman" aesthetic proved challenging for some lesbians' sense of identity because stereotypical butch attributes could be exhibited by straight, Maine women, similar to women's gender expression in the rural Midwest (Kazyak 2012).

Maine lesbians may not see their gender expression as particularly butch, but their gender expression is at risk of being "read" as butch by lesbians and by those outside of the queer community.

The overall gender aesthetic most common at Sisters, in Portland, and in Maine contributed to participants' ambivalence about feelings of home (Carrington 1999) within the space. This ambivalence manifested in two locations: in Portland's broader community and within gay and lesbian spaces like Sisters. Participants' discourses of safety in the home of Sisters highlight this ambivalence about community spaces as they exist (and when they exist), as well as the ongoing need for LGBTQ spaces.

A sense of home requires a community context, and LBTQ people in Portland understand themselves in relation to their city's local culture (Brown-Saracino 2018). Participants articulated an ongoing need for LGBTQ spaces. Portland is well known as a haven for (white) lesbians, as others have noted (Brown-Saracino 2018). Meg referenced this reputation when she explained:

> Like, for the most part, I feel very privileged and blessed to live in a community like Portland. But then, every once in a while, we'll be walking down the streets of Portland, and we'll get yelled at, or someone will say something, or we'll be in a restaurant and we'll get looked at funny or we'll be served weird by the server, the server will be odd with us, clearly uncomfortable . . . but then sometimes we'll be someplace and it'll be fine and it'll be like nothing; so when it happens it's like, [gasps] "What is that? What—what just happened?"

Other Sisters patrons, especially older lesbians, expressed memories of violence against LGBTQ people in Portland that still felt distinctly fresh. Younger Sisters patrons acknowledged that history by referencing the ways that Sisters was rendered invisible due to its location, lack of visible, external markings, and plexiglass-covered windows. For example, Alli explained how she learned from older lesbians that the need for physical safety was the root cause of Sisters' hiddenness: "Older dykes and stuff have always said that it's about safety, and about people not knowing, if people don't know where you are, they can't find you and do anything to you. Which is not always true, but people say the same things about why there aren't windows in gay bars." Patrons' sense of home within Sisters was both enabled and constrained by their sense of local history in greater Portland, where lesbians' integration into the local community existed alongside memories of violence and the ongoing need for safe spaces. For younger and older patrons, this experience of chosen family (Weston 1991) and community ownership and recognition was reinforced through the bar's evocation of family in its name: Sisters.

However, the home created in the space of Sisters was unique to Portland and the kinds of community that developed therein (Brown-Saracino 2018). As Sisters' name suggests, this family space was gendered, particularly as a space patronized largely by cisgender women. The family created within the walls of the bar was, to some, explicitly a *women's* family, and the type of women was prescribed. As Ann explained, what made Sisters a different kind of bar was the family feel that she believed women generated within its space:

> My perspective is that it's a women's bar and so that makes it wonderful and that makes it different. And when I go into another type of bar—it doesn't cater to women, it's just. . . I don't know how to explain it, it just, it's just different. . . . I think women are the nurturers and the carers, and all of that is brought together in this type of [bar] situation, and so you immediately feel it—it's just like going home, you know, to mom. You feel it.

To some bar patrons, the kind of femininity this family represented and constructed was comforting, welcoming, and familiar. The bar's family was seen as feminine not in gender expression, as noted above, but in essentialist ways, in the kinds of caregiving qualities women are assumed to possess. Ambivalence about Sisters as a homespace demonstrates the sense of exclusion experienced by femme and trans community members who did not fit with the kind of chosen family created within the bar, despite its name.

For some local queers, Sisters *never* felt like family, although they appreciated the need for a home like the one available at Sisters in the broader Portland community. Trans men and femme-identified participants especially felt alienated from the cisgender, soft butch culture of the bar. Logan described the spoken and unspoken "rules" at Sisters as being particularly alienating, stating that "it was really strict when I first got there, to me it was really strict. . . . I would never put up with the shit that I put up with in any other bar, if it hadn't been the only dyke bar in town. And you want to support it, and you want to see people, and blah blah blah." For Logan, ambivalence about Sisters as a homespace demonstrates a tension between, on the one hand, the desire to support queer community and "see people," and, on the other, an experience of invisibility, nonalignment, and "the shit" of unspoken community rules.

Max explained how his changing identity affected his sense of safety at Sisters. When I asked him how safe he felt at the bar, he sighed and offered the following:

> How safe did I feel . . . at Sisters? As a lesbian, safe, like, there was no question.

> There was, like, I never felt like we're going to have another Stonewall riot or anything like that. As a trans person, not so safe at all. I remember the first time going back to Sisters after like a three-month hiatus, and kind of identifying as gender-queer, and changing my pronouns, and, and, just, it was, like, ladies' night, or women's night only, or something like that, and another trans guy got a bunch of us together to go, and, quote, unquote, "protest," a.k.a. see if we can get in and just do what we did every single fuckin' Friday night before we came out, um, as trans. . . . And I remember we got in. And I just—I didn't have anything to drink, and I just shook the whole night, like, I couldn't calm my hands from shaking, and the whole day I didn't drink anything 'cause I didn't want to have to go to the bathroom, because the end-all and be-all compromise part of it was, "well, you still have to use the women's restroom. You can't use the men's restroom" . . . But, even now, talking about it, my heart races because it's not so much that I didn't feel safe, but the people making me feel unsafe, like, three months ago, were people that I would feel safer with than my family or cops or, or the Army or whatever, you know? And now, all of a sudden, they were against us; but they were us at the same time.

This long quote demonstrates ambivalence about safety in spaces that are, at least in theory, meant to be home for LGBTQ community members (Joseph 2002, 2017). Max's specific experience of coming out as genderqueer within the space of the bar demonstrates a painful sense of ambivalent community, compressed in the moment of reentering the space of the bar.

Several femme-identified participants noted the absence of visibly feminine lesbians at Sisters, another gendered dimension of ambivalence. Lyn stated that "when feminine-identified women would come in, there were often comments about how, like, 'Does her boyfriend know she's here?' And stuff like that." Jamie, a former Sisters employee and a white, femme-identified lesbian, told me that "when I first started working at Sisters, every body called me the 'straight girl.'" Casey expressed frustration that "there were definitely times in the later years that Sisters was open where I would be one of the only two or three people in the bar in a dress, and that was so often remarked upon." Because the "authentic" or allowable lesbian gender expression at Sisters was perceived as butch, a narrative of femme invisibility weaves through the stories of self-identified femme patrons. For femme and trans patrons, continuing engagement in Sisters as a *lesbian* nightlife space required an ambivalent acceptance of community norms and concessions (changing gender expression or avoiding the bathrooms) that was, for some, not sustainable.

These participants' comments suggest the ways in which LGBTQ community spaces must be persistently seen as ambivalent: simultaneously sources of community *and* spaces of alienation, of distancing, and of exclusion. Participants' experiences of Sisters as a home demonstrate ambivalence that, I argue, is always central to queer nightlives: a feeling of chosen family as a source of simultaneous inclusion and exclusion, of "us" and "against." Ambivalence must be considered in broader community contexts, too (Hanhardt 2013), as safety is constructed in relation to larger processes of inclusion and exclusion through local and national cultures and policy-making (Joseph 2002; Love 2009). While lesbians are well integrated into Portland's nightlife in general, gendered and racial queer community dynamics play out across other community spaces in Portland. It is also worth noting that these snapshots are from one moment in time: my interviews with former patrons in which they recalled their experiences at Sisters. In all cases, participants universally explained that they felt that the loss of Sisters represented *some kind* of community loss, even if the loss that they felt occurred before the bar closed.

REMEMBERING SISTERS: REGRET AND RELIEF

Participants also expressed ambivalence about the meaning of closed LGBTQ spaces, for example, in their regret *and* relief that such spaces have disappeared (Love 2009). The loss of this space was keenly felt by Ann and other lesbian participants in Portland. In discussing her decision to close Sisters, Ann remarked:

> I was seeing an era come to an end, and I knew there were gonna be people that didn't understand what it meant. And I felt kind of bad that way because I couldn't explain to them what it's going to mean, you know. They thought, "Oh well. It's just, you know, it's just closing. We'll all still be together. We'll all still be, you know, the best of buds," and all that, and I said, "You don't understand what a difference it's gonna make."

Other bar employees shared this sense of loss, even as they celebrated the idealized home that Sisters represented, like bartenders Jamie and Alex. Alex actively named the loss of these networks as the loss of family: "I miss what our community was then, 'cause our community definitely is not what it was then. Our community is not a family now. Yeah, there's a lot of great causes out there, but we don't come together. We don't. We don't do anything like, you know, back in the—I can't even begin to tell you how many fundraisers we had for individuals." Even Logan—who admitted that, if he "missed anything, it would be being that age, [not] necessarily Sisters!"—stated that "I do miss running into people in that kind of space, a queer space, I guess." Here, participants expressed a temporal sense of loss: an experience of queer family in the past, compared to queer isolation in the moment of the interview.

A final element of lesbian community that, to some, disappeared when Sisters closed was a sense of lesbian community history. As Alli explained,

> I think when you start talking about lesbian space, women space, or even dyke space, it can become very tricky. For a women's bar, how do you decide who gets in? . . . As much as I love Sisters, I would rather cut my arm off than go to the Michigan Womyn's Music Festival because of their history, but I recognize that a lot of dyke spaces, women-only spaces, have history like that, that's part of our history. It meant so much to me, it's hard to imagine that it wouldn't be beneficial to have a space like that now, for people who count on seeing older dykes and getting to know people that they wouldn't normally talk to. And being part of some kind of community.

For Alli, this connection to older generations of lesbians and to that sense of history was a critical function of Sisters, a function that has not yet been replicated in Portland. The trifold loss—of a sense of safety in community, of family and support, and of intergenerational contact—was a key element of participants' regret that Sisters closed.

While some participants expressed a sense of regret that these queer nightlife spaces closed, others saw their closing as a necessary pain or a sign of progress. Max described his sadness both at the loss of Sisters and at the loss of lesbian community that came with his coming out as trans, stating:

> I would say that the thing that I think is the most important piece of this interview, for me, is for people to hear how much Sisters meant to me as a young lesbian. That I got to see people like [Alex], and that I got to [meet] these lesbians who are successful, and had lives and friends and struggles and coping mechanisms, and were awesome. . . . And I am forever indebted for [that]. . . . And I think that's why it's so painful to be excluded from it, because it really meant and means a lot to me, and the exclusion, really, is very painful.

Max's sense of loss is also temporal (Halberstam 2005), occurring in the past and at the moment the bar itself closed, signaling a community that both "meant and means a lot." However, this ambivalence persists following the loss of Sisters.

Some participants emphasized trans patrons' lack of agency in being excluded from the lesbian community defined by Sisters. They placed responsibility primarily on older lesbians (including the owner) for not responding to the changing needs of trans patrons, specifically. Alli suggested that Ann needed to change, stating, for example, that "there were things she could've tried to do to get people to come in but she made some mistakes that alienated [trans folks]." Lyn suggested that "towards the end . . . that that's why they started losing business, actually, because the community was changing in a certain way, and the owners and the managers I suspect were having a hard time changing as well. For a lot of people, trans issues were a big deal in the use of the bathrooms." The regret that trans participants felt about Sisters' closure was more about this double exclusion that occurred prior to the bar's closing than about the loss of the space itself.

And yet, participants' ambivalence about these disappearing spaces is worth highlighting. I end this section with a quote from Max, who offered a religious framework for understanding the dual nature of the loss of Sisters:

> So it is sad, um, that Sisters closed. But I think about it, would I rather have Sisters be open and me not have, not be able to go when I wanted to go, or would I rather have Sisters closed? And it's like the—I hate to be religious for a second—but it's like the, you know the story of King Solomon? The, you know, the woman has the baby, and the other woman steals it and says, "well, it's my baby," and King Solomon says, "okay, I'll just cut the baby in half, and you can have half, and you can have half." And the real mother says, "don't cut the baby in half. She can have the baby." So this way, you solve by having all. But what we did was, we didn't—nobody came together, it was split. And then what we both ended up with was nothing. The trans community ended up with dialogue, but no physical place to meet to reinvent our community, and the lesbian community has no bar and no softball team from that bar. [chuckles] So, it just really sucks. It was the end of an *era*. So, anyway. That's a long fuckin' answer.

For Max, and for all participants, the loss of the physical place of Sisters represented the loss of a critical, community queer nightlife space, one that was experienced ambivalently in the past and in the moment of remembering.

THE FUTURE (OF) QUEER SPACES IN PORTLAND

While the loss of spaces like Sisters felt like "the end of an era" for some, participants also expressed ambivalence about queer futures (Joseph 2017; Muñoz 2009). In Portland, some patrons stated that they believed that (a reopened) Sisters would be an anachronistic space—that it served a purpose while it was open, but that it would be out of place or too challenging to operate in the current moment. Bar manager Alex stated: "You know, it's been four years since Sisters has been done. I saw what to do, and what not to do. I don't think I would want a Sisters, though. I think I would want my community [to] come together, because we don't—we segregate ourselves too much, still." Following Sisters' closure, a few community spaces emerged as locations of queer nightlife, notably a bar and performance space called the North Star and private spaces like community members' homes. As Logan explained:

> The North Star [which closed in 2010] has been the one place that has been open to anybody, extremely queer friendly, has a lot of great music; and it has more . . . poetry nights, and writing groups, and activities like that, and. . . . It has food and tea and stuff like that, and that's really important, 'cause it's really kind of a huge mistake to have just alcohol in a place where you're expecting a queer community, I think—or, really, any community.

For some participants, the privacy of friend groups and house parties recreates a partial sense of queer community that spaces like Sisters offered. For example, Beth and her partner spend less time in public spaces like bars and more time at private home parties and potlucks. Similarly, Max described his dinner parties as a community:

> I have had parties at my house, and I invite my friends over, and we create a community space. Sisters is community because you walk in, and there's familiar faces; but you might not know who those people are, you just know that they're familiar. And now, my friends group . . . is moving towards a place where we want to be stable and have dinner parties and watch movies. The bar is a social place, but our home is our friends' intimate place, um, in a platonic way, and so, that's kind of where I go, is nowhere. I stay home.

Perhaps communities of friends gathering in homes, long-standing examples of queer nightlife spaces even in urban contexts, are the most sustainable types of queer nightlife spaces in small cities, as commercial sites like gay or lesbian bars have largely disappeared. However, the loss of semiprivate, semipublic queer nightlife spaces like bars, with all the community ambivalences contained therein, also demonstrates a return to relative queer invisibility.

In the post-bar era, some patrons are satisfied with the local community they create with friends. Across community contexts, friend groups thus constitute a private kind of queer community. These spaces fill the need for queer community in some ways, but they should not be considered utopian queer spaces. Such friend groups can be impenetrable to community newcomers, for example, and they risk re-creating inequalities. Friendships tend to be homophilous, meaning that friend groups tend to share identity characteristics, and friendships across identity lines, especially race, continue to be difficult to maintain (McPherson, Smith-Lovin, and Cook 2001). And participants largely agreed that *public* queer spaces are still important. While these participants agreed that queer space is needed, their comments suggest that understandings of what the space "should be like" and what the space *means* differ and may be impossible to resolve (Joseph 2002). Still, some examples of flexible queer nightlife space in small cities may be broad enough to accommodate queer communities even as they lack institutionalization. In a second research site in a small midwestern city, a queer social group initially generated through the in-person social networking site Meetup resulted in small groups of queer friends visiting public parks, theaters, and bars that were not explicitly gay. Even in these temporary community spaces (Gray 2009), however, ambivalences emerge.

CONCLUSION

As of 2020, at the time of this writing, one self-identified gay bar and at least one gay-friendly bar exist in Portland. However, Portland has no lesbian bar, and the city's only gay club closed in 2016. Whether and how these ambivalences—the complex sense of home in queer nightlife spaces, regret and relief in the closing of these spaces, and speculations about the future of queer community space—play out in these new and old spaces should be considered in future research. While spaces hold celebratory queer potential, they must always be held in tension, in ambivalence, in their erasures. Queer community members' ambivalences reveal local norms and the boundary-marking processes that are inevitably central to queer nightlife.

For Sisters, and for my participants, there were two types of absences: marked and unmarked. The absences that my participants marked were specific to identities and local cultures: femmes and trans men both felt excluded from Sisters. Largely unmarked, with some exceptions, were the absences of people of color. Although Portland is a well-known liberal enclave, Maine vies with Vermont for the whitest state in the country by population. My research suggests that Sisters was not especially welcoming to LGBTQ people of color. For example, in the process of remembering these spaces, interviewees reinforce a kind of white, working-class aesthetic associated most clearly with L.L.Bean, as discussed above. This aesthetic differs from a midwestern white, working-class lesbian aesthetic oriented around other dimensions of gender expression (Kazyak 2012), and an analysis of these differences helps us unpack the ways that whiteness remains central to constructions of lesbian community and identity more broadly.

The rise and fall and rise of lesbian bars, gay bars, and (possibly) queer spaces in small cities suggest a need to examine the spatial and temporal dimensions of queer nightlives specifically in these communities (Forstie 2020; Stone 2018). The changing LGBTQ communities in these cities defy a kind of progress narrative that originates from theorization that focuses on urban queer communities, even as national discourses play out in highly local contexts. For example, lesbians in both River City, in the Midwest, and lesbian-friendly Portland, in New England, form a sense of community along lines of shared interests rather than identity (Brown-Saracino 2011). Trans men and femme lesbians experience lesbian and queer community as ambivalent home spaces in different ways across cities and regions. And what constitutes queer community in these cities remains in flux, including, for example, friendships, house parties, and LGBTQ-specific events. Understanding queer nightlife spaces in small cities critically helps us interpret changes in *urban* queer nightlives.

In addition to understanding the broader forces at work in small cities, researchers should also analyze the shifting power dynamics in *remembering* queer nightlife spaces (Drysdale 2015). There is the power to control the space of the bar, noted most vividly by Max and Logan, but there is also the power to *remember* the bar, and to determine which memories are noted as authentic. Logan, after relating a long set of what I felt were overwhelmingly sad and angry memories of the bar, stated, laughingly, "let's say something positive here," suggesting some awareness of the "correct" way to remember a lesbian bar. We might challenge our participants in the moment of an interview to consider the affective pressures to remember queer spaces in a certain (generally positive) way. And in our analytic work, we might read these narratives with ongoing skepticism (Brim and Ghaziani 2016; Browne and Nash 2010; Gould 2009). Approaching memories with a persistent sense of ambivalence and skepticism might help rural, urban, and small-city queer communities build more vibrant, flexible, and equitable spaces for the queer nightlives of the future.

Ms. Briq House in Her Own Words

Based on an interview conducted and edited by Kemi Adeyemi

My name is spelled B-R-I-Q and the Q is for queer and I say that at my show and people know that. And Suga Shaq is spelled S-U-G-A S-H-A-Q and the Q is for queer. I had my first show six years ago. It was called *Heartbreak Hotel*, and it was at the Can Can down in Pike Place Market. It was an all-POC burlesque revue on heartbreak and getting over it, and it was featuring all performers of color. Sold out.

Burlesque has a nuanced history. So, you have white women doing their thing, right? It was basically very beautiful, scantily clad women dressed in their finest, in diamonds, usually that a patron had purchased for them. It has very strong sex work history because it wasn't just like they were just dancing and that was it—there were a lot of other things. So, it originally started with women kind of making fun of high society and the rich women. Basically these are a bunch of whores who were like, *Oh, like look, I can be prissy and all these things—but it's what your husband bought for me.* It was like a joke, and it's really strongly theater based, which is why you get all the big costumes and the props and all that because burlesque is all about comedy. And then what was happening, though, was a lot of white women who were getting all the stage time and all these things, they were stealing movement from Asian women, Latina women, Black women, Indigenous women. They were going and seeing how they were moving and what they were doing, and they'd steal that movement and then make it popular.

In America, because we're fucked up here, when they did eventually start having performers of color it was really, really race baited. "Oriental Express" and all that bullshit, you know. It was hot and spicy when it was Latina women. Really promoting women of color who were mixed: *ooh, mulattos!* And, like, *She's a savage!* You know: *She was a savage but now she's a classy lady!* And all this bullshit around Black women. So when they started allowing women of color on the bill, it was still this really sensational way and they were still coming in through the back door. They were still not coming through the front door. They were still not on top billing. They were still being paid less. They were still being disrespected.

But women of color continued to press the boundary and push the issue and then ask for the same pay, and to ask the same recognition on billing, and to ask not to be sensationalized in that way. It took a long time. And even now there's like the Burlesque Hall of Fame but even their acknowledgment of women of color in the movement is very, very scarce. I mean, it's no different than any other history, like the history books that we've got in school: it's all about the colonizer and never about the colonized, and it's the same thing for burlesque. The very exact same thing for burlesque. So, they have some things, but our things weren't archived the way that white folks' were, things weren't preserved the way white folks' stuff was, things weren't written down or advertised that way—so there's some things but there's not as much.

Suga Shaq started because burlesque was great, I had a good time, but I wasn't seeing my people. And there were people coming up to me when I was sweethearting (which is like being like a stagehand for different shows) and also starting my career performing in Dr. Ginger Snap's production, which was a POC-centered burlesque show, like: *I've never seen anyone who looks like me onstage in this way. I didn't know Black people did burlesque. I didn't know this was a thing. Are there other people like us, people like you?* I wanted to create a space for folks of color who wanted to be celebrated in that same way, and I knew that there was history of it—even though you know our history is the last to be told, the last to be archived, the *last.* But I knew there was history of it and so I just wanted to create that in Seattle because I felt like what other place would it be better in? Of course it'd be better here because there are other folks of color who came before me, who were creating those safe spaces and eventually got called to other places. But it doesn't mean that the work stops. We have to continue it because we don't want other people of color coming here and feeling like they're alone.

So, I did it because I wanted to be able to curate and see people that were gender nonconforming people, all different genders, trans folks, nonbinary folks. I wanted to see fat folks. I want to see people with stretch marks. I wanted to see people of different abilities. I wanted to see everybody onstage, and I'm wanting to see them be POC, Brown and Black as fuck. And I knew that waiting around for other people to create—that was dumb. Why would I do that? Aite, no. I'll just create my own. That's how Suga Shaq started. A lot of people who don't fit society's normal standards of beauty or gender or those things are in Suga Shaq, are celebrated at Suga Shaq, because that's

Fig. 1. Portrait of Ms. Briq House. (Photograph by Fiona Pepe.)

what we're all about. Suga Shaq is very much about activism and very much rooted in the activism of the marginalized. Whether people know it or not. Of course we're sexy, but I'm all about stimulate and educate. That's my whole mission ever in life: it's always about stimulate and educate. So, I can bring people in with all of whatever they think they're getting from me. But then they leave with an education about something maybe they'd never heard of, they never thought of it, but they're willing to listen because I've already enticed them with my beauty or my sexuality or my whatever.

Whenever I host, I host and have a good time, but I also talk about things that are really important to me like sex work and sex workers' rights, and the beauty of polyamorous relationships, and BDSM relationships, and how BDSM teaches you about boundaries and you can explore that and put that into other parts of your life, and all of these things. I talk about my enjoyment of learning about sexuality and gender. I talk about my enjoyment of having people come and participate in Suga Shaq, and I educate people, like, *Hey, there are going to be people up on the stage who may not understand how to take them in. I don't want you to figure that out, I just want you to celebrate them. They can be different from anything that you've ever known. Just celebrate them because they're here and they're doing the work of sharing their bodies so you should be grateful even if you're unfamiliar with the type of person they are or what type of body they have, you should be celebrating them because they're here—and if you can't then get the fuck out of here.* So, people have been so intrigued by that and learning so much about that, that they'll just kind of like look closer to me for like, *Can I have like a one-on-one so I can figure this out?* Or even just wanting to learn burlesque, like, *Hey, like I want to know how to move my body better or be more comfortable in my body. You're a large person, I see that you have so much confidence* (which people feel like is such a compliment), *how can I have more confidence?*

People who know me from doing burlesque know me from doing burlesque, people who know me from doing sex work they don't know me for doing anything other than sex work, but a lot of people know me from doing both. Me doing burlesque opened the door for me to do sex work because I got to learn more about different lifestyles and different ways that people live in relationship. When you enter in, burlesque is such a sex-positive environment that opens the door for you to learn about all kinds of things. When I realized like some of these things that I naturally do or are natural things that I practiced when I was younger, I didn't have a name for it. I didn't know that's what it was called: it was called sex work. Once I had a name for it I realized I've already been doing that: interacting with people, setting boundaries and interacting with people around those boundaries in a way that's beneficial to both parties. You know, especially Black folks—Black folks, Black femmes—we've been doing all kinds of work. We've been doing feminist work. We've been doing queer nightlife work. We've been doing sex work. We've been doing all those things without those names for *years*. So I don't feel like I'm doing anything different than what I had already been doing. I just have a different vocabulary to express it . . . and to get better sponsors.

In the contemporary age, and even before, the sex work can include sex, but a lot of times it has nothing to do with sex at all. Like at all; like nothing to do with sex. And in the contemporary age it could look like just companionship. In the contemporary age it can look like a couple's session. In the contemporary, you can look like just a patron with the stripper or it can look like a lot of things: a dom with their sub, a top with their bottom. I mean there's so many different types of fetishes, and it can look so different than what people are assuming. You could see two people out at a park and there can be a sex work session happening and you're not even aware of it because it's not about the sex, it's about the connection. If the connection leads to sex, that's also beautiful, but that's not a necessity. It's not a prerequisite. A lot of people have a lot of things you want to talk about, a lot of *body* things they want to talk about, and they want to hire me because who will know better than a sex worker?

My particular sex work is very rooted in intimacy. Hookups are awesome. Hook up all you want to. Hook up, be safe, be responsible, be honest. But sometimes folks are just craving intimacy and so they're hooking up a lot of times and they don't actually want to hook up, but that's just kind of how other people want to operate. So, they go through the whole thing, but sometimes they just want the intimacy without the fucking, and so I'm a great person to call because they're like *I want to be able to be in a queer engagement and I want to be able to feel special and to feel this queer chemistry, but I also don't want to necessarily have sex. I want to feel close, I want to feel seen, I want to feel heard.* So, a sex worker who is familiar or is also queer, it's perfect because I'm not judging you. I don't give a shit about anything that you have chosen to do, because that was important to you. Matter of fact: I'm celebrating you for that.

Show

Dancing on the Edge, in the Silence

Trajal Harrell's *Antigone Sr. / Twenty Looks or Paris Is Burning at the Judson Church (L)*

Clare Croft

This is how it ends. A strip of gray marley, dully lit, bisecting the space. Once-full spaces near the stage's edge have emptied. The bed upstage is empty, too, its only inhabitant a tossed-off bedsheet that needs a trip to the laundry.[1] The light, the emptiness, the cleaning waiting to happen make the theater's stage look more like a barren club dance floor in post 4 a.m. light than a last moment at the end of an almost three-hour queer dance-theater spectacle. What kind of climax is this?

Yet, this is how it ends. The stage at the end of choreographer Trajal Harrell's 2012 epic *Antigone Sr. / Twenty Looks or Paris Is Burning at the Judson Church (L)* utterly lacks brightness and motion. No longer does a pulsing strip of light on that gray marley invite the five men of the work's cast to strut and sashay. No longer does the edge of the stage offer platforms for stunning solos that blend house's quick footwork, vogue's luxurious arm movements, and modern dance's sense of gravity. No longer does the bed hold gorgeous men, commenting dryly on the evening's action. All this seems like it should have culminated in something big, sexy, sequined, and loud. Instead, in the work's final moment, Jan Maertens's lighting design reveals the mundaneness of what moments before seemed a magic space.

But what this moment *looks like* cannot be equated with what it *feels like*. All that has come before still lingers. The work ends—not with the sexy climax, an explosion of a party that seemed maybe too obvious but also right—but rather with this paradoxically empty/full moment. To sit in the theater's darkness staring at the dull, blank stage feels an awful lot like stepping out of a just-closed queer club onto the sidewalk of an urban night-almost-dawn, the charged silence of a city nightscape. The transition from inside to outside affirms that, while what happened inside might be temporarily over, something of its energy and difference lasts. And that somewhat unnamable, maybe even unseen feeling can carry one into the nonqueer spaces, as well as get one back to the club the next night for another needed round.

This essay borrows these lessons from queer nightlife to explore how Trajal Harrell bends the space of the concert dance stage to reimagine the possibilities for affirming and supporting Black queer life in postmodern dance. Specifically, I examine how in *Antigone Sr.* Harrell exploits the transitional moments, especially those that interrupt expected climaxes, to illustrate the power available in the peculiar light of the always-threatening-to-recede, but also always-promising-to-return queer night. I argue that Harrell invites dancers—and audience's eyes—to play strategically along the edges of being seen, envisioning a difficult possibility of cross-racial engagement in queer dance space.

Antigone Sr. underscores the importance of the spaces between lightness and darkness through its repeated tactic of emphasizing the moments—like the concluding "work light" look—that follow climactic events. Harrell, his fellow performers, and Maertens's lighting ask the audience to attend to the charges that remain or are felt in moments of transition, moments where the simultaneity of what lingers and what disappears produces possibility. Harrell's epic dance-making shifts attention from the height of spectacle to what might happen on the other side of spectacle. *Antigone Sr.* is not a refusal of queer spectacle or a too tight nostalgic hold on queer spectacle. The choreography offers possibility via transition (even if these transitions are harsh) and seriality rather than only reproductions of well-known structures.

Antigone Sr. dances theories of spectacle that make a queer Black dancing body visible, while also recognizing that to be visible is a fraught goal for queer Black artists. In its choreographic invention aimed at an attenuated politics of Black queer visibility, *Antigone Sr.* is not just queer: it is *quare*, a term that queer Black studies scholar E. Patrick Johnson (2001, 1–2, 11) has offered to comment on queer's too-frequent erasure of racial difference. In shifting from queer to quare, Johnson seeks, first, to acknowledge the multiple raced and classed subject positions that form sexual communities, and, second, to note that these many physical expressions of sexual difference produce multiple meanings and politics of queer pleasure. Johnson's emphasis on race and on the meeting of bodies among difference provides a frame for comprehending what Harrell's work theorizes through dancing. Black queer pleasure may best reside on the edges of visibility.

The importance of the partial, the edge, and the collision of time and space in Harrell's choreography has led performance studies scholar Tavia Nyong'o (2018, 3) to place Harrell at the center of what he terms *Afro-fabulation*, which he defines as "the persistent reappearance of that which was never meant to appear, but was instead meant to be kept outside or below representation."

Nyong'o extends his argument, framing Afro-fabulations like those produced by Harrell, as both queer and Black in their relationship to fugitivity and their resistance to "reproductive, developmental, and accumulative time" (10–11). Building on Johnson's framing of Black queerness/quareness as having a particular relationship to visibility and Nyong'o's emphasis on Harrell's choreography as fugitive, I consider how these ideas manifest in the specific space of the concert stage in Harrell's *Antigone Sr.* I argue that Harrell's performance of Black queer visibility on/at the edge of representational apprehension intervenes in accepted notions and histories of US postmodern dance.

Antigone Sr. / Twenty Looks or Paris Is Burning at the Judson Church (L) is one of five dance works in Harrell's series, all of which have a title and a size label. Harrell began the project with his 2009 solo *Twenty Looks*, which he labeled *(S)*. The titles' two parts (name plus size) link conceptions of categories from drag ball competitions with those of the fashion world, making explicit how the two worlds, balls and fashion, have always been intertwined. In *Antigone Sr.*, Harrell continue this work, telling the Greek myth of Antigone through balls' creative categories and through a reappropriation of fashion iconicity. For instance, dancer Thibault Lac appears in fake Hermès scarves fashioned to create a costume for "Prince Realness," a rather queer reference to the battle between the two princes that catalyzes the tragic events surrounding Antigone.

Harrell's dramaturgical tendency to pair worlds to create spectacle extends into this pairing of vogue and postmodern dance in all the works in the series, including *Antigone Sr.* He has described the entire five-part series as being shaped around the question: "What if someone from 1963 had come down from Harlem to perform at Judson Church?" (Kourlas 2012). Harrell's phrasing of the question—which centers the Black queer performer and treats the largely white, postmodern scene as a site, interestingly echoes the image with which I began this essay: an empty scene awaits dancers who can re-ignite a space. By aligning this empty space with the Judson Church, the site usually credited by dance historians as the home of postmodern dance, Harrell presents the Black queer ball dancing body as having the agency to transform not just a space, but also a history. Judson, at least as it generally described in canonized dance history, questioned codified dance forms, insisting that the pedestrian and the nonspectacular could be dance performance, too—interventions that somewhat transformed who could be considered a dancer. One did not need dance training to dance at Judson, but Harrell's pointedly Black pairing of Judson and Harlem underscores one key limit of this reformation of who could be a dancer. Most of those involved in Judson were white.

A Black dancer's capacity to guide and transform a formerly white space is a key theme in *Antigone Sr.* The work features five dancers: Harrell, Lac, Rob Fordeyn, Stephen Thompson, and Ondrej Vidlar. Of the five, Harrell reads as the only Black dancer; the others are white to the point of almost glowing in Maertens's lighting. The piece moves across multiple sections that include the telling of Antigone and a number of solo, duet, and trio choreographies danced to an endless montage of nostalgic pop music, designed by Harrell and Robin Meier. (Cue Tori Amos's "Cornflake Girl.") Text and dance intermingle in more text-heavy sections that often deploy the mundane, task-oriented aesthetics familiar from postmodern dance. For instance, early in the work, for almost twenty minutes, Lac and Harrell sit on the bed onstage recounting, in deadpan voices, a long list of pairs of pop culture icons (Mary Kate and Ashley, Serena and Venus), as well as joking riffs on the linguistic pairings ("Victoria and her secret") that offer tiny insertions of humor into the work's otherwise flat affective field.

In terms of movement, *Antigone Sr.* draws on all its historical sources in a wild mélange, again blending white postmodern with Black vernacular dance. While the work's movement vocabulary is often functional—sashaying down the runway/catwalk or accomplishing tasks like taking string through the audience—several sequences offer full-out dance. In these moments, the dancers usually bounce (literally) in what looks like house footwork meeting the sixties Pony or slow, luxurious choreography drawn from vogue's slashing grace.

From its opening moments, *Antigone Sr.* stages a queer Black subject at its center, yet it also makes clear that not all that this subject has done or is doing can be fully comprehended. Harrell begins *Antigone Sr.* standing in the audience just in front of the stage, wearing a shirt and pants that do not look like much of a costume, if any. He is so casual that his address barely feels like a curtain speech, and it definitely does not feel like part of the performance. In this mode, he explains that the piece is too big for the theater, so the work has been modified to fit the space. He also adds that the cast is "still working" on the piece. Harrell's prologue invites the audience to imagine, from the outset, what might not be yet fully present in what they are about to see. *Antigone Sr.* trains its audience to imagine what cannot be seen because of space or time limitations, and this early, important training comes in a moment that seems not part of the show, a first transition.

Antigone Sr. uses transitions to do more than deliver significant spectatorial information. In the section that follows Harrell's pre-show speech, it is clear that it is the moments that follow obvious climaxes—rather than climaxes themselves—that deliver the work's Black queer spectacle. After Harrell finishes his opening remarks, the remaining four cast members enter.

Lac, with Harrell now onstage and at his side, invites the audience to stand and join him in the evening's "house anthem." Britney Spears's "Baby One More Time" blares through the theater. Initially everyone, cast and audience alike, sings along, a moment that seemingly brings the audience into a world in which queer investments can cross racial difference. The Black Harrell and white Lac lead the predominantly white but interracial audience in the boisterous sing-along. But then, as the cast turns the musical key toward a minor register and slows the tempo, cross-racial utopia fades. As the cast's voices grow increasingly mournful, audience members cease singing and then somewhat awkwardly take their seats. The potential for a loud, cathartic climax disappears, replaced by melancholy and awkwardness. Being all together feels, if not impossible, at least difficult. This is the first of many times in *Antigone Sr.* that a climax of queer, cross-racial ecstasy seems to be just on the horizon. But this climax never comes, and the moment of this realization is the moment that really matters.

The experience of an occluded cross-racial utopia orients the audience (or at least the dance historians in it) to the performance's animating question: "What would have happened in 1963 if someone from the voguing dance tradition would have come downtown to Judson Church to perform alongside the early postmoderns?" (American Realness Festival 2013). Harrell has said that the question interests him as a choreographic departure point not to imagine what would happen if he could go back in time, but rather to imagine a "historical impossibility" in a public space. He wanted to explore "how *together* as an audience we can use . . . historical imagination to see future possibilities. This idea of imagining together is something that performance can provide. . . . The show proposes a certain way to activate the viewer to be in this negotiation with me" (Harrell 2011, italics added). The act of seeing *Antigone Sr.* in a downtown New York theater re-creates a version of the scene Harrell imagines, putting a Black vogue artist—or at least a Black queer artist borrowing from that tradition—into a primarily white space. The stage gets marked as white through casting and the audience makeup. Working in these rich transition moments after near climaxes, we all navigate the awkwardness and partialness of racial integration. I am unsure whether this navigation helps one imagine future possibility as Harrell hopes, but I do feel forced to experience the complication of racial difference on terms proposed by a Black queer person.

There is never any doubt that in *Antigone Sr.* Harrell is the work's principal creator and its artistic, intellectual engine, even though he is just as often among the audience as he is onstage. In a moment that feels particularly potent in its centralizing of Harrell, the cast members tie strings to one of

Harrell's hands and then crawl through the audience, still holding the string and distributing it through the audience space. When the other dancers reach the back wall of the theater, Harrell raises his hands, lifting the strings above the audience to become not just *Antigone Sr.*'s protagonist and emcee, but its master magician. We are now in his space, even though his initial question imagines his coming into white postmodern space. To return to E. Patrick Johnson's evocation, this is quare space.

What if this *is* Judson? What if Judson is no longer the climax of postmodern dance, but is rather the never-fully-realized climax that *Antigone Sr.* can transition concert dance beyond? The consideration of *Antigone Sr.* as both Judson and post-Judson offers a compelling queering/quaring of the mundane and spectacle as choreographic possibility. Of the many practitioners associated with Judson—Steve Paxton, Deborah Hay, Fred Herko, Judith Dunn, and Robert Dunn, to name just a few—probably the best known figure is dance- and filmmaker Yvonne Rainer, who, in 1965, penned the "No Manifesto" while also making the piece *Parts of Some Sextets*. Rainer has long since disavowed the manifesto's aesthetic claims, but nonetheless the short script has become synecdochic with postmodern dance. It begins: "No to spectacle. No to virtuosity." Rainer refused what she saw as the ocular-centric and emotional excesses of modernism in favor of the pedestrian. This shift (at least for Rainer in her later work) had feminist implications and facilitated a particular relationship to the idea of choreographic transitions. Rainer's most famous work, *Trio A* (1963)—which had many iterations but is best known as a solo danced by Rainer—has either no transitions or is one long transition, depending on how one looks at it. Rainer—in a choice seen by many as a rejection of the male gaze—leaves the audience without a clear sense of what to look at while she dances. Everything is important, and nothing is important: see everything and nothing at once.

In a 2011 interview with Harrell, dance scholar Thomas DeFrantz noted that two conceptions of visibility also meet in Harrell's pairing of Judson and voguing. On the one hand, Judson highlights the question of visibility by refusing visual spectacle. On the other hand, drag balls, with their large-scale, eye-catching, bold movement vocabulary and reclamation of elite tools and characters, in DeFrantz's words, "idolize the possibility of being seen" (Harrell 2011). Of course, one can only refuse visibility if one has access to visibility in the first place. Harrell's work, by proposing the travel of a queer Black subject from Harlem to the Village, moves a drag ball figure into visibility and then ponders what could happen after this. How does the Black queer postmodern choreographer manipulate transitions as Rainer did? Can they? How can the queer dancing subject retain any sense of power, or imagine that their stage could exist again? What happens when the lights come on?

While Harrell names only Judson and drag balls as his historical sources, his choreographic and performance strategies draw on a wider repertory of interruptive work, particularly that of Black feminist artists. Harrell deploys what Daphne A. Brooks (2011, 179, 182)—speaking about vocalist Nina Simone and drawing from Houston A. Baker Jr.—calls *supraliteracy*, commenting on Black presence and absence in dance and performance spaces while also refusing to allow the white audience to wander in a romance of Blackness. Harrell is just as often in the edges of Maertens's lighting, dancing in the shadows, as he is in spotlight or at the microphone. Whereas the white voguing men in silky light easily become beautiful for the audience, Harrell often dances in a corner, offstage, or out of the lights. While the white members of the cast dance onstage near the work's end, Harrell has a one-man dance party in an offstage corner of the audience. In the space of New York's Abrons Arts Center, where *Antigone Sr.* has most often appeared, Harrell dances in a corner well beyond any space where the stage lights can catch him. His dark form registers more as energy than shape. The audience can see his pleasure in dancing but cannot really see him. The pleasure is his, not offered for those watching. To paraphrase Nyong'o, Harrell's dancing is an Afro-fabulation, demonstrating a queer, Black refusal of spectacle, existing just outside or below full representational (white) comprehension. Harrell's dancing, like much of *Antigone Sr.*, says "yes" to virtuosity, while also refusing to be the spectacle for someone else. To Rainer's 1965 "No to virtuosity. No to spectacle," Harrell has made an addendum: "No to virtuosity for others, for white eyes."

Harrell's solo locates him as a particular presence, a singular Black presence in the work. Elsewhere he uses the post-climax transition to comment on the audience's gaze both in terms of race and sexuality. Harrell comments as much on a straight gaze as he does on a white gaze by offering to his fellow dancers, the quartet of white men who join him in *Antigone Sr.*, a similar possibility of dancing in not quite fully seen light.

Near the end of the work, a giant queer dance party takes place, and it is easy to assume that this celebratory moment will finally end the evening. The dance party happens three-quarters of the way through the work and features all cast members strutting into space. Vidlar begins the party, doing a samba-like, prancing step with such vigor that his legs seem to threaten to leave the rest of his body behind. Light fills the theater: side light creates glaring, starlike shapes, and the house lights come up to half. As audience, we have been in our seats for more than two hours at this point without intermission; surely (I think) we have earned a place on the dance floor. The dancers suggest I am right: they cavort through the audience as Harrell sashays onto the stage, yelling at everyone to "Werk!" The soundtrack moves from the original 1984 version of "The Roof Is on Fire" to Zebra Katz's "Ima Read," a 2003 hit by the openly gay, Black, male rapper that was Katz's homage to the Harlem ball scene. The dancers, who have changed into togalike dresses made from ripped cotton—a gesture to the entire work's DIY aesthetic—first sing along playfully, then speak along earnestly with the lyrics of "Ima Read": "It's gonna be cohesive / It's gonna be my thesis / I'ma read that bitch." The space is full—full of light, the dancers' virtuosity, and an ambiguous mix of humor, solemnity, and play. It could all end right here. And the white and Black folks, at least all the queers, have found their way together again, and coming together feels surprisingly easy.

But the work doesn't end with this sonic, visual, and participatory high. Instead, the dancers' campy mimicry of "I'ma take that bitch to college" turns into a wail, and the lights dim. The sensorial excess is not a climax, but an entrée into the hushed section that follows. One by one, dancers appear in the barest but silkiest of light. Their forms are scarcely visible: part ghost, part shadow, all feeling. Warm white light from above washes over the dancers' bare torsos and arms, offering only hints of their physical shape: an elbow here, a shoulder there. Music plays softly, but the light and gliding dancing invite hushed silence. The stunning, buzzing, not-quite-silence absolutely conjures the moment of stepping out of a party into a vacant urban nightscape. There is a hum, a disorientation. A luxuriant sense of absent presences always lingers in *Antigone Sr.*'s excess. The hum means that the night happened even if you can't see it right now, and it might be just enough to get you to the next night.

Yes to climaxing *and* transitioning. Yes to not fully knowing. Yes to awkwardness (it means you're not assuming you know the rules). Yes to being on the edge of visibility, seen on one's own terms.

Note

1. All performance description is drawn from my live viewing of the work at the Abrons Art Center in 2013 as part of the American Realness Festival.

Una Peña en Párraga

Drag Kings and Cuba's Sexual Revolution

Matthew Leslie Santana

There was only one drag king performance at the 2016 Conference ("Jornada") against Homophobia and Transphobia in Havana. It consisted of a Black lesbian woman, Argelia, dressed as a man, Alberto, during the Conga against Homophobia and Transphobia, Cuba's version of the gay pride marches that take place all over the world. As the crowd waited in a staging area to begin marching, Alberto posed for photos, wearing light khaki pants, a burnt orange shirt, a tie, and a baseball cap. He then marched down the streets of Havana with the rest of us, occasionally holding on with one hand to the giant Cuban flag that participants escort along the route. Argelia had tried to convince the National Center for Sex Education (CENESEX), which hosts the Jornada, to include *transformismo masculino* (drag king performance) in the gala performance that punctuates the conference, but CENESEX had not agreed.[1] So, this cameo in the march was the extent of Alberto's participation that year.

When I caught up with Argelia at another event during the Jornada, we realized that I was leaving Cuba the day of her next *peña*, or informal performance. I was dismayed because I had only been able to see Argelia—who was at the helm of Havana's nascent drag king movement—perform once before, and I was back in Cuba beginning research for a dissertation on gender performance on the island. "Don't worry," she said to me when I told her I would miss her show, "voy a hacer una peña en Párraga antes de que te vayas" (I'll put on a *peña* in Párraga before you go).

This essay examines performances that took place at that gathering in order to imagine the possibilities that *transformismo masculino* engenders in contemporary Cuba. Since 2008, CENESEX has been engaged in a campaign—often referred to as Cuba's "sexual revolution"—to transform public opinion and government policy toward sexual diversity. This effort has changed the terrain of gender performance on the island, where it was once practiced in secrecy and now is the main attraction at state-run gay nightclubs and polit-

Fig. 1. Argelia, in drag as Alberto, at the 2016 Conference against Homophobia and Transphobia (Jornada) in Havana, Cuba. (Photograph by Matthew Leslie Santana.)

ical events sponsored by CENESEX. Drag *king* performance, however, has failed to gain traction in these more prominent spaces.

In a way, then, this essay is about some exclusions of queer nightlife. In Cuba, at least, the *transformismo* (gender performance) scene is dominated by men, and Black women in particular have been marginalized within both that industry and the queer nightlife spaces that sustain it. This essay turns away from the nightclub to follow Havana's *transformistas masculinas* (drag kings) to an intimate *peña* in a house on the outskirts of the city. After narrating that performance, I consider the place of *transformismo masculino* within the larger context of queer nightlife and sexual revolution in contemporary Cuba. I suggest that *transformismo masculino* conjures a different kind of sexual revolution, one that emerges from groups left out of mainstream discourses and promotes queer mobilization within a broader fabric of social and economic formations.

RUMBA AND TOURISM

Argelia organized the *peña* in her neighborhood of Párraga, which is roughly seven miles south of the central El Vedado area where my mother was born and where I was staying. I recognized the name of the neighborhood from stories my grandmother had told me; she had spent her adolescence living with a relative there. I was eager to visit, but I had never been, so I took careful notes on how to get there. These did little to help me when I eventually tried—along with my brother and my partner, who were with me in Cuba at the time—to make my way to Argelia's house from a friend's place in La Víbora, a neighborhood that is about halfway between El Vedado and Párraga. Unable to find a collective taxi or a bus that would get us close enough, I resigned to hiring a private taxi in what felt like a failure to me on the very avenues my mother and her parents had traveled in the middle of the last century.

The driver left us in front of the house with the number Argelia had told us, but it wasn't her house. Neither was the small cottage on the back of the lot. Argelia's place was tucked away in a small corner near the center of the property. The front door opened into the kitchen, and beyond that was a small bedroom with a door that opened to a small patio. She was making some snacks when we arrived, but she took a break to give us a tour. The place is slowly coming together, she told us, as she patches the roof here, lays some new floor there. We went back to the kitchen, and she showed us some of her artwork, mostly glass bottles she decorates with Afroreligious themes using papier-mâché, paint, and photos. These then serve as items to sell, to raffle off at shows, or to give to friends as gifts.

When Argelia finished preparing the food, we walked to her friend Nidia's house for the gathering. A few women were already there when we arrived, and we talked with them over rum and fortified wine purchased from a neighbor. Nidia's house was simple but ample. A small patio separated the front door from the street. The door opened into the living room, which had a sofa and a couple of chairs oriented toward the television in the corner. The kitchen was behind the living room and looked out onto it, and there were two bedrooms off of the central hallway. Nidia's living room would serve as the stage, and the performers would be using her TV and a small pair of speakers for the show. This is a common sound system in Havana, where people often carry USB flash drives (*memorias*) with them and accumulate songs and other media from friends or vendors. In a country with an extremely limited internet infrastructure, these *memorias* serve as a kind of Cuban intranet. By plugging the *memoria* into a television set, you can scroll through the contents and choose songs to play.

Argelia's girlfriend, Ana—also a *transformista*—was late getting back from work, so the show started with just two drag kings. The audience was composed of friends of theirs, mostly women they knew from Grupo OREMI, CENESEX's network for lesbian and bisexual women. Argelia emerged as Alberto, wearing dress shoes, slacks, a dress shirt casually unbuttoned, and a driving cap. He and Andy—the stage persona of Argelia's friend Diana—split the set, mostly lip-synching and dancing to love songs and salsa hits by Spanish and Caribbean artists like David Bisbal, Son by Four, and Luis Enrique. Using a hairbrush as a microphone, they took turns interpreting each song, stepping in rhythm with the music, making measured gestures with their free hands, and contorting their faces into earnest and impassioned expressions along with the music.

Toward the end of this half of the show, however, Alberto and Andy performed to "La Gozadera," a *guaguancó* by the famed folkloric ensemble Yoruba Andabo. The *guaguancó* is a type of rumba, and it is a partner dance intended for a man and a woman, often associated with the *vacunao* gesture (see Daniel 1995). In the *vacunao*, the man thrusts his pelvis toward the woman, and she tries to block his approach by shielding herself or turning away from him. As the song began, Alberto took the lead, lip-synching the opening lines, while Andy danced next to him. When the chorus and percussion entered, Andy lip-synched the refrain, and Alberto fell into step with his movements. At one point, Alberto handed the microphone to Andy, surrendering the lead to go in search of a dance partner. His eyes landed on my brother, Bobby, and he extended his hand, inviting Bobby to rise and dance with him. Bobby—always a good sport—danced as he could with Alberto, gamely mimicking Alberto's movements to the beat of the rumba. Eventually, Alberto swayed around Bobby, enticing him closer. When Bobby became distracted by a *pregón* (a call from a street vendor outside), Alberto seized the moment and thrust his pelvis at him in a rather unsubtle rendition of the *vacunao*. Far from being skillfully deflected, Alberto's thrust landed squarely on my brother's hip, and the audience erupted in laughter and applause.

Alberto and Bobby's dance subverted a number of power relations that shape *transformismo* and queer nightlife in contemporary Havana. Social dance is, to be sure, an important site in which such relations play out. As Celeste Fraser Delgado and José Esteban Muñoz (1997, 9) describe, "dance sets politics in motion, bringing people together in rhythmic affinity where identification takes the form of histories written on the body through gesture." Given their focus on "Latin/o America," it is no surprise that their introductory essay turns quickly toward the rumba and its history as an example of the kinds of moves that made cultural retention possible through slavery (10–11).

The mere presence of the rumba at this house party distinguished this space from both the gay nightclubs and the political events where *transformismo* is often featured. In *transformismo* performances that take place in gay nightclubs, the rumba is often elided or, when present, mocked. Though drag shows in Cuba are indeed highly dependent on Black expressive cultures and artists (like Celia Cruz, La Lupe, Whitney Houston, Beyoncé), the rumba seems to be too local, too folkloric, too Black for the transnational marketplace that is the gay nightclub in Havana.[2] At political events featuring *transformismo*, by contrast, the rumba often takes its place as an example of national culture (see Daniel 1991), serving as the opener and closer for shows that include drag queens, singers, and dancers. Whether it is excluded or bracketed, then, the rumba is kept in a sphere distinct from most mainstream *transformismo femenino* (drag queen) performances.

At this drag king *peña*, however, the rumba was lovingly, thoughtfully performed, even as it was put to do another kind of racial and sexual work. First, Alberto offered a queer reimagining of the rumba when he plucked my brother, rather than any of the women in attendance, from the audience. His carefully placed *vacunao* further inverted some important relations within queer nightlife in Cuba. In one way, Alberto and Bobby's dance could be read as a dramatization of the racialized practice of *jineterismo* (hustling) in postsocialist Cuba. *Jineterismo* refers to a wide range of activities within informal economies—including sex work—that Cubans engage in with foreigners. In queer contexts, fair-skinned foreign gay men often come to Cuba in search of *pingueros*—butch tops who are disproportionately young and Black—and use the audience of a drag show as a space to find them. Male sex work (and *pinguerismo*) is one reason cited by Cuban police and authorities for a more general criminalization of Black masculinity, particularly in Havana's city center.[3] This industry and its legal ramifications are a central element of Havana's queer nightlife, as Cubans, particularly Black men, are forced to deploy tactics to evade abuse from the police.

I also see the dance, however, as a duet between Argelia, a Black lesbian drag king, and Bobby, a fair-skinned diasporic Cuban. In this way, their rumba was acting out an inversion of and variation on the dynamic in which fair-skinned foreign men come to Cuba in search of *la mulata*, the mixed-race woman who has served as a symbol of the nation since independence and who is still used to sell the island to tourists. The very tourism sphere that props up Havana's queer nightlife scene is itself predicated on foreign men's conquests of *mulata* women. In Argelia and Bobby's rumba, however, a Black lesbian woman positioned herself as the leader, the instructor, the one who—at the opportune moment—landed her *vacunao* on a fair-skinned visitor. The performance was indicative, then, of the social capacity of *transformismo masculino*, which Argelia and others use as a tool to advocate for the needs of Black lesbian women in postsocialist Cuba.

BALADA AND HOMOEROTICISM

Argelia's girlfriend, Ana, was several hours late getting home from work, and eventually we decided to go looking for her. After a short walk with Argelia through her neighborhood, during which she greeted a handful of neighbors, we found Ana at the bakery where she was employed, exhausted after a long shift. The bakery was run out of the front of someone's house, and the upstairs kitchen served as Ana's workspace. The owner of the bakery was paying Ana the equivalent of one *peso convertible* a day for her labor, and even this payment was often delayed, she told us.[4] Still, this salary would have put Ana's earnings roughly in line with the average state salary at the time. After talking with Argelia for a few minutes, Ana sent us on our way and promised that she would be home shortly. As we were walking back to Nidia's house, Argelia told me that she would soon start working at the bakery, too, at least until she and Ana could work out a way to make enough money on their own terms.

Ana finally arrived at the house a bit later than we did, and despite her grueling day at the bakery she changed her clothes and got ready to perform as Dany. Dressed in jeans, a dress shirt, a vest, a long tie, and a baseball cap, Dany danced and lip-synched to "A Puro Dolor," a sentimental ballad by the Puerto Rican salsa group Son by Four.[5] Alberto served as a backing vocalist, and he swayed in rhythm in the background as Dany sang the amorous first verse. Though the lyrics of the song are meant to suggest heterosexual desire, Alberto and Dany's interactions complicated this meaning. Watching Dany perform, Alberto would drift toward him flirtatiously, with lust in his eyes, and Dany would dutifully rebuff him. After a little while, Alberto's eyes would eventually drift once again toward Dany, drawing attention to the song's homosocial triangle and dramatizing the erotic charge between the two male performers. Again, Dany would scold Alberto for this, trying to make him snap out of it.

The women in the audience delighted in these moments, knowing full well that Argelia and Ana were lesbian partners offstage. These games also riff, however, on the latent (yet blatant) homoeroticism already present in the ensemble Latinx pop songs to which these women often perform. Take the video for "A Puro Dolor," for example, in which the members of Son by Four perform the song in a dimly lit room, surrounded by a group of instrumentalists. The woman to whom they are singing is nowhere to be found; instead, the men form a wall of homosociality, sincerely belting their feelings to one another. In turning lustfully to Dany during their duet, Alberto laid bare the homoeroticism underlying such songs.

In performing this routine as Afrodescendants in Cuba, Argelia and Ana also disrupted a deeply rooted association of Black men with heterosexuality and homophobia on the island. This is part of a larger association of Blackness with masculinity, one that also leads Cubans to interpret dark-skinned Black women as butch while erasing the presence of Black queer men. This attitude overlooks a vibrant queer of color world in Havana, the capital city of a country that is, despite census data that suggests otherwise, majority Black and mixed race. Gay nightclubs that exist outside of the tourist infrastructure in particular draw a much higher proportion of Afro-Cuban patrons. Not coincidentally, fairer-skinned gay Cubans often describe these establishments as dangerous or lowbrow, trafficking in the aforementioned associations of Blackness with masculinity, criminality, and violence.

Argelia and Ana intervene in these logics through their performances. Their emphasis on homoeroticism within male-dominated musical genres associated with heteronormative love disturbs broader investments in normative masculinity on the island in favor of staging masculinity's anxieties and desires. These performances are not a mere play on latent homoeroticism between men, however. This critical commentary on masculinity is in service of a larger project of advocating for Black lesbian women in the context of queer social life in Cuba and a sexual revolution that centers and has disproportionately benefited gay men.

SON AND REGIONALISM

Toward the end of the night, Alberto emerged from one of the bedrooms transformed again, this time wearing a straw hat evocative of the Cuban *guajiro* or countryman. He scoured his *memoria* and selected "Como baila Marieta," a *son* by the late Afro-Cuban *tres* player and singer Faustino Oramas, better known as El Guayabero.[6] In her performance, Argelia embodied an old rural Cuban man: after deftly swaying her hips to salsa and rumba earlier, here she stiffened her stance, restricted her movements, and strained her face to resemble a Cuban *viejito* (old man). The audience laughed along as Alberto mimed some of the more comedic lyrics in the verses, which relied on wordplay and evoked rural life in the Cuban countryside. This performance was unique in the course of the show, as it lacked either the amorous charge of the sappy love songs or the more virtuosic movement of the dance numbers. Instead, Argelia engaged in a kind of multidimensional drag that hinged on a transformation not only of gender but also of age and region.

Nevertheless, the performance of this *son* fits within a larger scheme of this troupe to enact diverse Cuban masculinities. The rural *guajiro*, then, lives among the *rumbero*, the *reggaetonero*, and even the foreign crooner. Moreover, however, I see Argelia in this performance highlighting the salience of regional divisions in contemporary Cuba. Oramas is from Holguín, a predominantly white city in Cuba's largely Afro-Cuban Oriente, or eastern region. Rebecca Bodenheimer (2015) has argued that regionalism is a crucial marker of difference as it, like race, threatens the coherence of narratives of Cuban national unity, an important element of Cuban revolutionary rhetoric since the late nineteenth century. I would argue that this marker operates on various levels: Cuba is shaped not only by the internal division between Havana and the provinces but also by the division between Havana's city center and its predominantly Black *repartos* (outlying neighborhoods), which have not witnessed the kinds of postsocialist development that have transformed, for example, El Vedado.

Alberto's performance of Oramas, then, ought to be understood within a context in which Argelia, a Black lesbian woman, lives and works in the *repartos* of Havana. It points to a racialized class division in a postsocialist Cuba that has witnessed uneven economic development that expresses itself both racially and spatially. Havana's drag king movement has emerged from and found support in the *repartos* and away from the tourism economy at a time when access to capital from that sector determines one's ability to live with dignity on the island.

TRANSFORMISMO MASCULINO, QUEER NIGHTLIFE, AND SEXUAL REVOLUTION

Once the sun had set and the mosquitos had come out, we lingered for a while to chat and then began our journey back to El Vedado. Argelia and Ana insisted on escorting us to a more central part of town where we could catch a collective taxi. We walked through the dark, humid night and caught a bus to Mónaco. Once there, Argelia and Ana waited until we were able to hail a car that would get us to El Vedado, and we said a final good-bye before my brother and I headed back to the United States. Arriving in El Vedado, my brother, my partner, and I caught one more bus before making our way to the house where we were staying. Our winding trip—two long walks, two bus rides, and the wait for and journey in the collective taxi—was the same one that Argelia and Ana made each time they went to a CENESEX event in El Vedado during the Jornada.

This is the distance between mainstream queer nightlife scenes in Havana—which are centered in El Vedado—and *transformismo masculino* in Cuba's capital city. This divide is illustrative of widening racial and economic disparity since the fall of socialism. Cuban cultural critic Roberto Zurbano (2014, 71) has suggested that Cuba's dual currency system—a tourist currency and a local currency—created "two contrasting realities," one in which white Cubans enjoyed access to capital from abroad and another where Black Cubans saw "a reversal or paralysis of the great social mobility that propelled them from 1959 to 1989." Numerous feminist critics have pointed out that women—especially Black women—have also been excluded from or exploited within the more lucrative tourism sector on which the dual currency scheme is based (e.g., Abd'Allah-Álvarez Ramírez 2016; Torres Santana 2020).

These economic changes along with Cuba's sexual revolution have transformed the structure of queer nightlife in Havana. The state-run gay nightclubs that dot El Vedado would have been unthinkable before the CENESEX-sponsored movement. Nevertheless, they are yet another example of the kinds of racial, sexual, and economic stratifications that have come to define Cuban society after socialism: the nightclubs are geared toward foreigners, they generate capital within the tourism industry, and they have been reluctant to welcome Havana's *transformistas masculinas*.

Such critiques build on other observations about CENESEX and its sexual revolution. Frances Negrón-Muntaner (2008) and Abel Sierra Madero (2014), for example, have described the movement as a kind of *transformismo* or *travestismo* (transvestism) of the state, in which the Cuban government is attempting to rehabilitate its homophobic image while accumulating more citizens under its aegis, thus limiting possibilities for grassroots protest and dissent. Tanya Saunders (2009, 2016) has been more specific about the ways that CENESEX elides racialized experiences of queer people and racialized histories of queer mobilization. One of Saunders's (2016, 154) interlocutors, for example, points out that CENESEX owes a debt to hip-hop group Krudxs Cubensi for its role in spearheading conversations about racial and sexual diversity at a time when there was no official dialogue on either topic. Saunders (2009, 170) further critiques CENESEX for its failure to adequately support Grupo OREMI, the center's network for bisexual and lesbian women. During Grupo OREMI's heyday in 2005, 150–200 women would gather "for antiracist social critique, lesbian empowerment, and socialization." Overwhelmed by the interest in the group and fearful of negative public response to lesbian public affection, CENESEX downsized the group in fall 2005. Saunders (2009, 170) describes this move as complicit in "a racialized sex/gender system that continues to impede Black lesbians' ability to participate fully in Cuban society as autonomous subjects."[7]

At CENESEX events, it is clear that the center is eager to differentiate its sexual revolution from the US gay rights movement. Dr. Mariela Castro Espín, the director of CENESEX, has tried to distance the movement from, for example, a singular focus on marriage equality (see Lavers 2017). Chants during the Jornada of "Socialismo sí! Homofobia no!" (Socialism yes! Homophobia no!) also favorably distinguish Cuba's sexual revolution from the US gay rights movement's comfortable ties to corporate money and global capital. Other slogans take aim at US foreign policy more generally, like "Me incluyo! Me incluyo! Abajo el bloqueo!" (I include myself! I include myself! Down with the embargo!).

Argelia's *peña* in Párraga points to a potent possibility for how a Cuban sexual revolution could indeed look very different from the US gay rights movement. Genuine discussions about how sexual subjectivities are inextricable from racial formations and intensifications of global racial capitalism would be a stark counterexample. To be clear, it would be inaccurate to characterize these women as working entirely outside of CENESEX's efforts. Many of them enthusiastically participate in CENESEX's programming as members of Grupo OREMI, and they often communicate positive feelings about the organization and their role within it (see White 2017, 168–71). Instead, I want to imagine them working alongside and beyond official channels to accomplish social goals that go beyond mainstream discourses of sexual diversity.

Transformismo masculino emerges from the artists' positions as poor, Black, lesbian women from the *repartos*. In the context of a sexual revolution that has disproportionately benefited gay men, *transformismo masculino* comes decidedly from the labor of lesbian women. As Argelia put it in a 2017 interview, "the main premise of my work is to empower women, to give visibility to women" (Fernandes 2017). At a time when Cuba is witnessing a renewed racialized disparity of wealth, *transformismo masculino* is spurred on by a woman who describes herself as Black and poor. Argelia and her collaborators rely on Afro-Cuban music to do this work, like their performances of the rumba and the *son* above. Finally, within the geographically uneven development of Havana and Cuba, *transformismo masculino* emerges from and finds support in Havana's *repartos*. Even if they are on the outskirts of both the city and official discourses of sexual revolution, *transformistas masculinas* in Havana are already demonstrating what another kind of sexual revolution might look, sound, and move like, what it might be able to do.

Earlier drafts of this essay were presented at Harvard University's Department of Music lunch talks, Drama Colloquium, and Graduate School of Arts and Sciences Gender and Sexuality Workshop; the annual meetings of the Society for Ethnomusicology and the Southeastern Council of Latin American Studies; and the Tepoztlán Institute for the Transnational History of the Americas. I am grateful for comments at each of these meetings. I am particularly indebted to the careful reading of Krystal Klingenberg, Michael Uy, and Kareem Khubchandani, whose suggestions inspired substantial revisions.

Notes

1. The usage of *transformismo* and *transformista* in Cuba most closely mirrors that of "gender performance" and "gender performer" in the United States, although these phrases are not direct translations. I use "gender performance" throughout to denote

the vast field of *transformismo* in Cuba, but for clarity I use "drag king" to describe an artist performing masculinity (*transformista masculina*).

2. See Berry (2016, 30–33) for a more in-depth discussion of the relationship between rumba, folkloric performance, and Blackness in postsocialist Cuba.

3. See Hodge (2001), Allen (2011), and Stout (2014) for more in-depth discussions of queer sex work in Cuba. See Hodge (2014) for a discussion of criminality, race, and gender performance in Cuba.

4. As of 2020, Cuba still operated on a dual currency system in which the value of the *peso convertible* or CUC—a tourist currency—was equivalent to the US dollar and is worth roughly twenty-five pesos in the local currency, *moneda nacional* or CUP.

5. The group also recorded a salsa version of the song, but the duo here performed to the ballad version. *Balada* emerges from bolero, a genre often associated with drag queen performance in the Spanish-speaking Americas (see La Fountain-Stokes 2008).

6. *Son* is a distinctive Cuban genre with working-class Black origins. It is characterized by, among other features, a final *montuno* section that involves rapid fluctuations between the chorus and improvising vocalists or instrumental soloist (see R. Moore 1997, 89–91). The signature instrument of the *son* is the *tres*, a metal-strung plucked string instrument smaller than the modern guitar with three courses of double strings spaced widely from one another (see Sublette 2004, 336–38).

7. While Grupo OREMI certainly operates on a smaller scale now than it did in summer 2005, it is still to a certain extent a space for lesbian and bisexual women to gather and have critical discussions about race, class, gender, and sexuality.

Muxes Have Crossed the Border

Altivas, Celebration, and Walls That Bleed

Noé López

> There are stories never forgotten,
> stories that time cannot carry away,
> they are written on the wall,
> in her heart. It's useless to paint,
> a thousand colors won't erase her memory.
> She knows this well:
> It's not that the pain subsides with time,
> It's that one learns to live with the pain.
>
> —Irma Pineda, CUE' YOO (The Wall)
> Translated by Wendy Call

Muxe: The Zapotec word for a gender that is neither man nor woman.

In an Armenian elementary school hall that resembled a basketball court in West Hollywood, people gathered for a Zapotec *vela*, a celebration. The women dressed in traditional Zapotec dresses with ribbons tied to their braided hair, dresses colorful as valleys of flowers that bleed pink, red, yellow, and purple. The circular tables around the dance floor were decorated with *manteles* of white and purple colors. The ceiling was decorated with pink, green, and yellow flags tied together with many ropes. The DJ played the music of the Isthmus of Tehuantepec, especially "La Zandunga," a *son istmeño* as Zapotec people call it. With the *son*'s rhythm—one, two, one, two—the mayordoma, the organizer of the *vela*, entered the place. Her little daughter and her husband were by her side; they were then followed by a procession of Muxes along with men and women dressed in traditional Zapotec attire. Men wore black pants and white dress shirts, while women and Muxes wore traditional gala dresses.

Maritza Sánchez was announced as the Muxe to be crowned queen of the celebration. She entered in a Zapotec blue dress along with her *novio*, her partner. Maritza arrived to the dance floor with her face and her back straight while gracefully moving her body to the rhythm of the music. When Maritza danced, she held the front part of her dress and moved it delicately side to side and up and down. Such posture distinguishes Tehuanas (Zapotec women from the Isthmus of Tehuantepec) as *altivas*, meaning "prideful" or "arrogant." An *altiva* knows that the garments—Zapotec gala dresses and golden jewelry—that decorate her body represent the beauty of her culture. Maritza danced as an *altiva*, a prideful Muxe. Photographers and journalists surrounded Maritza as she entered the dance floor, desperately trying to capture pictures and videos. I sat next to the stage accompanied by my two nieces. We watched with amusement the glamorous scenario, as the queen entered the dance floor.

As the ceremony continued, the DJ played an audio-recorded narrative of Maritza that described her life growing up as a boy in Santa Ana del Valle in Oaxaca, Mexico. She is the only Muxe among her three siblings—one man and two women. In her narrative, Maritza detailed her transformation from a man to a Muxe, the moment when she embraced her femininity and her native culture in Mexico and the United States. Such transformation was influenced by her life experiences in rural Oaxaca, crossing the US-Mexican border, and settling in Los Angeles, California.

She was the queen of the night. She was the subject of the curiosity of others who came to the celebration to see her crowned. People were dancing, eating, and clamoring to take pictures with their smart phones. It seemed like joy was everywhere, in every table and in every corner. Celebration was key in people's pride of Zapotec culture; Maritza and other attendees described it as "accepting" and "open" of third gender people.

Nostalgia was in every song, in every dress, in every plate of *botanas* (appetizers), the food the mayordomo, the mayordoma's husband, was distributing. Nostalgia was the longing of Oaxacan fiestas, Tehuantepec music, and the language of the people. Attendees told me: "Pues allá en Oaxaca, las fiestas son más grandes" (in Oaxaca the parties are bigger). They said it as if this party will never be enough and that it will never measure up to the ones in their land. It seems that it doesn't matter where parties take place nowadays. Nothing will equate to the joy at a party in Oaxaca. Nostalgia doesn't exist there. But the purpose of this chapter is not to explain why nostalgia doesn't exist in certain places. I won't describe how this *vela*—in an Armenian school hall in West Hollywood—should be experienced or argue how "decolonial" it is (Tuck and Yang 2012). This chapter is not to satisfy your curiosity, your hunger for details, or the enlightened obsession for truth and knowledge of those deemed strange. The United States has a long tradition of making strangers criminals, and criminals are entitled to their own secrets (Shah 2011). The purpose of this chapter lies in the often-ignored fact that this celebration is also pain, a pain only the colonized understand. It is not an open invitation.

CELEBRATION, AND WALLS THAT BLEED

History was present in the walls of the Armenian school hall. I don't know exactly why the 2014 mayordomos chose this venue for the *vela*, but its walls tell a complex history. The school stands as evidence of Armenian migration to the United States, a partial consequence of the Armenian Genocide in the early twentieth century, commemorated annually by Armenians in Hollywood (Suny 2015). The venue reminds me of Zapotec poet Irma Pineda's words: "walls drain stories" (Pineda 2001). In her Zapotec poem "The Wall," Pineda describes how walls provide and maintain spaces for pleasure, happiness, and intimacies, but also drain stories of violence, sadness, and traumas. I think of such "draining" as "bleeding" instead, because the walls of the Armenian school "bleed" violence and colonialism, the appropriation of land through conquest, and the continuous settlements on Tongva land. "Time is ungenerous" to the wall, Pineda writes, "it brands her skin and wounds her visceral."

The Tongva people were the first inhabitants of the land where the Armenian school is situated. As with the Zapotec people, the Tongva were also called Indians by European colonizers that arrived on the continent in the sixteenth century. The land of the Tongva people was later called California and was occupied by Spanish missionaries, Mexican hacendados, and then the United States after the Treaty of Guadalupe Hidalgo of 1848.

On the night of the *vela*, immigrant people celebrated Muxes—the third gender of the Zapotec people from southern Mexico. Like the Armenian and Tongva people, the Zapotec people have histories that bleed. These stories are of land dispossession and violence. Since the Mexican nation-state was created, Zapotecs have been at the forefront of counter insurgencies against it. For instance, Zapotec José Gregorio Meléndez was the leader of multiple rebellions (1827–53) for the autonomy of the Isthmus of Tehuantepec from Mexico (Guerrero 2014). He battled against the army of Benito Juárez, the acclaimed Indigenous president of Mexico. This history of rebellion and anti-nationalist ideologies allowed the Zapotec people to survive and reinvent their culture despite Mexico's settler colonialism—the occupation of Indigenous territories and the commodification of Indigenous bodies for labor.[1] As Pineda's poem claims, these "are stories never forgotten, / stories that time cannot carry away."

Walls bleed so many stories. The history and location of the Armenian school create possibilities to reflect on the structural processes that shape the lives and bodies of Indigenous migrants in the United States: migration, colonialism, and violence. Such processes are reflected in the fantasies journalists and media have of Muxes, fantasies that create a homogenous account of the Indigenous third gender body. These fascinations obsessively position the Indigenous third gender as an alternative to "modern sexualities"—that is, the gay, lesbian, and bisexual identities dominant in liberal nation-states. *VICE*, the *New York Times*, *National Geographic*, Univision, and Televisa, among others, are fascinated with Muxes. The cameras then become a dominant gaze that "captures" images of the native to distribute them as delightful *botanas*. Along with the images come assertions that the colorful seasoning is "decolonial"—which, in my opinion, appeals to the hazardous hunger (oftentimes unconscious) for pure Indians (or Indianness) untouched by history. Such enchantments occlude historical processes of exclusion and political systems that Muxes collude with as colonized subjects. For instance, these reports do not mention that certain Muxe organizations support the Partido Revolucionario Institucional (PRI), known as one of the most corrupt political parties in Mexico, often accused of the massacre of Indigenous people in events such as the Acteal massacre (1997) and the Ayotzinapa case (2014). The fantasies that construct Muxes as a homogenous identity create a colonial image of the Muxe as Other and savage, different from modern sexual and gender identities (Trouillot 2003). Homogenous constructions of Muxes do not complicate their history and complex agency as human beings and colonized subjects. Such reportages take away the various subjectivities of Muxes as well as their complex experiences in Mexico and the United States (both settler-colonial states).

INDIGENOUS DIASPORAS AND THE SETTLER'S TOOL

I don't intend to fantasize about Muxes or to write about Muxes so that you, the reader, feel invited to "Visit Oaxaca!" as many Oaxacan governmental slogans encourage US tourists to do. Rather, I reflect on their struggles and the future of other "queer" Indigenous diasporic bodies, especially non–third gender bodies in non-Zapotec Oaxacan Indigenous communities. Therefore, I position my own body as an Indigenous Ñuu Savi (Mixtec) "queer" person in displacement in the United States. But I have to be clear on my use of "queer." It is not a call for an identity. Rather, I use it for a lack of a better term.

"Queer" is a gaze: it is the settler's tool to try and make sense of the Other (Lorde 2007). Natives will always be "queer" to the eyes of the settler. It is a tool that makes colonialism a structure, not an event. Colonialism is a "queer" process. It is a process that establishes walls of difference between the settler and the Other. It is a complex description, or an attempt, to refer to my body, and bodies like mine, as strange and impossible: an aberration within contemporary colonized cultures but also exotic, and "erotic," to the dominant settler gaze (Smith 2010). I refer to "queer" as in a strange, broken, pre-Hispanic relic within the ruins of a contemporary archeological site. An artifact fit for an exhibition glass in the liberal multicultural academy. "Queer" as in a fetishized commodity trafficked in the political economy of knowledge (Rivera Cusicanqui 2010). "Queer" as in a *transborder life*, trans everything (Stephen 2007).

Many of us Indigenous diasporic peoples living in the United States are still struggling for gender and sexual equality; not in the nation-state liberal sense but in the context of diasporic cultural formation. Muxes as dissidents call on us displaced Indigenous people to envision our future beyond the constraints of ideological nationalisms, institutions, or the tourist eyes that constantly watch us. Mexican nationalism reproduces racist colonial ideologies, heteronormativity, and patriarchy with conceptualizations like the "Mexican family"—a family that supposedly started when Hernán Cortés and La Malinche had children. Such settler ideologies continue to be imposed as Mexico reaffirms itself as a nation, as the owner of Indigenous land.

Therefore, I want you to see that the Vela Muxe is more than a celebration, a show for outsiders, or an innovative, homogenous, epistemological model of "decolonial" identity. It is a political festivity with the potential to conceptualize the future of heterogeneous Indigenous diasporic cultures.

As an Indigenous Na Savi migrant, a non-Zapotec Indigenous person, I admire the Muxe queen. I find stories of me in Maritza's laugh, her posture, and her pride. Witnessing her, I find my displacement and my daily struggle against heteronormativity. My strange—not normal—body is reflected in her narrative of migration and struggle. I too migrated from Oaxaca, Mexico. I also imagined myself being applauded as Maritza once dreamed—as I will explain later in this chapter. I also felt rejection. I also felt ashamed and confused. I felt hated not only as "queer," when people used derogative names against me because of my sexuality, but also as an Indigenous person within Mexican spaces. My grandmother, for example, told me to learn Spanish and speak it fluently so that I wouldn't get called *indio* (Indian). The Vela Muxe challenged these complex discourses of displacement and rejection.

The Vela Muxe is meant to be a community celebration. It is not an individualistic demonstration of sexual identity. It is not a coming-out party either. Its many Indigenous attendees have felt excluded from family, community, and nation-state. I did not see Muxe stories in books dedicated to the history of Mexico. When I was growing up in my town in the Mixteca region of Oaxaca (seven hours away from Maritza's hometown) and in Southern California, I did not see people like Maritza celebrate whom they are. I only knew of the Mexican transgender neighbor I had when I was living in the South Side of Oxnard, California; she was judged and hated by other neighbors and my family. At some point, I myself hated her because she represented my shame. I didn't want to be like her. I did not want my family to think I was one of her kind.

The Vela Muxe created a space that granted possibilities for the future of diasporic Indigenous cultures. For instance, my two teenage nieces that accompanied me to the Vela Muxe also felt admiration toward Maritza. I am reminded of a time at my family's dinner table when my two nieces argued with their uncle, my brother, for gender and sexual equality because they described to him how Maritza Sánchez was crowned. "Those people are crazy," my brother said. "Don't you mean this society is crazy, *tio*?" one of my nieces replied.[2]

The Vela Muxe affords us the opportunity to reflect on the future of Indigenous cultures from Mexico that have been dispersed across the United States—from Los Angeles, California, to Salem, Oregon, to New York City. I ask myself, "Can we Indigenous immigrant people write new pages for our future?" What I really mean here is: What is our future? What is the future for the children who like my nieces think that our society is "crazy," and therefore challenge the reproduction of heteronormativity within our Indigenous families and communities? Do we tell them they need healing, that they are breaking our culture and traditions apart? These are questions I have no answers to.

When Muxes cross the border, they mark the path for the social, political, and cultural transformation of Indigenous diasporic communities. Muxes mark the path for the critical redefinition of a future where Mexican nationalism will not hunt us. Our future is to rethink who we are as men, women, Muxes, and displaced Indigenous peoples living in the United States. Muxes, with their pride and elegance, provide steps for us to learn how "to live with the pain."

MUXES *ALTIVAS* MAKE AN ENTRANCE

Immigrant Muxes, like Maritza, dance to the music of their people and their land. They dance to the Zapotec song "Son Paulina." Zapotec poet Andrés Henestrosa wrote "Son Paulina" to honor Zapotec femininity. The song goes: "As Paulina dances, / she does not step on the floor, she steps on my heart." As Muxes dance, the floor trembles, and with it, the memories of childhoods and life wounds are opened. They step on our hearts.

In Maritza's celebration, her future shines bright with the memories of Oaxaca and her childhood, when she lived as a boy dreaming of being loved. The sorrow of such wounds made the *vela* more meaningful as Maritza danced to Zapotec songs. The way she held her dress and danced as an *altiva* while looking at the men and women in the audience inspired everyone that watched her. Muxes had arrived in West Hollywood. I felt it. I am sure many attendees felt it too.

I believe our diasporic future is reflected in the dances of Muxes because they require us to witness them, and they make us reflect on our desires, memories, and longings. To enjoy our music is to reject centuries of racist and sexist violence that our bodies, masculine or feminine, have endured.

Muxes have arrived in West Hollywood. They crossed the US-Mexican border. Of course, journalists and their cameras were there to witness, but the cameras won't capture the "bleeding." The cameras won't picture how Maritza, when she was a boy, would step onto a rock imagining it was a stage where she was being applauded and accepted by the ones she loved. Those cameras won't picture the cattle she was herding in Santa Ana del Valle, her pueblo in the Oaxaca Valley. The cameras won't picture the mountain trees, the flowers, the feeling when you don't know how to name yourself or when Mexican people yelled *indio* or *puto*. The cameras won't capture her hopes to be accepted as a third gender or her decision to be a Muxe in two racist and homophobic societies. The cameras won't picture the memories of those loved ones she said good-bye to when she came to the United States. The cameras won't picture her crossing the border as a Zapotec, native, Muxe, *joto*, and *maricón*. Those cameras won't picture how Maritza learned to love herself.

Muxes dancing in West Hollywood challenge the fantasies that the cameras and news outlets have created to portray them as a homogenous "Indian" third gender people. They challenge the articles published days after. The *Latin Times* wrote: "Meet the Muxes: Mexican Indigenous Community Where Sexual Diversity Is Celebrated since Birth" (Saldana 2015). The article excludes the embodied experiences of Muxes. It doesn't include Muxes' Indigenous and "queer" perspectives, it excludes their traumas and memories, and it creates a fascinating Indigenous subject to be observed by outsiders.

Migrant Muxes in West Hollywood challenge the dominant gazes toward their bodies. They speak. Zapotec writer Macario Matus (2010) said in an interview:

> Yo cuando viajo a Nueva York, a Italia, o a Francia, me hablo solo como un loco desposeído dislocado y hablo solo en Zapoteco. Ahí en la vía apia de Roma . . . solo. En Manhattan, solo. Y hablo Zapoteco porque los extranjeros todos vienen aquí y hablan y gritan. Pero, ¿y por qué yo no voy a gritar en su país?

Matus writes about his travels in different countries: the United States, France, and Italy. He claims to recite poems in Zapotec as he walks the streets of Manhattan and Rome. He recites poems in Zapotec because when American, French, and Italian foreigners visit Oaxaca, they speak in their languages. Matus asks: why should I not speak Zapotec in the countries of these people? Matus challenges power difference between Western and non-Western, modern and so-called premodern. Matus challenges history and dominant literature by reciting the translations of English poetry in Zapotec when in Europe and the United States.

Like Matus, Muxes in Los Angeles speak who they are. They dance it. They celebrate it. They smile. Despite the homogenous representations of their identities, and the racism and homophobia in Mexico and the United States, Muxes have crossed the border, and they are here to tell us that they are "global divas" (Manalansan 2003). They appropriate gay West Hollywood. They pose for the cameras. They inspire bodies like mine. They tell us what an Indigenous diaspora is: a fabulous, critical, and fucked-up mess with the beauty of always longing for the land and the people we left behind. Their stories now are part of other stories that continue to "bleed," such as the Tongva history, Armenian Genocide, Mexican and US colonialism, and Indigenous resistance. Muxes have crossed the border. They have their ordinary burdens, their pain, but at the *vela* they embrace their border life with style and celebration.

Notes

1. Although I provide my own definition of the concept (as it applies in this specific case), I borrow ideas from Patrick Wolfe (2006).

2. "Crazy" here is ableist language used to disregard, devalue, and oppress people or actions that are not part of dominant social and physical normalizations. My nieces challenged such language by defending Maritza and the Vela Muxe. Their argument also indicates the heterogeneity of Indigenous migrant families and communities.

From the Club to the Fiesta

Drag and Folklore in La Familia Galán

Enzo E. Vasquez Toral

THE FIESTA DANCE FLOOR

Born in the late 1990s, La Familia Galán (the Galán Family) is a drag collective based in La Paz, Bolivia. A self-proclaimed "group of cross-dressing activists for sex and gender rights" (Aruquipa Pérez 2016, 451),[1] La Familia Galán is not your typical drag family: it was initially composed of individuals of different gender and sexual identities who adopted the Galán surname for their drag personas in response to the conservative discourse of early 2000s Bolivia that defended the "biological family."[2] Since its inception, its members have explored cross-dressing in different artistic, intellectual, and political forms including gay nightclub performances, LGBT marches,[3] contests and parades, visual art exhibitions, plays, a TV show, gay pageants, and production of magazines and academic texts, among others. Especially important to their craft is their engagement with Bolivian folklore, in particular their participation as dancers in folkloric *danzas* (dance-dramas)[4] at Catholic patron-saint festivities such as the Carnaval de Oruro (Oruro's Carnival) in Oruro, and the Fiesta del Gran Poder (Fiesta of the Great Power) in La Paz.[5]

Fiestas and carnivals are multiple-day cultural expressions across Latin America and the Caribbean that include dance parades, Catholic processions, food, contests, and music, and that are often read as syncretic or hybrid products of Catholic and Indigenous influences. At the same time, they are participatory and political acts with their own systems of production and logics that are not "discontinuous with political order, but rather as expressions of an alternative political order, one very much its own," thus establishing a form of "fiesta politics" (Marino 2018, 22). In this respect, fiesta politics are related to gender and sexual norms that are the product of long-standing patriarchal traditions. For example, in the past women were prevented from participating as dancers in certain *danzas*; instead, select men cross-dressed as women's dance characters for many decades.[6] In the spaces of the dance spectacle, Bolivia's famous *entradas*—parades where *fraternidades* (fraternities or dance troupes) showcase their dances around an established route—stand as the imaginary dance floor where performances "cross-dress" the streets of Bolivia to (un)mask the underlying tensions of gender and sexuality.

What does it mean for a drag collective to participate in fiestas and bring identity expressions usually attached to queer nightlife into this heteronormative space and the gendered performance seen in *danzas*? How are Andean gender views and hetero-nationalistic folklore being contested as La Familia Galán redefines the dance floor of the fiestas as a more inclusive space? In reading these epistemological encounters, I rely on the late performance studies scholar José Esteban Muñoz's (2009, 65) assertion that "dance is an especially valuable site for ruminations on queerness and gesture," and anthropologist Zoila Mendoza's (2000, 4) proposition that *danza* performance in the Andes "is a key public context in which identity is defined." Additionally, I draw inspiration from Giuseppe Campuzano, the late artist and founder of the Transvestite Museum of Peru, who saw Andean expressions such as those in folklore as forms of transvestism.[7] By queering the fiesta space, I argue that La Familia Galán rechoreographs fiesta parades as an extension of the dance floor of gay nightclubs, using aesthetics such as androgyny and costumes usually not found in the daytime fiesta in order to defy heteronormative views engrained in Andean folklore.

BEFORE *LAS GALÁN*

Cross-dressing by LGBT individuals has been present in fiestas for decades, although it has not always been as visible as it is today. Danna Galán (David Aruquipa Pérez), a drag performer and one of the leaders of La Familia Galán, helped illuminate this larger history in his *La China Morena: Memoria histórica travesti* (2012), which includes several testimonies by 1960s *transformistas* (female impersonators).[8] The book focuses on the cross-dressing character of the China Morena (Morena Woman) in the Morenada *danza* of the Carnaval de Oruro.[9] As Aruquipa Pérez unveils, Carlos Espinoza ("Ofelia") was one of the first *transformistas* to perform as a China Morena. Espinoza, a well-known Oruro costume maker, modified the traditional China Morena *figura* (figure or character), drawing from vedettes and TV figures of the 1960s to create the China Morena version that is better known today (Aruquipa Pérez 2012, 53). He shortened the skirt's length, extended the boots up to the knees, and added provocative cleavage and a wig. Additionally, most *transformista* dancers used makeup instead of the old China Morena's mask that formerly symbolized the hiding of a heterosexual (cross-dressed) man in this female dance character.[10]

With some alterations, the celebrated *transformista*-modified figure of the China Morena became a presence that is embodied by cisgender women today. In 1975, dictator Hugo Banzer allegedly prohibited the presence of *transformistas* in fiestas after an incident in La Paz that became known as "The Kiss of Barbarella." Peter Alaiza ("Barbarella") was a well-known *transformista* who danced as a China Morena in the Fiesta del Gran Poder. Supposedly, in 1974, he decided to come up to the seating area where Banzer and other government officials were watching the fiesta parade and gave the dictator a kiss on the cheek. Banzer accepted the kiss as he thought that Barbarella was a cisgender woman, but the press revealed Alaiza's sexual identity when it covered the incident (Aruquipa Pérez 2012, 69). Although Barbarella's kiss was never given as a reason for the *transformista* ban, there is a popular belief—a folkloric queer myth—that this was the case. Oruro *transformistas* recount that this incident paved the way for cisgender women not only to replace them as China Morenas in both Oruro and La Paz, but to do so in the queer *versión vedetizada* (vedette-ized version), as it caught the masculine eye of both spectators and leaders of dance troupes. In other words, the presence of China Morenas in many Morenada *fraternidades* today is a queer legacy and an appropriation. Given the publication of Aruquipa Pérez's oral history book, dance troupes and fiesta-goers are now more aware of this genealogy although with different degrees of acknowledgment by traditional (male) folklorists.

Members of La Familia Galán dressed as China Morenas in 2012 to create awareness about the queer origin of this character. Their take on the China Morena greatly resembled the current version performed by cisgender women, but with a drag twist that included heavy makeup, high-platform sparkly boots, tight corsets, and colorful costumes. Costume colors are usually chosen yearly by dance groups, but the Galán version of the China Morena wore the colors of the Bolivian flag. Hence, they used their nation's official colors to honor a *transformista* past not written in national history, as they stood and pranced, demanding attention from the spectators. Their hip movements and their delicate arm swings imitated dance steps characteristic of this female dance character, but their presence inscribed the aesthetics of the queer nightlife in the daylight of the streets of La Paz.[11]

Fig. 1. Alicia Galán, Paris Galán, and Danna Galán pose as China Morena in La Paz, Bolivia, 2012. (Photograph courtesy of Varinia Oros.)

ANDROGYNY AND THE WAPHURI GALÁN

Although the original mother of La Familia Galán, Diana Sofía Galán, performed in gay nightclubs and was a well-known *transformista*, she was not fond of the label "drag queen." Alongside Paris Galán (Carlos Parra), Danna Galán introduced the term and adapted it as part of a more irreverent aesthetic—including "androgynous figures, zoomorphic creatures, drag queens with colorful wigs and galactic costumes"—that quickly became synonymous with La Familia Galán in street marches and interventions, and gay events in La Paz (Aruquipa Pérez 2016, 456). In 2002, members were able to transfer some of their drag explorations to a character they called the Waphuri Galán when Paris was invited to dance as a traditional Waphuri for that year's Carnaval de Oruro (Carlos Parra 2017). The Kullawada (Weavers *danza*) is an allegory of the *hilanderos* (weavers) and is performed in *bloques* (dance groups) that consist of several dancers. This dance has long featured a cross-dressed character known as the Awila (Grandmother), a parodic representation of an old woman, which is still danced by heterosexual men in a form of ritual cross-dressing. Whereas the Waphuri, a masculine figure who wears a mask with a long phallic nose, is the *capataz* (foreman) of the group of weavers and is said to represent a Spanish manager, the embodiment of power (Sigl and Mendoza 2012b, 186).

When Paris was invited to dance as Waphuri, she brought three friends from La Familia Galán—Alén Justiniano (Malena Galán), Alberto Noriega (Calypso Galán), and David Aruquipa Pérez (Danna Galán)—and proposed they dance together as a group. Although the Waphuri usually dances alone at the front of a *bloque*, Paris wanted this show of mutual support. Uncomfortable with the heaviness and masculine look of the costume they were meant to wear, they decided to design a new one. Inspired by the torero-like tight costumes used by late Mexican singer/*divo* Juan Gabriel, they made their own black costumes with pearl decorations that consisted of short and tight coats, a pearly *rueca* (distaff), tall pointy hats inspired by the old Waphuri but with sparkly decorations, black-and-white pants, and boots with a small heel. In revamping the original character, they created a showstopper that spoke to the style of gender bending through clothing associated with queer nightlife. Although they did not wear makeup or perform as their drag queen personas, their presence was an intervention that drew attention to a new form of Waphuri that has since become a staple of La Familia Galán and many fiestas. For instance, new queer Waphuris have emerged in other Kullawada dance troupes, while more traditional ones have retained the original masculine version. In addition to appearing in fiesta spaces, this character has garnered national attention, as was the case in 2012 when Miss World Bolivia, Mariana García, decided to dress as a Waphuri Galán as her national costume in the international pageant, for which La Familia Galán helped her prepare by coaching her on dancing and costume design.

Despite some continuing resistance from traditional folklorists, the Waphuri Galán has become more noticeable and celebrated for their increasingly extravagant costumes every year. For instance, Danna Galán created colorful costumes in black and pink for the 2017 Oruro Carnival and the Fiesta del Gran Poder, and Paris Galán danced in a black and rainbow costume.[12] The 2017 costumes had similar elements as the 2002 Waphuri Galán, but with additional developments adapted throughout two decades: they now use heavy makeup, a corset, a women's blanket tied around their waist, higher heels on their boots, and a colorful Viennese mask, among other ele-

Fig. 2. David Aruquipa Pérez (Danna Galán) and fellow dancers as Waphuri Galán in the Fiesta del Gran Poder in La Paz, Bolivia, 2017. (Photograph by Enzo E. Vasquez Toral.)

ments that feminize their appearance. Particularly, I read the mask, which they only carry in their hands, as a reminder of their former invisibility in the fiesta space. The mask, in Latin American gay politics, was in past decades a tool to negotiate visibility. For example, in the 1993 Buenos Aires Pride Parade organizers distributed masks to those who did not want to be recognized while marching (Quiroga 2000, 1). Similarly, in La Paz, the 2003 and 2004 gay pride parades were subtitled, "Masks against Prejudice and Misconceptions" to symbolize the anonymity of the participants (Aruquipa Pérez, Entenssoro, and Vargas 2012, 228). The old Waphuri used a mask at all times, but the dancers of La Familia Galán refuse to hide their faces and hold their masks only as an accessory to mark their sassy hip and hand movements. In doing so, they symbolically undo the mask as a marker of queer invisibility and retool it as if it were a queer hand fan.[13]

During my long hours watching the 2017 Fiesta del Gran Poder parade from the side of a busy street in La Paz, I came across other Kullawada dance troupes with their own traditional Waphuris. However, when the Waphuri Galán appeared, I felt transported to another dance floor; the daytime of the fiesta parade was suddenly inhabited by Waphuris that energetically danced to amplify and queer ritualized dance steps to show off their costumes. They waved their masks up and down to create a sense of fabulosity, bringing attention to themselves in the sea of dancers. This style destabilized the gaze of the many spectators who, like me, were used to seeing a different type of masculine Waphuri, even just ahead of them in the parade. As Marcia Ochoa (2014, 211) has proposed, the spectacle is "one register through which individuals can signify." The (re)signification of the Waphuri that La Familia Galán has done by revamping it not only serves the "spectacularity" of the fiesta, but also transports elements from the outside and hidden world of queer nightlife to inhabit the fiesta's language of performance and register as a continuum. As I have noted elsewhere, this makes the Waphuri Galán "a hybrid embodiment of two spaces" (2020, 98).

By repurposing queer nightlife aesthetics, the Waphuri Galán defies heteronormative notions of gendered *danza* performance. Anthropologist Eveline Sigl argues that the Waphuri Galán brings together feminine and masculine elements and thus becomes an ambiguous character that is a "drag character" (Sigl and Mendoza 2012a, 465). I read the Waphuri Galán similarly, but to me the figure is more androgynous than female drag: its transgressive power lies precisely in its ambiguity. In other words, it is not drag as female illusion but rather an androgynous performance where gender cannot be pinpointed, thus intervening in a space like Bolivia where the gender binary permeates and rules daily interactions. Furthermore, by being androgynous, the Waphuri Galán undoes gendered performance in *danza* characters, who are expected to be either male or female. Aruquipa Pérez (pers. comm., 2017) mentions that La Familia Galán wanted to reverse the macho characteristic of the original Waphuri by *mariconearlo* (queering it). In this effort to *mariconear* folklore, the Waphuri Galán represents a masculine Waphuri lost under an androgynous look that evokes the freedom that queer individuals feel in the way they dress and act in nightlife spaces.

By showing a character that cannot be said to be fully man, woman, drag queen, or *transformista*, the Waphuri Galán represents the queer dancing that was only welcome in underground gay venues but is now acclaimed by spectators in the open spaces of fiestas. Theater and performance studies scholar Angela Marino (2016, 159) argues that the durational aspects of the fiesta establish a "fiesta time" that "blends the extraordinary with the ordinary" and "embraces and integrates the moment of staging art as parallel to displaying art." In relation to the time of the performer in parade performance, theater studies scholar Christian DuComb (2017, 87) proposes to consider it as "a continuous and reiterative 'space of time,' a mobile stage filled by the movement of the group of which one is part." The Waphuri Galán embodies this liminal temporality that serves as a continuity of a different queer space, thus creating its own queer stage and time as an extension of the queer nightclub dance floor and the night hours. For La Familia Galán, fiesta time is a queer space of time whose stage is inherently mobile as it aesthetically evokes more than one space.

WAITING FOR THE WAPHURI

As I stand in the middle of the crowd in the 2017 Fiesta del Gran Poder, I witness a great deal of impatience among the spectators who await the Waphuri Galán's appearance. "There, they are coming!" is what I hear as Danna dances down the street leading a group of Kullawada dancers alongside two other Waphuris. As they get closer, the audience starts screaming their names and asking them to approach the security line on the side of the street for photographs. Others decide to go into the street as security lines are not strictly enforced; I do the same, feeling a gravitational pull toward a familiar presence and celebratory affect that I had only experienced on the queer dance floor. Multiple journalists in the middle of the parade space stop them with cameras to get a live televised interview or shoot the perfect picture of their costume. Despite some development of LGBT protections in recent years in Bolivia, to which some members of La Familia Galán contributed as activists, their celebrity treatment is due to their artistry and not an acceptance dictated by the law: they have created a new "fiesta law" that not only includes but also celebrates their queerness.[14] Although some may see the Waphuris as mere attractions of the fiestas, the transgressive power of the Waphuri Galán lies in bringing the pleasures and poses of queer nightlife to the masculinized spaces of folklore.

Fiona Buckland (2002, 9) sees the dance floor as a "space of participation, [where] the boundary between audience and actor is already blurred." In reading improvised dance practices as creations or acts of queer worldmaking, Buckland relies on an understanding of the queerness in these practices to include "strategies and tactics that deconstruct heteronormativity"

(5). In the space of the fiesta parades as enabler of an imaginary dance floor, the audience and dancers are separated; spectators technically should watch from their improvised seating on the side of the streets. Similarly, *danza* performance is ritualistic in nature, prescribing certain choreographies and dance steps. Despite these restrictions, the presence of individuals such as members of La Familia Galán catches the attention of audience members, who approach them and break spatial codes. These new shared codes are dictated by La Familia Galán's embodiment of an anti-heteronormative gesture, as its members create with their costumes and subtly modified footwork and hand gestures a queer style of being in the fiesta, a style that is similar to their style of dancing and dressing in queer nightclub dance floors and the events where they started to perform as their drag personas. La Familia Galán allows for the audience not only to watch but to insert in the fiesta schema other artistic expressions that are only familiar to the LGBT community: spaces of improvised dancing and borderless dance floors. In this transformation of the dance floor, the members of La Familia Galán are not only dancers to be watched, but also agents of visibility. They create new stages on which to perform, and a new stage in the hetero-nationalistic narrative of Bolivian folklore, where queerness is a defiant presence. Visibility, as a first step, becomes vital for them in the fiesta to carve a space for queerness.

Although earlier LGBT dancers had cross-dressed in fiestas (while closeted, while trying to "pass" as women, or while out but in a state of fear), La Familia Galán has claimed a space for the queer individual to share a common dance floor. After the 1975 prohibition took place, a lot of *transformista* performers were not allowed to perform in urban areas but were welcomed in rural or smaller celebrations (Parra, pers. comm., 2017). La Familia Galán has, however, found a stage in the bigger urban spaces where tourism and commercialization of folklore abound: its members claim a space where they can be seen in order to defy economies of embodiment and difference. As Chilean writer Diamela Eltit (2007, 123) has argued about La Familia Galán as a group, they are not "a counter-culture unit, instead, they are intensively cultural, allowing for signs to flow and travel among bodies, decentering in that way the official mandates towards normalization and standardization." By embodying the Waphuri Galán, La Familia Galán dancers ask for the coming together of the folkloric dance floor and the queer dance floor by extending nightlife elements that were not part of or not supposed to inhabit public spaces. In this way, they make folkloric practices also part of queer expressions inside a nation that still does not fully accept them as individuals deserving of equal rights.

Notes

1. Unless otherwise specified, all translations in this text are my own.

2. La Familia Galán initially included individuals across many LGBT identities; however, most active members today who are based in Bolivia are gay men.

3. I use the LGBT acronym because TLGB (trans, lesbian, gay, and bisexual) is the preferred form in Bolivia. The term *queer* or *cuir* (Q) is usually not used in Spanish, although this term has received some traction through academic—and sometimes activist—discourse elsewhere in Latin America. For more on queer/*cuir* in this region, see Falconí Trávez, Castellanos, and Viteri (2014), Lanuza and Carrasco (2015), and Domínguez Ruvalcaba (2016).

4. *Danzas* are folkloric cultural expressions that are composed of different characters who dance to a song for long periods of time in a particular space, choreography, or parade route. Characters are both male and female, sometimes wear masks, and can be distinguished by their costumes and dance steps; however, each character can be played by several dancers who wear identifiable costumes and dance side by side to create a group identity attached to a single character type. In this exercise of dancing, the identity of the performer is usually taken over by the ritualistic dancing of their character. *Danzas* are considered to be dance-dramas because the characters represent a particular identity in relation to race, ethnicity, or provenance, which is inserted into a larger narrative of the story that the dance troupe is trying to portray. I use the Spanish-language terms (e.g., *danza*, fiesta) throughout this text as their most approximate English translations do not fully encapsulate the cultural specificities of the original terms.

5. Oruro's Carnival is celebrated every February in honor of the Virgin of Candelaria. La Fiesta del Gran Poder is celebrated every late May or early June in honor of Our Lord Jesus of the Great Power. Both festivities are categorized as UNESCO Masterpieces of the Oral and Intangible Heritage of Humanity, receiving this designation in 2001 and 2019, respectively.

6. Some of these traditions have ceased, and cisgender women are now allowed to dance, for instance, in the Tunantada *danza* in Peru, which was an all-male affair until around the 1970s. Other *danzas*, such as the Diablada in Bolivia, have retained specific cross-dressing characters but allow cisgender women to dance as others.

7. Campuzano claimed that "toda peruanidad es un travestismo" (everything about Peru is transvestism). I extend Campuzano's assertion to read a shared Andean identity with Bolivia, specifically in relation to fiesta performance in both countries. For more on this museum project, see Campuzano (2008).

8. The word *transformista* is used in many parts of Spanish-speaking Latin America and the Caribbean. In Bolivia, the word is used to describe female impersonators regardless of their sexual orientation or identity, although they are usually gay men or trans women. The word *travesti* (transvestite) is sometimes used interchangeably with *transformista*, although the former refers, in most cases, to members of the trans com-

munity; nevertheless, in recent years *travesti* is being replaced by "trans" to account for transgender and transsexual identities more globally. Conversely, for instance in the case of Venezuela, the word *transformista* is mobilized to account for a trans woman identity (Ochoa 2014, 3).

9. Other cross-dressing characters in this festivity include the Awila (Grandmother) in the Kullawada *danza*, and the China Supay (Devil Woman) in the Diablada *danza*.

10. Given that Espinoza is a well-known figure in Oruro, his presence created a following of *transformistas* who danced as China Morena alongside him. At one point, every Morenada dance troupe wanted to have a *transformista* perform with them as they became the fiesta's showstoppers.

11. Aruquipa Pérez recounted to me in 2017 that he only found out about the existence of the 1960s China Morena around 2009, years after he and some members of La Familia Galán had started to delve into folkloric performances. People in fiestas would mention that these performances reminded them of the *transformista* China Morena, and that resemblance encouraged Aruquipa Pérez to start his oral history project.

12. Since 2017, Danna and Paris have separated and now dance as Waphuri Galán in different dance troupes. In doing so, they have each brought new Waphuris from in and out of La Familia Galán to perform with them. In spite of this separation in the fiesta space, La Familia Galán remains as an activist collective and a family.

13. The tradition of masks in folkloric dances in the Andes has been studied from various anthropological perspectives in relation to identity construction. For an example of such works, see Cánepa Koch (1998).

14. Following a series of neoliberal governments, the early 2000s was marked by the rise of Indigenous and social movements in Bolivia that led to the 2005 election of Evo Morales as the country's first Indigenous president (2006–19). In this context, sexual minorities in Bolivia saw an opportunity to gain a voice in many initiatives and obtain certain rights. Although marriage equality has not been granted, other laws have benefited LGBT populations. First, passed in 2010, Law 45 ("Law against Racism and Any Form of Discrimination") included a ban on discrimination against sexual orientation or gender identity; particularly, it defined homophobia and transphobia explicitly. Second, passed in 2016, Law 807 ("Gender Identity Law") has allowed transgender and transsexual individuals to change their gender identity in official documents. Because of their activist work and professional careers, some of La Familia Galán members have served in different NGO and government positions. For example, David Aruquipa Pérez (Danna Galán) was the general director of Cultural Heritage in the Bolivian Ministry of Culture from 2006 to 2010, and Carlos Parra (Paris Galán) was elected as alternate for departmental representative for La Paz in 2015 and assumed office in 2019.

From Streetwalking to the Catwalk

Red-Light Nightlife and the Girls of Daspu

Gregory Mitchell

> In the front lines in the battle of the sexes, prostitutes are "the only street fighters we've got."
>
> —Carol Leigh, echoing Ti-Grace Atkinson

PUTAS ONTOLÓGICAS, GOOD OLD-FASHIONED WHORES

The lower-class *putas* storm the stage of Circo Voador (Flying Circus), the premiere concert venue in Rio de Janeiro's trendy Lapa nightlife district. Yesterday they were walking the streets, enduring pitying looks and scorn from tourists and abuse from police. For now, they soar. The first woman hits the catwalk, stomping like she's wearing Gaultier. She instead displays clothing from the fashion line Daspu as the *baile funk* music blares through the whole neighborhood. Nearly two thousand twentysomethings sing along to the Daspu theme song, a pounding piece filled with sexually explicit lyrics rich in both filth and clever Lusophone wordplay:

Daspu é uma puta parada.
Daspu é uma parada de puta.

Daspu is a fucking cool thing.
Daspu is a whore's thing.[1]

The next model, a Black woman in blue fishnets, black-lace fingerless gloves, and a baby blue and white checkerboard dress modeled on a chef's apron enters to applause. DJ Marlboro's lead guitarist—who wears only a speedo and a pair of cartoonish oversized sunglasses—nods in admiration as she passes. This may be the most happening place in Carioca nightlife tonight, but what exactly is it?

Fig. 1. Daspu models dance with partygoers at Circo Voador. (Photograph by Gregory Mitchell.)

Daspu, founded in 2005, is the fashion line of Davida, a prostitute rights organization in Rio de Janeiro founded by Gabriel Leite, a prostitute and political organizer originally from São Paulo. (Although Davida is part of the larger sex worker rights movement, its members usually prefer to use the word *prostitute* and to reclaim the word *puta* in their performances.) Leite decided to launch a fashion line with outfits that would be designed in collaboration with and modeled by prostitutes and their allies. And it's this fashion line—its discursive effects, its ability to use nightlife spaces to cross from the abject to the respectable, and its ability circulate precariously as a stand-in for marginalized sexual subjects—that I take up as the subject of this essay.

REFASHIONING CARIOCA NIGHTLIFE, ONE GARMENT AT A TIME

No lazer, na folia, na pista ou na luta
Trepa zen, veste bem, goza bem na costura

At play, at the party, on the dance floor or in a fight
Fucks all chilled out like, dresses well, cums right on the pussy's lips

Leite, a charismatic Trotskyite who fell ill shortly after the show and who died of cancer in 2013, wanted to reclaim fashion: to take it back from the upper classes and to use it to assert the whore's claim on the city of Rio. Leite called this line Daspu, which means "from the whores" but also serves as a pun on São Paulo's high-end fashion line Daslu. Daslu, famous for providing a helipad atop its store so that its wealthy customers could buy its insanely expensive clothes without having to see (let alone walk among) the common *gentinhos* (little people), took offense at the pun and threatened to sue. The "little people" loved the Daspu versus Daslu storylines in the media, where the wealthy, fashionable, and arrogant Eliana Tranchesi, head of Daslu, sought to use her considerable clout to destroy these upstart whores for daring to make even a small joke. Shortly thereafter, in 2005, in an unrelated matter, three hundred federal agents raided Daslu's store and offices in the aptly named Operation Narcissus and arrested Tranchesi (Parra-Bernal 2005). She was eventually fined R$236 million (at that time, US$112 million) and sentenced to 94½ years in prison for organized crime, smuggling, and tax evasion (D'Agostino 2009). Thus, Tranchesi, a wealthy heiress and a symbol of Brazilian elites and "good society," was revealed to be the less moral party by far. Her meteoric fall seemed a fitting ending to the legal struggle between Daspu and Daslu, even though it was caused by her own hubris and crimes rather than the scrappy prostitutes' collective.

Nevertheless, all the press paid off, and Daspu was a hit. Its prostitutes worked the catwalk at São Paulo's fashion week and were featured on runway shows in Milan in collaboration with an Italian designer. They were featured on a telenovela and popular talk shows, given spreads in *Marie Claire UK* and *Brazil Vogue*, and blogged about in the United States on *Jezebel*. Part of the appeal of Daspu's brand is that compared to the skinny supermodels of Daslu, it is far more inclusive, featuring women and men of all ages, shapes, and colors. Ironically, this inclusivity has led some commentators to argue that Daspu's use of fashion and nightlife is glamorizing prostitution and turning it into an overly simplistic celebration of diversity, sexual and otherwise. As Leite explained to me, "We are not glamorizing prostitution because prostitution is already glamorized. The same person who denounces prostitution as immoral also sees a certain glamour in it. What we're doing is simply putting these two sides in dialogue." Her partner and Daspu's communications director, Flavio Lenz, nodded, adding: "I think using that word *glamorizing* is a trick to really say, 'Stay quietly in your corner, you are the victim of this society. Do not come here to talk to us. Stay in your place and don't threaten us.' Because glamour has to do with elevation, with leaving your place in low society. So it's very threatening for some people to see prostitution elevated."

Debates about the visibility of prostitution in Brazil elevated in 2005, when George W. Bush and the Republican-controlled Congress threatened to renege on US$40 million in USAID money owed to Brazil unless it agreed to publicly condemn prostitution, which remains technically legal there. Perhaps emboldened by its newly cemented status as the political powerhouse of Latin America and the world's eighth largest economy, Brazil told the United

Fig. 2. A model poses for the media at a Daspu fashion show. (Photograph by Roberta Valerio.)

States in shockingly undiplomatic language what it thought of the US neocolonial efforts to dictate its policies on public health and sexuality. Instead of condemning prostitution, Dr. Pedro Chequer, director of Brazil's National HIV/AIDS Commission, condemned the Bush administration:

> We can't control [HIV] with principles that are Manichean, theological, Shiite, and fundamentalist. . . . [The Bush mandate would be] an interference that harms the Brazilian policy regarding diversity, ethical principles and human rights. . . . We view prostitutes as partners in this effort [to combat HIV], partners who are efficient and competent . . . and we have a commitment to work with this group and respect them. . . . Obviously abstinence is the safest way to avoid AIDS. But it's not viable in an operational sense. . . . If we increasingly focus the prevention of AIDS along these lines, we are generating carnage, a slaughter. It's not a realistic vision. (Rohter 2005)

At the center of the controversy were organizations such as Davida that provided sexual health resources to Brazilians and that were to benefit from the promised money. Although Brazil's response earned a moral victory that was cheered globally by many activists, public health workers, and scientists, Davida found itself with a challenge: how to effectively get its message out to prostitutes and the people of Brazil, all with practically no money? Unable to move discursively through the halls of power, the message depended on circulation through public spaces and nightlife venues. Daspu frequently staged runway shows in public squares during rush hour and in bookstores and cafés, where it caught crowds unaware and used fashion to force the prostitute's body and subjectivity into bourgeois public spaces. Daspu isn't especially good at monetizing. Nowadays, its online store is untended and closed. It does not retail at Brazil's malls. It mainly sells T-shirts (some didactic, but mostly clever) at its shows. After Leite's death, the organization struggled to stay alive. So while Daspu doesn't do much to fill up Davida's coffers, it has generated new ways to reach audiences as it integrated itself into the city's nightlife, and it continues to put on small-scale shows and to offer pop-up shops to sell its T-shirts.

The shirts themselves focus on wordplay. For example, one in bright orange declares that "All over Brazil, it's legal to be a whore," but *legal* is also slang for "cool," giving the shirt a message of affirmation. Thus, it's both "lawful" and "cool" to be a whore, the shirt says, making dual claims on workers' legal rights and the need to reduce stigma. However, dozens of slang terms for prostitutes (some amusing, many offensive) fill the body of the shirt: *vaca* (cow, because it stands on the side of the road), *roda-bolsinha* (purse-twirler), and *couro de tambor* (leather drum). Another shirt is in the style of a soccer jersey (with the player number 69 on the back). The familiar soccer logo has had the silhouette of a sexy woman added, and the slogan reads "para ser brasileiro não é principiante" (To be Brazilian isn't for beginners), which is a play on a famous saying that "Brazil isn't for beginners." But *principiante* also means "virgin," so Daspu is winkingly saying on this athletic shirt that being a Brazilian man isn't compatible with being a virgin while also offering the solution of a Daspu woman selling sexual services. Another shirt features Mary Magdalene's saying "For she hath loved much," playing on the chaste love of faithful Catholics and the not-at-all chaste love of Mary's clients. This was one from a line of shirts featuring inspirational women who were (or who were rumored to have been) prostitutes at one point, including Edith Piaf and Coco Chanel. Such shirts also offer Daspu's artful wit. And so by playing with fashion in this manner, the organization also reveals a part of its ontology: prostitutes live within a conventionally gendered, patriarchal world and are subject to its norms and oppressions, but they still exercise agency through fashion and nightlife. Prostitution doesn't have to mean abjection or silence, and so they use the catwalk to, quite literally, refashion their place in the world.

What I find most interesting is how this fashion circulates in Rio's nightlife and blends into the phenomenological—the realm of the experiential, the perceptual, the sensuous. That is, where does the prostitute's body end, and what does it mean for their clothes to circulate independently of those bodies? What does it mean for those clothes to leave the bodies of prostitutes and travel on the bodies of customers? The fashions that a Daspu model wears are certainly part of the *puta* herself. Yet without her, they are not particularly interesting or useful. If just anyone designed these clothes, the items would not connect the same way. Few people would want to buy them, and, certainly, *Vogue* wouldn't be featuring them. But the prostitute was also uninteresting and uninspiring to the media (and to the fashion world) until she put on these Daspu clothes. So the Daspu model is more than just herself and more than just the clothes. To have the fashion "work," to have it connect with audiences, it needs to be from both the world of fashion and the world of the *puta*. So what happens when the clothes are worn by nonprostitutes? What happens when someone takes that part of the whore's being and puts it on their own body before taking it for a walk in public?

On the one hand, the fashion becomes a pedagogical tool. The didactic T-shirt that explains in small text the legal differences between decriminalization, legalization, and abolition is almost purely informative. But what of the T-shirt with the litany of synonyms for prostitute? One must consider who the wearer is, speculate about their subjectivity and positionality and politics, and imagine what signal they wish to send by wearing this T-shirt. Are they a prostitute? Do they care about prostitutes? Would they patronize prostitutes? Is this person mocking prostitutes? Is it just a joke? Are they even aware that prostitutes designed and made this shirt? What conversations might happen between strangers as a result of wearing Daspu clothes? It is from these tensions that class dynamics in the Lapa nightlife district—with its mix of partygoers and prostitutes, beggars and bourgie bohemians, dancers and drunkards—are laid bare.

THE BEST DEFENSE IS AN AFFECTIVE OFFENSE

Som e sexo para o povo!
A cabeça tá erguida, o peito aberto por esporte
Aqui meu respeito, que não tem ninguém de bob
Se você quiser um "cat" não se esqueça do din-din
Porque a parada é profissa e princesa são "as mina"

Sound and sex for the people!
Head erect, chest out
Here's my respect, no one's a fool
If you want a blow job, don't forget your cash
Because this is professional and these girls are princesses

And so, while Daspu's real audience is the prostitutes of Rio's seediest neighborhoods, its actual customers are hipsters and bourgie bohemians. In Rio, it has become trendy to throw after parties, raves, and gay nights in brothel venues and red-light areas. Daspu is aware that hipsters are skimming a feeling of being "*puta* chic" and transgressive off of the sexual labor of women whom they don't care about, but Daspu sees itself as infiltrating rather than being appropriated by these young people. After the Daspu show in Lapa, a somewhat drunk young Brazilian woman approached Leite and gushed about what a fan she was. "Your book changed my life!" she explained, speaking of Leite's autobiography. Her friends pored over the merchandise with delight, while she got on her knees in front of an embarrassed Leite in obeisance to ask for words of wisdom.

Perhaps too cynically, I found myself wondering what exactly this wealthy-looking white student on vacation in Rio for carnival connected with in Leite's story of poverty, discrimination, and alienation from family and society. But Daspu occupies a precarious affective space—teetering between a productive disruption of social order and acquiescence to late capitalism's demands on fashion industries, gender, and normativity. It is brazenly adversarial and unapologetic. The clothes are tight and sexy and clever, but they are clothes *by* prostitutes, not *for* prostitutes. The models take pleasure in discomforting part of society and also in titillating their audiences. They stir up strong affective responses, but they also emphasize their political message of social inclusion and equal rights for prostitutes. And so, the fashion becomes the spoonful of sugar needed to force the medicine down the throats of the privileged classes. Daspu realizes that, ironically, if it wants the opportunity to reach the masses, it needs to sell T-shirts to the crowds that can afford to attend shows at Circo Voador.

It is through such circuitous routes that Daspu is able to reach genuinely new audiences and not simply preach to the choir. And Leite was not afraid to go after new or hostile audiences. Laura Murray (2012), an anthropologist who made a documentary about Leite called *A Kiss for Gabriela*, laughed as she recalled their adventures together on Leite's last trip to the United States:

> Gabriela came to Washington, DC, and we went to NOW [National Organization for Women] and the Feminist Majority Foundation and some of the feminist groups that think sex workers are just "women in prostitution" or, worse yet, "prostituted women," that they have no agency. And the representatives of these groups were changed, I swear. By the end of that meeting, NOW wanted its own Daspu fashion show. And they loved the wedding dress that

Fig. 3. A model poses for the media at a Daspu fashion show. (Photograph by Juan Guerra.)

> was made from condoms and bedsheets from the "love motels." That dress completely changed how they were thinking. They thought it was brilliant. So, yes . . . [laughs] she can even convince the Feminist Majority Foundation!

Murray's anecdote speaks not only to Leite's charms, but to the ability of prostitutes to fill a unique affective space. Who else rubs against such disparate sectors of Brazil's highly stratified and unequal society? They have access to the hearts and secrets of middle-class businessmen and powerful elites, but all too often they dwell in poor areas and on the margins of society. Theirs is a rather unique category—rivaled perhaps only by the country's live-in domestic servants. But by taking to the catwalk and filling Rio's nightlife spaces, they gain access to new social modalities, and their bodies also obviously circulate beyond the catwalk, moving virtually via the television, internet, and print media that cover the shows. And through their clothes.

As Murray (2012) explains,

> You have bourgeois kids, children of powerful people, circulating in elite spaces in these shirts. It's a conversation starter. It makes a statement by wearing it. It has that potential not only in the fashion show venues. But when I wear mine, I have people stop me and say, I have one too. It's underground enough that you're in the know, you have something that's cool, but people wear it and they feel they are part of a community. It's a political statement.

The clothes, in addition to being a form of political speech, are also an extension of the whore's body, even if no prostitute from Davida ever wore that individual T-shirt. The clothing circulates, going into spaces where not all prostitutes can. In this way, Daspu's fashion, its catwalks, and the photo shoots in magazines and newspapers, as well its increasingly "hipster" and "bourgie" customer base means that Daspu is able to (literally) thread its way through multiple, complicated, and competing sectors of Brazilian society, disrupting social order even as it gives in to certain demands of late capitalism. The mainstream fashion industry, as an extension of the ever-segmenting late capitalist marketplace, demands a knowable subject so that the consumer may be marketed to with hyperprecision.

And yet, *putas* don't circulate without restriction. I've seen prostitutes thrown out of hotels and restaurants. I've experienced all too many sudden and mysterious restrooms being suddenly "closed for repairs" at establishments when I've patronized these businesses alongside prostitutes. Anti-immigrant laws and anti–sex trafficking laws aim to restrict and confine prostitutes so that they cannot cross borders to work even when coming from and going to countries where sex work is legal (Agustín 2007; Piscitelli 2006, 2007). When early evening rolls around in Copacabana and the prostitutes begin to fill up the tables in front of the beachfront restaurants and bars to cruise for clients, I've watched dozens of middle-class families scoot over to make room for them without showing the slightest scorn even as the middle-class children scamper about underfoot. So there is a certain acceptance of prostitutes. But there can be rigorous policing of sexual mores, too. At a university near the city of São Paulo, a woman wearing a short pink dress caused nothing short of a full-blown riot among seven hundred students. She had to be covered in a professor's coat and escorted out by armed police amid shouts of "whore" and chants of "Let her out, professor! We want to rape her" (North 2009). The university blamed the victim and expelled her for having "an unprofessional demeanor," until an international outcry prompted a reversal. Foreign observers would be wrong to think that all of Brazil is as sexually permissive as movies, television, and other carnival-obsessed media portray it to be. Fashion and sexuality can still combine to form a great threat to patriarchal gender policing. So while prostitutes and other sexually transgressive women do circulate in Brazilian society, exercising this ability doesn't necessarily come without cost.

Just as sexually transgressive people who wish to exercise their rights to circulate and move freely through society must pay a price, so too do consumers face an abundance of societal demand. The fashion industry can, as we all know, be harsh and unrelenting toward women. Here is not the place to rehearse a complete list of the alleged crimes the fashion industry has perpetrated, but no doubt readers are familiar with them and know already that they range from encouraging eating disorders to destroying women's feet to harshly objectifying women under a putative "male gaze." As such, it may seem odd for any women, let alone prostitutes, to choose fashion as their point of entry for waging a campaign for equal rights. But Daspu doesn't simply adopt the industry's oppressive standards, even though its clothes are sometimes quite revealing. Daspu disrupts these demands not by rejecting them outright, but by subversively toying with them. So models walk the catwalk without concern for age or weight or race. They refuse to index who in the show is a prostitute, and who is an ally, an academic, or a student intern. Its T-shirts may be offered in a tailored or baby doll–style version for women or a conventional men's cut, but the content eats away at gender normativity. A woman may have a shorter, tighter T-shirt, but it may feature Mary Magdalene or Edith Piaf or Coco Chanel or any number of others from the series of inspirational women who were once prostitutes. And so by playing with fashion in this manner, Daspu also reveals a part of its ontology. Prostitutes live within a conventionally gendered, patriarchal world and are subject to its norms and oppressions, but they still exercise agency.

But the Daspu catwalks also do more than this. They point us toward another element of fashion and its power to reshape the way we experience ourselves. Among scholars in the humanities who study identity and politics, the tendency is to reject the notion of a static, rigid, essential inner or "authentic" self. Instead, we understand identity to be highly flexible, contested, reflexive, contradictory, and located at least as much "outside" as it is "inside"—that is, in our interactions, exchanges, bodily comportment, self-presentation, and actions. We no longer see our emotions and affective responses as simply originating from the brain and manifesting through the body. Rather, they reflect and refract within our bodies and those of others, shaping and being shaped by our relations to our social world. As such, scholars since the 1990s have started to pay an enormous amount of attention to philosophical questions about bodies and identity (or subjectivity, to be more precise), and especially to the role of desire in connecting them. Elspeth Probyn (1996) describes this line of inquiry as the "sociology of the skin" and sees our desire for belonging as "becoming-other."

The body is a site of contestation, where social forms are manifested and identity worked out. In the case of Daspu, one can see this process clearly at play. Fashion is performative and does *not* signal an authentic inner identity that manifests a corresponding innate form. (There is nothing genetic that forces an academic to wear tweed or a hipster to put on thick glasses.) Rather, fashion is our visible effort to portray that which we desire to be read as, and therefore become. It is our desire for belonging, and belonging is located as much on our outside, on our surface, on our flesh, as it is in our heads. In this way, clothes are an extension of our bodies; they are prosthetics that we take off and put on, but part of this same "sociology of the skin." But at least as much as they reflect how we feel, clothes also affect how we feel, as can be attested by anyone who gets that extra strut when wearing that perfect pair of sexy jeans or by anyone who has worn pajamas past noon and discovered they just can't be productive. So for Daspu models to put on their fashions and take to the catwalks is a bold and performative demand for recognition and respect from society. But those customers who put on these clothes are also engaging in Probyn's (1996) desire for "becoming-other," for making a claim on the world. And in that way, they are taking that piece of the prostitutes' skin, that part of identity that exists "outside," and rearticulating that social body in new ways.

If the distinction between the interior and exterior of the body is somewhat arbitrary, then a mass of people circulating in Brazilian society in Daspu clothing is a networking of individual bodies, but also a social body—a body politic of the *puta*. Framed this way, the fashions are not merely a circulating echo of prostitutes, but a circulating of actual prostitute subjectivity and its attendant desire for respect and inclusion. Fashion marks a new journey for the "whore's body": a new way of being in the world that is more diffuse, yes, but also potentially more effective. And through fashion's dispersal, through this transformation into a sort of weapon of mass ontological destruction that can more effectively challenge conservative sectors of society and circulate with less personal risk, we can see fashion's potential for truly radical politics. Admittedly, activist fashion usually falls short. (Consider the ubiquitous Livestrong bracelets, the anti-choice philanthropist Nancy Brinker and her numerous pink campaigns for breast cancer awareness in memory of her sister Susan Komen, or Bono's RED project.) But it doesn't *have* to be crass commodification or mere publicity stunt. When activist fashion is designed and executed properly, it can powerfully remake us by changing the way we operate within and relate to the world around us, including to those on the margins who find new ways to circulate in and articulate themselves to society.

Note

1. My thanks to João Gabriel Rabello de Sodré for assistance in parsing the lyrics. I also owe a debt of gratitude to Josh Buznitsky, my undergraduate research assistant, for his help with this chapter.

We Are Not Special, We Are Just Here

An Interview with Alexandre Paulikevitch

Meiver De la Cruz

Alexandre Paulikevitch is known in Lebanon for being an activist and a dancer. Paulikevitch is part of an ever-growing cohort of male and genderqueer belly dance performers in transnational dancer-generated circuits who are decentering the male gaze as the central focus of a feminist and queer response and analysis in belly dance. His embodied aesthetic and performative strategies blur boundaries of perception and redefine categories, demanding new ways of watching and consuming belly dance, queerly. Born in 1982 in Beirut, Paulikevitch moved to Paris in 2000 to pursue a degree in theater and dance from the University of Paris VIII. In 2006 he returned to Beirut, where he creates, through his teaching and performance, spaces of reflection and artistry for what he calls *Raqs al Baladi* (dance of the homeland, or village), his preferred terminology for a dance most commonly known in the Arab world as *Raqs al Sharqi* (Oriental/Eastern dance) and in the West as "belly dance." Paulikevitch's insistence on referring to his work as *Baladi* differentiates his craft from the cosmopolitan *Sharqi*, which has adopted orchestral Western instruments and balletic movement, and which circulates in competitive global spheres. *Baladi* remains something that Egyptians do at home and in social gatherings. He has put his *Baladi* dance on international stages, on television, and in museums, reframing it as contemporary dance, while simultaneously using it as a public, dynamic, and performative investigation of sexual and gender politics in Lebanon. This transcript is compiled from three different interviews conducted with Paulikevitch between 2017 and 2018 and draws attention to how dance becomes a means of staging pleasure and critique on three different stages: the contemporary dance circuit, underground ball culture, and cabarets in the Middle East.

Fig. 1. Alexandre Paulikevitch in *"Elgah": Watch Me Move Resistance!*

CITY, CHOREOGRAPHY, AND VIOLENCE

DE LA CRUZ: You write in the introduction to your piece *Tajwal*, "To walk in the city is to oscillate between exaltation and total frustration. I am constantly verbally solicited: seduced, mocked, harassed, celebrated. My body and the city merge and clash. My walks and flâneries through urban pathways turn into observatories and directories of these transactions." Will you tell me more about how you think about relationships between dance, city, and violence in the piece?

PAULIKEVITCH: The narration comes from thoughts on degendering the body. I start the piece with this walk, which for me, it's my walk with this feminized item that is the high-heeled shoe. I finish, I take it off, and I do the same walk again without the shoe. It's not what is outside the body to tell us what is man, what is woman; it is in the body. The piece changed since the version you saw. In the version you saw I start the piece walking in high heels. In the new version, this personage comes back with only one shoe and crippled—this passage was added later, an apparition, "entrée . . . sortie." When I do the piece outside of Lebanon I am naked in these scenes. There I can't be fully nude onstage.

DE LA CRUZ: I love how you make the audience focus on this one arm, articulating a snake arm, repeatedly, and intensely, for a while.

PAULIKEVITCH: This is a meditation on the mutilated body. I go from the basic idea that if we lose a sense, others will strengthen. If I lose sight, my hearing will become more sensitive to compensate. In the piece if I lose an arm, the other one will become more articulate. I want to ask how does the mutilated body re-adapt or adjust to the loss of something, if that body wants to do this dance, now that the symmetry is gone.

DE LA CRUZ: Why do you dance?

PAULIKEVITCH: We are resisting bigotry and trying to maneuver the censorship bureau, in the arts, specifically. Beyond the policing of our bodies by society, [by] the moral police, and by law (and what is imposed by law on us), we are resisting the lack of freedom, and the lack of possibilities to exist and think. We are resisting not being able to be. We are not special. We are just here.

CLUB CULTURE, MINI BALLS, AND HOMOPHOBIA

DE LA CRUZ: In Jocelyne Saab's documentary you talk about the risk of imprisonment for homosexuals, and the sodomy test, putting an egg into the anus, to see if it is flexible, that people must endure. There's a moment of you in the documentary holding a sign at a protest, "Your test is torture."

PAULIKEVITCH: [after a pause] I don't like labels. I'm not here to label.

DE LA CRUZ: What does this feel like? And how do you sustain yourself, emotionally and spiritually, with all the constant confrontation?

PAULIKEVITCH: Meiver, Habibi, you know this, if you were still living in the Dominican Republic it might be the same for you. You don't think a lot about facing it, you do it, because you live in it, and you know how it is, you have been in the schools, etcetera, and you know the system, how it functions and where you can provoke, where you can confront, and when you should erase yourself from the equation and be more low profile. My guarantee is the huge international community that I have. This week I did Dutch TV, and I still have an interview with the Germans this week. This is a bit [of a source of] security for me. This is what makes me ready to take the role of the one that will engage in a public display of gayness or anything provocative. And the other thing is that I am also a figure for the

LGBT [community] in Lebanon. I have been here for a long time facing things. I'm one of the ones that opened things up for everyone, and made it possible for this generation to do their mini balls. They acknowledge that. They know that Alex is a force to reckon with. I'm an inspiration for a lot of people, and this gives me a lot of power. When it's too much, I go into nature or stay at my place. I live in isolation a lot.

DE LA CRUZ: You were recently a judge at Beirut's second mini ball?

PAULIKEVITCH: Yesterday we had the second mini ball, with categories: Eleganza Extravanganza, Lip-Synch for Your Life, Star Impersonation, and the fourth category was Freestyle. And we battled, bitch! I am gonna send you a picture later on. I was all in full latex.

DE LA CRUZ: A drag ball scene has also begun in the Dominican Republic, in Santo Domingo, where I am from, through the "Draguéalo" parties, which observe similar categories—

PAULIKEVITCH: Coco Montrese is Dominicana! Last year's ball started and the euphoria of *Drag Race* gave the new generation a new drive and I'm grateful for this happening, because there is a resurgence of *paillet* [sequins], feathers, glitter, all the flamboyance we enjoyed—

DE LA CRUZ: When was this earlier moment?

PAULIKEVITCH: In the nineties. We had so many after the Lebanese Civil War. There was fear but there were lots of extremes. Two club names I recall were B018 and Acid, which was also Orange Mechanic—they all closed. And they started not letting drag queens into clubs. Loud gays were asked to leave—for twenty-six years. That [the feathers and sequins] was killed by internalized homophobia, by those bears and muscle men that don't let any femme queens bloom and feel threatened by them. They arrived to kill all the diversity and joy of the gay community. But with the balls, it's full of kids. They are all between eighteen and early twenties—very unaware of local history and all the fighting we did. They think they are liberated, but the mini balls exist in total secrecy. I tell them that they exist because there are people who worked for it, and it's not because of RuPaul that you are able to do this.

MEDIA, CABARETS, AND RESPECTABILITY

DE LA CRUZ: Will you tell me about the online debate you had with an Arab-speaking American dancer?

PAULIKEVITCH: She has had a harmful impact for dance, because she has gone multiple times on television to articulate a common and frequently used narrative that she's "one of the good ones."

DE LA CRUZ: What is that narrative?

PAULIKEVITCH: To show that you are clean, that you agree with everyone, that there are some dancers that are not [morally] good and give a bad image to the dance. You have to point out cabarets, that the good girls don't go to cabarets. You should say that you have never danced in a cabaret to be respected. Because if you dance in a cabaret you don't dance in weddings, nor have the possibility to dance in a five-star hotel, with a contract. So you have to be clear that you don't dance in cabarets and that you are against those places. And that you respect Egyptian law and don't wear costumes that are too low in the front, that you will cover your belly button. Even if who fucking cares about covering the stupid belly button! But you have to show that you are a narrow-minded person. The more narrow-minded the better.

DE LA CRUZ: How do you define what is the cabaret in the Arab world, and how it is different than other venues? How is that line drawn?

PAULIKEVITCH: Cabarets are how poor people can have access to entertainment because this is the main difference with the five-star hotel. Five-star hotels are not for everyone. One drink in a five-star hotel can be the salary of a month for a farmer or lower-class person. So the cabaret is the popular place, that's to start. The cabaret, in terms of the difference in presenting the dance, is that you have multiple dancers at the same time, prostitution is clearly there. Customers interact with dancers, and are incited to drink more by dancers. The dancers will come to your table and try to tell you to drink more, to get you to spend more. In a five-star hotel nobody will push you. There is prostitution there too, but it is hidden. So that maybe you have to buy a car for the dancer to go out with her. Also in a cabaret you don't come with your band to perform. Although there are exceptions: Aziza is a cabaret dancer, and she has her band.

But you don't need to be so professional so as to have your own band, the costumes don't need to be so impressive. It can even be a top with jeans. But it depends on the cabaret. There are cabarets at many levels.

DE LA CRUZ: Is all this press coverage helpful? Does it translate into helping produce your shows, especially when there are so few formal funding mechanisms for the arts?

PAULIKEVITCH: Not at all. It gives me more prestige, I think. So when I have a show, I have a full house. That would be the added value of my international press coverage: "Oh, Alex is important." We have the inferiority complex of the colonized, you know?

DE LA CRUZ: Yes!

PAULIKEVITCH: So you know, "Alex was on French TV," then that's important. But for me being on national TV here is way more important. People say "Alex was on Netflix," and you know that I didn't even see it?" [we both laugh.]

DE LA CRUZ: Why do you stay in Lebanon, if it's so difficult?

PAULIKEVITCH: I am making history in Lebanon, Meiver. I am opening new horizons, definitely, for the dance. I am a pioneer and I have a lot of respect here. My name is very strong, and I don't have that elsewhere. Money can't buy this.

After

Public Notice from the Fucked Peepo

Xandra Ibarra's "The Hookup/Displacement/Barhopping/Drama Tour"

Juana María Rodríguez

On a crisp San Francisco evening in summer 2017, Oakland-based Chicana performance artist Xandra Ibarra transported us through a wormhole of time and space to inhabit a lost realm of queer feeling she called "The Hookup/Displacement/Barhopping/Drama Tour."[1] Advertised on Facebook, the event was organized as a walking tour of queer Latinx and "lezzie" historic sites lost to gentrification in San Francisco's Mission District. The posting read:

> I can still hear the music, feel los dedos, smell the sobacos and see the drag queen mugre on the walls of our old neighborhood haunts EVEN after they resurfaced as sterile establishments. I KNOW you can too . . . you just need a little motavation. Let's invade, resurface, and imprint our titties, besos sucios, and pleasures on the phantom walls of our adored queer nightlife venues![2]

The language of the invitation announces exactly for whom this event was created: those of us willing to transform her sensory incantations—the pungent stench of armpits (*sobacos*), the sticky filth of *mugre*, the sloppy wetness of dirty kisses (*besos sucios*) into a performance of radical presence, a reaching for joy and one another. Ibarra's invocation of "our adored queer nightlife venues" summons an imaginary space of queer Brown commonality. It enacts an open invitation to join the party and the movement for another kind of sexual future. Identification here is not about ethnicity or sexuality or even a common history; instead, it is about a shared sensorium, a collective recognition of belonging that might endure in the afterlife of gentrification. As ghosts, haunting the phantom spaces that we once called ours, we were invited to hear, smell, taste, feel, and see what is no longer there—to inhale the funk of another moment, to call forth another future of what could have been, and to occupy a present space of Brown belonging.

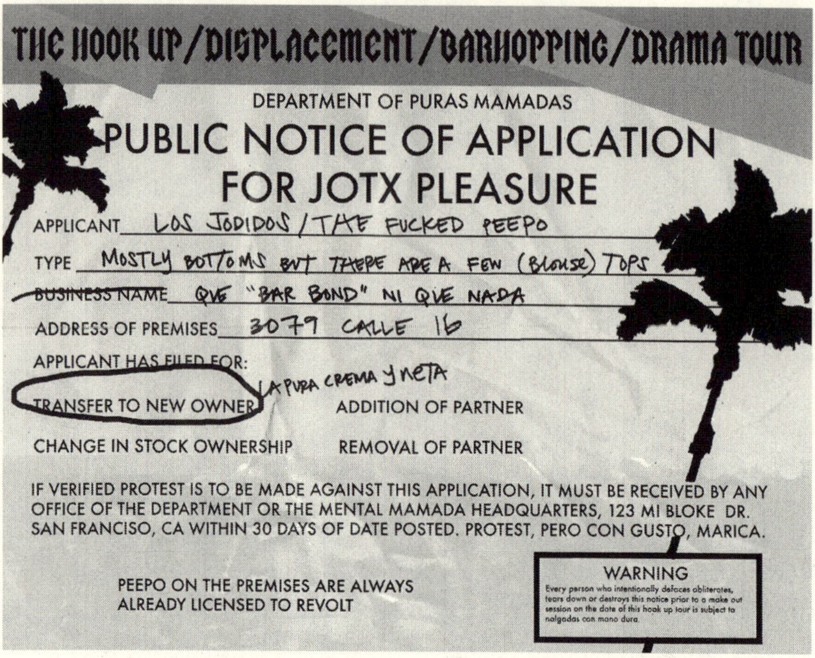

Fig. 1. Xandra Ibarra's counterfeit city notice, Public Notice of Application for Jotx Pleasure, advertising an upcoming performance. (Courtesy of Xandra Ibarra.)

As part of the Facebook invitation, Ibarra created yellow counterfeit city notices for change of ownership, the telltale signs that a property is changing hands. Under the authority of the "Department of Puras Mamadas" (Pure Blow Jobs, Pure Bullshit), Ibarra ridicules the city's power to sanction urban amusement and takes over the regulatory function of the state to issue her own "Public Notice of Application for Jotx Pleasure."

This application for queer racialized recreation projects an imagined future, a proposed plan to re-create something new for those priced out of the gentrified landscape of what was once a beloved queer Latinx neighborhood. This application is issued in the name of "Los Jodidos/The Fucked Peepo," and we see Ibarra translate one vernacular form, Los Jodidos, into another vernacular invocation of a racialized public, the Fucked Peepo. The new owners are listed as "*La pura crema y neta*," a wordplay on *crema y nata*, a reference to elite social class, the cream of the crop, but *neta* with the *e* is an urban Mexican colloquialism that signifies something definite and legit, turning elitism back on itself. Under "Type," language shifts again to a new twist on a familiar queer idiom: "mostly bottoms but there are a few (blouse) tops." Finally, as it mimics the toppy disciplinary function of the state, the notice comes with its own threat of punitive action, stating that anyone "who intentionally defaces, obliterates, tears down or destroys this notice prior to a make-out session on the date of this hook up tour is subject to nalgadas con mano dura." These spankings or *nalgadas* playfully transform *la mano dura* (the hard hand of the law) into an erotic encounter intended to titillate rather than castigate.

In a few short lines, the wording constructs a public that is invited into the scene through multiple overlapping registers of linguistic play, the language of the state, a hyperregional, urban Mexican-inflected Spanglish, and queer idioms that reference sexual play and positionality. Juan Flores and George Yúdice (1992, 220) write of Spanglish, "Interlingual puns, multi-directional mixing and switching, and the seemingly limitless stock of borrowings and adaptations attest to a promiscuous joy not only in excluding and eluding the dominant and exclusionary, but in the very act of inclusion within a newly constituted expressive terrain." Inclusion in Ibarra's performance of linguistic play is not predicated on transparent access to specific static cultural codes but rests on a willingness to delight in figuring out meaning together. Ibarra's invitation hails not a definable set of queer or Latinx bodies but the possibility of radical Brown communion, a "you" that might respond to Ibarra's call, that might actually show up to roam the streets of memory, mourning, and imagination—together. This is community as sensuous feeling.

Of course, the displacement and drama elements of the tour have a much longer history. San Francisco remains the traditional land of the Yelamu Ohlone people, part of a larger interconnected network of Indigenous communities in the region (Voss 2008, 48). Jodi A. Byrd et al. (2018, 14) remind us that the dispossession brought about by gentrification in the historical present is not a new phenomenon, but instead amplifies and extends "the lethal confluences of imperial conquest and racial capitalist predation." Joanne Barker (2018, 33–34) makes the point even clearer relative to articulations of a "new" financial crisis: "the dispossession of Indigenous territories de-exceptionalizes the crisis. . . . Dispossession is not anecdotal but formative." The Ohlone were the original "fucked peepo" of what is now called San Francisco; the rest of us, including Latinx queers, may be the most recent group to be displaced from this geography by the whims and fluctuations of racial capitalism, but that is because we were only the most recent squatters on a land that was never ours. Founded by settler colonialism and lived through dispossession from spaces of belonging, queers, including queers of color, need to practice being gracious and grateful guests, attentive to the histories and struggles of the lands we occupy, allies to the Indigenous guardians who labor alongside us in our shared resolve to create more livable, sustainable worlds. In his posthumously published *The Sense of Brown*, Muñoz (2020, 2, 118) characterizes Brownness as "a being with, being alongside" and suggests "performance is a mode, a protocol, a path toward an attunement to the brownness of life and the world" (2, 11). He writes, "The story I am telling about a sense of brown is not about the formation of atomized brown subjects. It is instead about the task, the endeavor, not of enacting a brown commons but rather about knowing a brownness that is our commonality" (2). Like Muñoz, like Byrd and Barker, Ibarra invites us to see the Brown that is already here under the sediments of historical erasure, even after it has been resurfaced, erased, or forcibly disappeared.

Like a medium at a séance, Ibarra summoned us, and we arrived. The event performed its own form of intergenerational touch, gathering together a small, ragtag band of aging Latinx memory-seekers; an equal number of younger queer performance artist and activist types, many newly arrived to a city they had dreamed of making their own; and anyone else who wandered into the fray. In his essay "Sex Time Machine for Touching the Trancestors," Julian Carter (2018, 696) describes the radical queer potential of intergenerational sensuous exchange, "transfer[ring] our queer sexual culture to one another directly, body to body." But generational differences also transform our connection to histories of living, dying, and fucking as queers. Even as our collective grief and outrage had brought us together, those of us in attendance did not all share the same connection to the dearly departed. Ibarra herself has lived in the Bay Area less than a decade, having arrived from her hometown of El Paso, Texas, via Seattle. Most queer spaces we visited that night had already closed before she and many of the other attendees had arrived in the city. But this was not just an invitation to languish in nostalgia or memory; Ibarra was calling on the fleshy presence of our bodies to invade, resurface, and imprint our carnal pleasures—our titties and *besos sucios*—onto the phantom walls—suggesting that all we need is a little *motavation*, *mota*, or marijuana, being the newly decriminalized substance responsible for the incarceration and deportation of so many minoritarian pleasure-seekers.[3]

That most of us assembled that night cannot afford to actually live in San Francisco—that we commuted in from less desirable and picturesque locations for the party, just like we might commute in for work—is precisely the point. If we take seriously Barker's (2018) invocation to think "territory as analytic," then the economic, social, cultural, and sexual consequences of generational forms of racialized displacement emerge in sharp relief. In the mid-1700s at least ten thousand Indigenous people and forty distinct tribelets resided in what we now think of as the San Francisco Bay Area; as of 2018, according to the American Community Survey, the combined population of American Indians, Native Hawaiians, and Alaska Natives in the region is currently less than 1 percent of the total population, even as the data erases any tribal specificity of the current native Ohlone people of the region. In the past ten years, 25 percent of African Americans have left San Francisco, exacerbating decades-long "redevelopment" that began in the 1960s and turned "urban renewal" into "negro removal" (Jackson and Jones 2012, 62). The Latinx population of the city, which stood at 60 percent in 2000, is expected to fall to only 31 percent by 2025 (Bowe 2015). Just like the bars that have been renamed and rebranded, the bodies that once wandered these streets have been erased and replaced with younger, cleaner, whiter, more affluent versions of our sad queer Brown selves. The whitening of San Francisco means that the queer sexual pleasures of urban living—street-corner cruising and alleyway smashups—are becoming increasingly inaccessible to queers of color, who no longer have easy access to nightclubs, play parties, bathhouses, street fairs, city parks, and performance venues. But Ibarra had told us to "come thru—even for one drink, one beso, one lick," so we were there, hugging old friends and fellow survivors, but also dancing, grinding, and—yes—licking a new generation of displaced, depressed, and determined queers salivating for an escape from the soul-crushing beige boredom of suburban life.

The first stop on the Drama Tour was the iconic Esta Noche (1979–2014). Known as "Mala Noche" to regulars, it was the last queer Latinx bar to close in the Mission, replaced by something called the Bond Bar. There is something particularly cruel about this new naming; a bond invokes both collective attachments and a certificate of financial indebtedness into the future. In contrast, Esta Noche, *This* Night, names the immediacy of the present for ourselves, for pleasure, for the chance to get lucky. Of the numerous sites on the Drama Tour, Esta Noche was the longest lived, and its closure was most deeply felt. It also experienced its own fifteen minutes of gay (white) fame, when it was featured in the short-lived HBO series *Looking* (2014–15). In his essay on the bar, "The Dirt That Haunts," Iván A. Ramos (2015, 135) describes what it *used* to be: a bar catering "to a queer Latino microcosm of culture, adoration, and desires." But that night, in the urine-soaked alley, Esta Noche came alive again and hosted a spectacle for those that happened to notice, that turned to see what all the commotion was about, before heading on their way to their farm-to-table dinner, or to the doorway where they would spend the night. There in the alley, against the wall where so many of us had grinded our queer desires onto the crotches of strangers, Ibarra projected, among other things, excerpts from the 1994 film *¡Viva 16!* by Valentin Aguirre and Augie Robles, a visual reminder of the vibrant club and street scene that had once existed at the corner of Sixteenth and Mission. In that moment, the mobile surfaces of our bodies became the phantom walls, a screen for the projections of a past filtered through the heady haze of an urgent present.

Produced in 1994, *¡Viva 16!* commemorates what was then fifteen years of Esta Noche's presence there, on a corner that it shared with La India Bonita, another gay Latinx club commemorated on the Drama Tour. In the 1980s and 1990s, queer Latinx immigrants came to San Francisco—whether from the agricultural towns of California's Central Valley, or as sexiled refugees from Havana, Mexico City, or San Salvador—thinking they had arrived at the promised land, a place to live and die together, a land of queer salsa, hunky vaqueros, and multilingual sexcapades. This film functions as a looking back in time, produced with the urgency of documenting a community in death's grip. In 1994, AIDS was the leading cause of death for all Americans between the ages of twenty-five and forty-four. Yet, even as *¡Viva 16!* documents a fading past, it also foreshadows a prescient future. The following year, 1995, is credited as marking the beginning of the tech boom in the Bay Area and elsewhere, when Netscape had its initial public offering (IPO), quickly followed by IPOs from Amazon, Yahoo, and eBay. That year also marks the introduction of what came to be known as the AIDS cocktail, effectively rebranding HIV infection and AIDS as manageable conditions for those who could manage—meaning for those who were educated, employed, and connected to the dominant white gay male scene in the city.

Like the Drama Tour itself, the queer Latinx community that *¡Viva 16!* documents performs its own intergenerational bond, drawing on the psychic resources of past pleasures as a way to cope with looming death and displacement. In his essay on this film, Andrew Shaffer (2017) names this queer layering of time as *temporal flirtation*, another invocation of what Elizabeth Freeman terms *erotohistoriography*. Freeman (2010, 120) writes, "As a mode of reparative criticism, erotohistoriography honors the way queer relations complexly exceed the present, insisting that various queer social practices, especially those involving enjoyable bodily sensations, produce forms of time consciousness—even historical consciousness—that can intervene into the material damage done in the name of development, civilization, and so on." Twenty-three years after the film's premiere, its projection onto the walls of

Fig. 2. Outside of La India Bonita, on the route of "The Hookup/ Displacement/ Barhopping/Drama Tour." (Photograph courtesy of author.)

the alley, screened onto the bodies of those of us in attendance, created a kind of sensory communion with the dead—allowing us to dance, mingle, and flirt, if just for a moment, with the floating presence of friends now gone, with younger versions of our own aging bodies, and with a community that has once again been forcibly disappeared. Dancing in solidarity with the Indigenous ghosts of the past and in queer Brown kinship with a vision for a Black and Indigenous tomorrow yet to come, there in the present of that now, our bodies performed our righteous refusal to just fade away.

As with club nights of yesteryear, most of the action on the Drama Tour actually happened in the alleys, not in the bars. The music inside the Bond Bar was too generic and painfully happy, there were no heartbreak boleros, or lustful Latin beats to get hard for. So we brought our own boom-box jams and claimed the moonlight and misery of the city sidewalks for ourselves. But honestly, rather than a raucous, spirited mass protest ready to seek revenge for the shattering loss of our bars, our neighborhood, and our scandalous nocturnal delights, for the generational violence of dispossession and displacement, I admit we seemed sort of sad and rather silly, trying just a bit too hard to make a party out of a funeral, dancing to some club version of "I Will Survive," an aspirational manifestation of cruel optimism if ever there was one. But having shown up to haunt the hipster corridors of a city that no longer has a place for us, we did our best to push back against the daily strain of living in pleasureless times.

Ibarra's mobile public performance was not merely a homage to what once was; it called on us to occupy the present, to make an embodied claim to collective Indigenous, Black, Brown, queer sensual indulgence, to impress our perverse desires for alternative sexual futures onto the surfaces of a gentrified urban landscape. The raunchy, in-your-face, sexual spirit of the Drama Tour performed what Lauren Berlant (1997, 62) terms "sex acts on the live margin," "sex acts that threaten because they do not aspire to the privacy protection of national culture, nor to the narrative containment of sex into one of the conventional romantic forms of modern consumer heterosexuality." As the procession traveled to the four other spots designated on Ibarra's Drama Tour, Ibarra memorialized their lives, offering us inexact dates for their brief existence among us—La India Bonita (1970s–1996), Amelia's (1978–91), the Lexington Club (1997–2015), and Osento's Bathhouse (1979–2008) and we responded as best we could to Ibarra's encouragement to keep it *bien sucio*, real dirty. So we swapped tequila-flavored spit on the streets, mixing fury and desire to do the work of being publicly perverse, of baring breasts and ass cheeks in the name of other ways of inhabiting queer life forms and geographies of belonging.

In her essay on the Latino queer analytic of *lo sucio*—filth—Deborah R. Vargas (2014, 724) writes, "*Lo sucio* smells, acts, and tastes like those deemed collateral genders within a social world invested in the fiscal benefits of normative sexual intimacies . . . the magnificent refuse of surplus while in refusal of vanishing." At each location, participants performed our collateral genders: we set up altars in the nearby alleys, leaving behind flowers, carnival beads, dildos, tarot cards, and empty condom wrappers, chalking up the sidewalks with pink and purple messages of our love and hate. Along the way, we stopped to shout at the new skinny blond residents in Spanish, snap selfies, refresh our *motavation*, and make out on the streets in showy displays of our ongoing commitments to *puta* life. All the spaces of *jotería* in the Mission are gone, but so too are all the "lezzie" spaces, the feminist bookstores, the bars, the bathhouse, erased from the newly sanitized city made safe for tech workers and their bright white families of urban pioneers.

That the time of pleasure that was being invoked on the Drama Tour was also the height of the AIDS pandemic in San Francisco is precisely the point. Like colonialism, criminalization, and AIDS, the ghosts of gentrification per-

Fig. 3. Xandra Ibarra midperformance. (Photograph by Robbie Sweeny.)

Fig. 4. Xandra Ibarra midperformance. (Photograph by Robbie Sweeny.)

form their own slow death of disappearance and erasure. AIDS taught us how to mourn and grieve, but the crushing sadness of that historical moment also enacted a radical refusal to abandon pleasure in the name of grief, respectability, or political pragmatism.

Today, against a backdrop of wildfires, mudslides, earthquakes, and racialized disasters, unchecked development continues to devastate the local environment and wreak havoc on the fragile poetry of ecosystems gasping to find enough clean air and water to survive. Forced evictions, criminalized homelessness, skyrocketing rents, unsustainable environmental policies, and a lack of community services combine with the notoriously racist, sexist, ageist, ableist hiring practices of the tech sector to feed a growing income gap and opportunity gap for those shut out of the new bro-based economy that has taken over the city, fueling the never-ending needs of the tech sector for more yoga studios and vegan burritos. That Ibarra's event was organized and documented on Facebook—where only 5 percent of the entire workforce is

Latinx, in a state where 39 percent of all residents are Latinx—forms part of the cruel contradictions that today's activists are forced to inhabit. However, that night, Ibarra's public staging of desire, drama, and displacement revealed the trace of other potential futures hidden beneath the shiny veneer of tech progress. Like spirits summoned from the great beyond, those of us close enough to answer Ibarra's call showed up for ourselves, for the ancestors we hold dear, for one another, and for an alternative vision of living and loving—of enacting queer ways of inhabiting the stuck-together palimpsests of dispossession and possibility. That night we smeared our sad, diseased and trauma-stained fluids over the power-washed sidewalks of stolen land, to make a fleshy spectacle of our broken hearts, our stubborn commitment to pleasure, perversity, and our own aliveness serving as the ultimate revenge against those who plot our erasure.

Notes

1. Warm thanks to Xandra Ibarra, Julian Carter, Ren Ellis Neyra, and Joseph Pierce for their thoughtful contributions to my thinking for this essay. The germ for this piece appears as a coda to the reprinting of "Activism and Identity in the Ruins of Representation" published in *AIDS and the Distribution of Crises* (Cheng, Juhasz, and Shahani 2020).

2. Translations are my own: *los dedos*, the fingers; *sobacos*, armpits; *mugre*, filth, generally old encrusted filth; *motavation*, a neologism of *mota* (marijuana) and motivation; *besos sucios*, dirty kisses.

3. Legal cannabis has already become a new source of wealth for many, even as those who have criminal records, including for possession, are excluded from profiting from this new green economy, with the predictable racialized consequences.

Remember the Time

Black Queer Nightlife in the South

E. Patrick Johnson

Once upon a time, in a land far, far, away, deep down the goody trail called the South, there used to be these things called Black gay dance clubs. They were magical spaces where the bump and grind of crotches, the funk, stench, sweat, and overperfumed bodies fueled the high you were already on on the dance floor. Yaaasss, Mama! Twirling, spinning, and dipping to deep house, giving face, grace, and undeniable shade, the queens' bodies sashayed, shanteed fiercely to the rhythms that made the children go, "Umph! Umph! Umph! You bettah WERK!"

And then there were none. The wicked witch of gentrification came and destroyed the queer playground. Sassy queens in stiletto heels pushing poppers gave way to yuppie mothers in flats pushing baby strollers. The loud, thumping bass of house faded into the distance, replaced by the sound of bulldozers and cranes making way for the next high rise or trendy restaurant that no Black queen could afford (or self-respecting one would dare to enter). Hetero- and homonormativity be damned. But from the ashes, the queers will rise again. Just follow me.

This essay chronicles the rise, demise, and resurgence of the Black gay dance club in the South. Although I describe prototypes of the Black queer club from the time of slavery and the twentieth and twenty-first centuries, most clubs covered in this essay emerged from the late eighties to the present. Specifically, I discuss the social and cultural conditions under which many Black gay clubs in the South came into prominence and, after years of prosperity, were shut down due to gentrification or were transformed into something different altogether. I also discuss the role they played in the Black queer community and in Black queer worldmaking as a refuge from the hostility of Black institutions such as the church and family, as well as from white gay spaces. Finally, the essay is peppered with personal reflections from my own experiences of Black southern queer nightlife.

WE HAVE COME INTO THIS HOUSE: BLACK QUEER SOUTHERN WORLDMAKING

Because of its geography and the fact that even today it holds expansive swaths of open fields and farmland, the South lends itself to creating makeshift spaces for expressions and affirmation of libidinal desire. Discussing how slaves stole away for leisure, historian Stephanie Camp (2004, 61) argues that during slavery the southern landscape actually provided an opportunity for the enslaved to engage in "illicit" social activities: "Despite planters' tremendous effort, enslaved women and men routinely 'slipped away' to attend illicit parties where such pleasures as eating, dancing, drinking, and dressing were among the main amusements." Because homosexuality as an identity emerged postemancipation, one can only speculate about such spaces for enslaved queers.[1] At the turn of the twentieth century, Black sexual dissidents began to create spaces where they could be free to socialize away from the surveillance of family and heteronormative society, particularly given the stigma of homosexuality in Black communities, which often led Black queers to be, in the words of Black gay writer Craig G. Harris (1986), "cut off from among their people."

The important research of performance studies scholar Shane Vogel (2009, 46) indicates that in the North, and specifically in Harlem during the 1920s, a Black queer nightlife scene emerged in the form of the cabaret—defined as "a central institution of American nightlife"—where queers could sign and signify their sexuality as a way to push back against the "racial uplift" narrative so prevalent among Black elites at the time. While no similar entity existed in the South for Black queers during the early twentieth century, the spaces that did exist were, like the cabaret, associated with "deviant sexual practices, particularly women's prostitution, homosexuality, and black/white relations" (Vogel 2009, 10). Indeed, the "juke joint"—or what one might think of as a makeshift club—was one site, particularly in rural southern places in the 1930s and 1940s, where all manner of queerdom might manifest. Playwright and performer Sharon Bridgforth (2004, 9) captures this scene brilliantly in her performance novel *love conjure/blues* at a "ho house"–cum–juke joint located somewhere in the Mississippi Delta where the clientele comprises "mens womens some that is both some that is neither." One of those people present in the "jernt" is a "wo'mn named big bill," a gender nonconforming musician who, along with two other queer performers, mesmerize the audience with their music:

then suddenly/the three
of them hit a note
all at the same time/ aaaaaawwwwwwhhhhhh
went the sound and i declare some kind of hunger-
spirit swept through the room.
took everybody's mind in one swoop.
after that
wasn't nothing but bodies feeding the feeling till
sunday sunrise just before first service. shiit. we still
rest-broken from all that business. (9)

This moment in "figure's flavors," as the juke joint is called, represents not the bourgeois sensibilities of the Harlem cabaret, but rather the carrying on of working-class queers in the Deep South conjuring the spirit in a makeshift club, their "bodies feeding the feeling" of ecstasy brought on by music and song.

While Bridgforth provides a fictional account of Black southern nightlife spaces, George Eagerson (a.k.a. Countess Vivian), a Black queer man born in New Orleans in 1912, provides a glimpse into Black queer life in the 1930s and 1940s that speaks not only to a vibrant Black queer subculture, but also to Black queer ingenuity among the Black sex workers:

> Julia Pimpay and several others . . . put on dresses and dance[d] and hustle[d] at night. They wouldn't have nothing in the room but the bed and the one chair. . . . And you have somebody in that room right there and we used to call them "creepers" and they would get a trick and they would creep in the door, creep to come in the door. And while the trick was busy doing his business, they [would] go in his pocket and steal his money. That went on for God knows how long. . . . That's why they didn't have nothing in the room, because if it gets [to be] too big a haul, then they have to get out of there . . . because the people would go get the police. And then many, many, many times the person that got robbed wouldn't even go get the police because they would be ashamed to go and tell the police that they were up there with these black hookers, if they didn't know he was a sissy; they thought it was a woman. And even if it was a real woman they didn't want people to know that they was in there . . . with these blacks. Because . . . at that time blacks and whites wasn't close. Of course, they're not all that close now. But then, too, they were further apart than we are today.

So sometimes these were white men picking up these hookers?

Well, not sometimes, always. Always white, no black men, Honey. No black men. Even the black women that hustled, they didn't fool around with them black guys.

Why, because they didn't have any money?

That's right. That's right. You go where the money is. (E. P. Johnson 2008, 485)

Speaking to the racial politics of New Orleans in the early twentieth century and signifying on those same politics today, Countess calls out the white men who supposedly do not know that they are tricking with transgender hookers, while also commenting on the socioeconomic status of Black queers who become "creepers" to make ends meet. These hookers were tricking not with Black men but with white men because "you go where the money is." In a subsequent interview, Countess shared his knowledge of how many transgender hookers rented houses called "crypts"—two-room, shotgun houses in the French Quarter—that they left unfurnished except for a bed and a chair; this allowed them both easy access to a trick's wallet and a quick escape to another place once their scheme was discovered. In her history of Storyville at the turn of the twentieth century, historian Alecia P. Long (2004, 1) notes that after the Civil War, New Orleans "became a tourist destination that encouraged and facilitated indulgence, especially in prostitution and sex across the color line." Few historians, however, recount the city's transgression of same-sex prostitution across the color line.

Ordained "Countess" by a Black Russian drag queen named Olga, Countess Vivian was a part of a thriving Black queer community in New Orleans that took advantage of the loose sexual moral codes of the city and deployed them to resist racist practices meant to undermine their very existence. At the same time, these Black sexual dissidents created a supportive community around sex work that sustained them not only financially but socially. The houses (crypts) that the trans sex workers cultivated to do their business also emerged as a site for a broader spectrum of queer nightlife that entailed socializing as a community around music and dance. Indeed, the crypts detailed by Countess Vivian are the prototype for the "house party," which is still popular today, especially among Black southern queers of a certain generation.

House parties functioned not only as an agent of racial solidarity against racism, but also as a communal site where Black people could love and support one another. Similarly, Black queers who were ostracized by their heterosexual counterparts adapted the practice to provide a space to escape homophobia and to build their own sense of community. House parties were also a form of income for the host, who often charged an admission fee. In addition to selling drinks (most often without a liquor license), the host would sometimes also sell food. In Durham, North Carolina, for instance, Jeff Smith, born in 1918, hosted house parties. Jeff narrates:

> I had parties. I made good money, too. I would furnish whiskey. This lady that had a whiskey house, she told me what to do. She said, "Always have food. Keep 'em eatin' and that'll keep 'em from gettin' drunk quick. They'll eat more." . . . And they didn't get drunk. See, most people get drunk because they don't eat. If you keep your stomach full, you can drink a lot—'fore you fall out.
>
> Sometimes I had parties every weekend. And on a holiday weekend, I might have one on Friday night and one on a Saturday night, too. But you see, you didn't have this crack and stuff. I wouldn't try to have one now. It's a different kind of person now. See, along then you didn't have to worry about all this fighting and stuff. . . . But back then, anybody that come along could come in.
>
> I had a DJ. My DJ was living with me. So, it made it easier. He was good. He knew how to mix.
>
> *So, people danced at your parties?*
>
> Yeah, that's what they were for. [laughter] It was for dancing. My DJ was really good. He lived with me. He didn't have anything else to do. So, he would mix music. (E. P. Johnson 2008, 499)

Smith's parties were "legendary" in the sense that queers from across the state of North Carolina as well as from neighboring states like Virginia and South Carolina would travel to Durham to attend them. Smith held these parties for fifty years, from 1948, after he came home from World War II, until 1998. During this period, the clandestine nature of these parties provided a space for Black southern queers who lived in conservative towns and small cities to party without fear of harassment. It was also a place where one could find out who the queers in the neighborhood were.

DIVAS TO THE DANCE FLOOR: BLACK GAY CLUB SPACES

As Jeff Smith notes, things began to change when crack cocaine came on the scene in the eighties, along with amyl nitrite (poppers) and other recreational drugs that were used among gay men. At the same time, white-owned dance clubs began to cater to Black gay patrons during this period because they discovered the underserved market. Nonetheless, these white club owners deployed racist marketing schemes to entice Black gay patrons by designating a particular night of the weekend as "Black night." They also still engaged in racist entry practices such as requiring multiple forms of identification for entrance and hiring extra security to monitor the parking lots.[2] Eventually, however, what started out as a designated Black night turned into two and three nights a week as Black patrons took over some of these clubs, showing up on the "regular" nights, which eventually drove the white patrons away, thus making these clubs de facto Black in terms of patronage while still being white owned. The takeover of these clubs, the establishment of a few Black-owned bars, and the emergence and spread of house music from Chicago to the South created a booming business of Black queer clubs in the South, especially along the southeastern corridor from Washington, DC, to Atlanta, Georgia.

Several things distinguished these white-owned clubs on "Black night" and the all-Black queer clubs, most notably the blurring of secular and sacred African American traditions. One reason for this blurring of the sacred and secular, according to Black gay activist Craig Washington (2013, 75) is that "what distinguishes Southern Black gay men from their non-Southern and non-White brothers is the pervasive role of the church in their everyday life no matter how homophobic or accepting that church may be. This role is not necessarily interrupted by one's acceptance of queer identity or participation 'in the life.'" Call-and-response, hand clapping, catching the spirit, and speaking in tongues—performance traditions integral to Black church services—were mixed with shade throwing, voguing, bumping and grinding, and general nightclub theatrics.

Gospel music, which shares a rhythm (4/4 time) with house music, would often be remixed, such as gospel singer Shirley Caesar's "Hold My Mule," Tramaine Hawkins's "Fall Down (Spirit of Love)," and Vickie Winans's "Don't Throw Your Life Away." Or the DJs would play gospel-infused house classics such as Aly-Us's "Follow Me" and Dennis Ferrer's "Church Lady," which would give the children life on the dance floor. Moreover, the DJ, whose role was similar to that of a "minister of music,"[3] controlled the "spirit" in the room, keeping in tune with the energy in the room to determine which track to spin, but also sometimes coming down from the DJ booth like a preacher stepping down from the pulpit and into the congregation, to entice the children to leave their burdens on the dance floor. In an interview with Craig Washington (2013, 81), clubgoer Antron Reshaud Olukayode says that he "think[s] of the DJ as a therapist or spiritual healer. In a way. Not with words but with music. I'm sure he or she understands what we go through as a community. Like that house music, infusing the gospel with the secular. . . . I tell the DJ all my problems with each dance step I take and he turns that into music and makes me release. That is why the DJ cannot fuck up." So important is the role of the DJ that many clubs depend on particular legendary DJs for holiday weekends like Memorial Day in Washington, DC, and Labor Day in Atlanta (the weekends of Black Gay Pride in each city, respectively). Indeed, DJ Sedrick Drayton, who is perhaps one of the most famous Black queer DJs on the East Coast and who still spins today, travels the Southeast spinning at clubs in small cities like Fayetteville, North Carolina, and large ones like Atlanta—and has done so for over twenty years.

Finally, the type of dance that occurs in Black queer southern clubs blurs the secular and sacred. The same body movements that one might see in the choir stand and down at the altar of the church might also be incorporated into dances at the club, especially raised arms with palms extended upward, pulsing to the bass of the music, or fancy footwork in double time to the pounding of a tambourine. The slip and slide from Holy Ghost spirit to (homo)erotic ecstasy is made manifest through dance. Perhaps Washington (2013, 82) sums it up best when he writes:

> To dance is to speak using one's body, to consummate that which is summoned with us, to embrace and share the erotic, to heal, to reveal, to perform and to be. . . . For a people multiply oppressed and rich in improvisational and traditional language and spiritual agency, this primal act of exaltation accrues value. . . . Dancing in the relatively safe environs of the club facilitates release, self-expression and communal bonding that is elsewhere forbidden, limited or if indulged in the unsanctioned open, at varied risk. In these contexts, to dance is not only to have fun. To dance is to overcome. To dance is to be free.

The freedom through dance that Washington describes exists because, as I have argued elsewhere, the club *space* provides for a different experience than the pre-scripted church *place* (E. P. Johnson 1998). Thus, while queers may covertly assert their gender and sexual identities and proclivities in the church place, they may do so in the space of the club with a different level of freedom—or judgmental surveillance.

As previously described, these Black queer spaces served a particular function for their patrons regardless of whether they were white-owned clubs with a designated Black night or Black-owned clubs with majority Black clubgoers every night of the week. In urban cities like Washington, DC, and Atlanta, similar to house parties like the ones Jeff Smith hosted in Durham, queers in the club hailed from near and far, with many patrons traveling hundreds of miles to partake in the secular/sacred festivities on the dance floor.

In Washington, DC, the Southeast and Northeast districts were known for a number of Black gay clubs, some of which were Black owned. These included the Edge, the Bachelor's Mill (the Mill), and the Delta Elite Social Club (the Delta). The white-owned Edge nightclub had Black night on Fridays and was famous for its go-go dancers and well-endowed strippers. The Bachelor's Mill, located on the corner of Eighth and L streets SE by the Washington Navy Yard, opened in 1988. It is a small "dive" bar that caters to an older, working-class crowd. It has two floors. I have not been to the Mill since the early 2000s, but back then on the first floor you were likely to walk in on patrons playing a game of bid whist or spades, and old timers kiki-ing and shooting the shit about the good 'ol days over the bar's very strong drinks. Downstairs is the dance floor, where there are usually folks grooving to a mix of house and old-school R&B. And even smaller than the Mill was the Delta Elite Social Club, which was located in the city's Northeast district in a strip mall. It was open on the weekends, and it segregated the genders into "ladies' night" on Fridays and "men's night" on Saturdays. The Delta, where one had to traverse a steep set of stairs from the street entrance down to a basement to enter, was known for hip-hop and "go-go," a popular music form that is derivative of funk and that originated in Washington, DC, in the sixties. But if you wanted to dance—and get your life!—Tracks was the place to go, especially on the nights when DJ Sedrick was spinning.

Tracks was perhaps one of the most popular and largest nightclubs in the Washington metropolitan area, boasting the region's largest dance floor at the time, and it also included a huge bar that sold food, and a large outdoor space with a volleyball court with beach sand. It was known for its spectacular lights and sound system. Singers such as Gloria Gaynor, Thelma Houston, Crystal Waters, the Village People, Robin S., Martha Wash, and CeCe Peniston all played at Tracks. Owned and founded by white Denver-based businessman Marty Chernoff, Tracks opened its doors in 1984 in DC's Southeast district in what at the time was thought of as a dodgy neighborhood. The bar was gay every day of the week, but as its popularity grew, a few straight people began to frequent the club for the music and the famous acts. It was never an "all-Black" space as much as it was a diverse group of queers, though again, when DJ Sedrick played there, it was blacker than usual.

I cut my queer teeth at Tracks in the early nineties. During my first visit to Tracks in 1990, my first time at a gay bar, I was still quite closeted. I remember being so nervous about being there—despite the fact that I was there with friends—that I kept throwing *back* Long Island iced teas until I began throwing *up* in the lobby of the bar, not being able to make it from the dance floor to the bathroom. Embarrassed both by and for me, my friends took me out of the club and back to the apartment of the friend where we were staying, put me to bed, and went back to the club. Before I was too drunk to stand and had to be whisked from the club, I did dance to DJ Sedrick's mixes. In those days, he would burn cassette tapes of his mixes for patrons on the spot. I still, to this day, have the remix of Shirley Caesar's "Hold My Mule" that he burned for me.

According to Craig Washington (2013, 86), "the 80s set the dawning of Black gay clubs in Atlanta." Indeed, for many years Black queers from around the country flocked to "Hotlanta" to experience Black queer nightlife, most of which was downtown. One of the first clubs to open was Loretta's on Spring Street, or what the children referred to as "Lo-Lo's." Loretta's was Black owned and, similar to the Bachelor's Mill in DC, had a working-class clientele. Arguably more dancing took place outside of Loretta's on the street than did inside on the dance floor. Notorious for its strong drinks, deep house, and fights, Loretta's was legendary among Black gay nightclubs in the Southeast. Loretta's was one of many clubs from the 1990s to the 2010s where Black queers danced, had drinks, or hooked up. These included Jungle, Backstreet, Fosters, and Bulldogs, among others. And. Then. There. Was. Traxx.

Traxx in Atlanta is the other significant nightclub that played a role in my burgeoning queerness "back in the day." Again, DJ Sedrick was a key attraction for me and others. Founded in 1983 by young Black gay businessman Phillip Boone, Traxx was one of the first Black-owned gay clubs in Atlanta. Traxx, like Tracks in DC, was a mega club, with not just one dance floor, but two. As it was for so many of my generation, dancing at Traxx was for me a formative experience, especially coming of age in the shadow of HIV/AIDS. My trips to Traxx also changed my life because it was the first experience I had where queer nightlife and church blurred. In 1998, I published an essay titled "Feeling the Spirit in the Dark" that chronicles the ways in which sexuality and spirituality blur. In that article I provide the following description of the inside of Traxx and my experience on the dance floor:

> Inside, the club is sparsely decorated, which makes it appear even larger than its 3500 square feet. The entrance is on the second level, which overlooks the dance floor and resembles the second floor of a shopping mall. My friends and I squeeze down the staircase and descend into the sea of bodies onto the dance floor. There is barely enough room to breathe, let alone move. Every inch of the space is filled with a body—fat bodies, thin bodies, hard bodies, soft bodies, warm bodies, sweaty bodies, every body imaginable. Clearly, the body is on display: There are drag queens in skintight hotpants and platform shoes. There are "butch" men donning their black leather jackets, aligning the wall like two by fours holding the structure together. There are "queens," dressed in tight black jeans and black chiffon blouses unbuttoned to their navels, who are constantly pursing their lips while looking over the tops of their retro "cat-eye" shades; there are older men (in this club anyone over 45) sitting on bar stools, dressed conservatively in slacks and button-up shirts sipping their scotch and sodas while looking longingly at the young bodies sauntering across the dance floor. The hip hop contingent is sprinkled throughout the club in their baggy jeans, ski caps, sneakers, and black shades, some sucking on blowpops while others sip Budweiser. And then there are those like me and my friends who are dressed in designer jeans (Calvin Klein) and tight, spandex muscle shirts, performing middle class (acting bourgeois)—as if we actually have two nickels to rub together! You can smell us coming because we sprayed and resprayed cologne behind our ankles, on the small of our backs, and, of course on the front of our chests and all around our necks. We're beyond reproach. We manage to dance—spoon fashion—against the seemingly thousands of flying arms, legs, and butts. I dance with the same man all night—Kevin—a friend of a friend. Kevin and I don't mean to be exclusive dance partners, it just works out that way. We dance close. Every now and then we back off from one another as far as we can and then come together again. We kiss. We bump booties. We hold on to each other for dear life as the beat of the music, the smells of Drakkar, Cool Water, Eternity, and Escape, CK-One, the sweat drenching our shirts, and the holy sexual spirit that presides works us into a shamanistic state of euphoria. Time stands still. (E. P. Johnson 1998, 408)

And time did stand still. I was never able to capture that moment again—not even through the performative language I used to describe the experience. Many of the friends with whom I danced that night are no longer with us, which makes the words that DJ Sedrick chanted that night as he took to the dance floor with his mic in hand even more prophetic: "Look around you. Somebody that was here last year ain't here tonight! Look around you! Somebody that was dancing right next to you ain't here tonight!" And like the many bodies that were vibing, sexing, and hooking up on the dance floor, many of the clubs that facilitated this communion are also gone. Look around you.

AND THEN THERE WERE NONE

During the economic boom of the late 1990s through 2007, many neighborhoods where these clubs were located became vulnerable to higher rents and taxes, or the clubs—as was the case with many of the clubs in DC—were forced out because of eminent domain (see Fatzick 2015; Ha 2010). And as the country experienced a conservative backlash during the George W. Bush administration, local governments especially in the South became increasingly intolerant of the presence of a particular kind of queer nightlight. In downtown Atlanta, for instance, a series of gay bars were forced to close their doors because of increased surveillance around liquor licenses, police raids, and escalating rents. Between 2003 and 2009, six clubs in Atlanta closed, including Loretta's and the original Traxx. What emerged in their place was a new "all inclusive" club that appealed to straights and queers. This rebranding was more respectable and sanitized all the sexiness out of the club spaces, as exemplified in this online description for Club 708 Restaurant and Grill, which opened in the space that formerly housed Loretta's:

> Club 708 Restaurant & Grill, formerly known as Loretta's, is the first in Atlanta that initially attracted black males and females with an alternative lifestyle preference. Today, Club 708 Restaurant & Grill caters to all races, in the gay community. The Restaurant is known as the most original gay spot in Atlanta. Even though, Club 708 Restaurant & Grill caters to those with an alternative lifestyle, others come to the club for the great music, which consists of hip-hop, R&B, house/club music and the friendly sociable atmosphere.[4]

Trying to thread a needle very carefully, the owners engage in pandering to "all races, in the gay community" as well as "others" who "come to the club for the great music," while placating the historically Black clientele of Loretta's. Rather than use the term *gay* or *queer*, the ad traffics in the offensive "alternative lifestyle." Sadly, this is what is left of the rough-and-tumble transgressive space known as Loretta's. Traxx is now "Traxx Girls at Club Miami," a Black lesbian space on Friday and Saturday nights.

Almost all the bars in Southeast and Northeast Washington, DC, were either closed or bulldozed to make room for the new baseball stadium for the Washington Nationals. Tracks closed its doors in 1999, having switched owners a few times in the preceding years. Chernoff, once again owner of the club, decided, "Like everything else, Tracks' time had come. You can't hang on to the previous concept and expect it to move into the next decades and next generations" (Chibbaro 2013). And with the stroke of a pen, Chernoff sold the building to a developer who built a new office building that now sits where Tracks once was. As of this writing, the Bachelor's Mill remains open, but it has softened a bit over the years to attract a broader range of patrons. While folks still play cards, outside alcohol is not permitted and some younger gay men attend. But its fate is uncertain. The building where it is located was sold in spring 2018 at public auction. Currently, the Bachelor's Mill is the last remaining Black-owned gay club in Washington, DC. For thirty-seven years, the Delta catered exclusively to Black queer people, but it was forced to close in 2014 due to the escalating rent in the gentrifying Brookland neighborhood where it resided.

I take away a number of things from this phenomenon. First, the Black gay nightclub in the South is always already bound by the political economy of the city. In other words, even from its emergence in the early 1980s, the Black gay nightclub was motivated by white capitalist ventures, whereby businessmen wanted to capitalize on the demand for a niche market. Gentrification and sexual policing—which occurred throughout the country, especially in urban areas, and had a chilling effect on gayborhoods—detrimentally affected all-Black queer spaces. Second, changing trends in musical tastes, sartorial performance, and gender presentation have decidedly changed the clientele of Black gay spaces that currently exist. House music, once the music of choice among many Black queers, has been replaced with hip-hop and rave music, which appeal to a younger crowd. House heads have to seek out clubs on a particular night when the music is played or, ironically, have reverted to hosting house parties where they have control of the music. Third, class distinctions have further created cleavages in the Black queer scene, especially in urban areas, where the number of middle-class and upper-middle-class Black queers has risen. Those who have ascended to such status often balk at the thought of attending places like Loretta's, where one might dance until drenched with sweat or be offered a chicken wing with a bottle of Zima, preferring instead a more bourgie affair, where the closest one would come to sweating would be while doing the wobble and sipping on prosecco. And, finally, the advent of social media outlets such as Facebook, Snapchat, and Twitter, in addition to hookup apps like Grindr, Adam4Adam, and BGCLive, among others, has shifted the spaces where Black folks build community from brick-and-mortar spaces to virtual ones.

And yet, from the ashes, the Black queer club rises. Despite the disappearance of many of these Black queer club spaces of the past, new ones continue to emerge, though not nearly at the pace they did in the 1980s—and nearly all the new spaces are a one-night-a-week affair. Mixx Atlanta, near Piedmont Park, for instance, has a "Hip Hop and R&B Night" (code for "Black night") on Fridays. Bulldogs, which has been around for close to forty years but was mostly known in the past as a place for white men to pick up Black men, now caters to a mostly young, Black crowd. Indeed, as with most queer things, the pendulum of time swings both ways. Ultimately, I agree with Craig Washington (2013, 84) when he suggests that no matter what, the club will always exist as an important site for Black southern gay men because "it is here that men go to be with others like them, to see and be seen, want and be wanted, whatever the outcomes, to be fully, freely themselves."

As the South continues to shift demographically due to increased reverse migration from the North and Midwest, it will be interesting to see how queer nightlife evolves. One thing for sure: the children will continue to carry on and remember the time.

Notes

1. For discussions of Black queer desire among slaves, see Nero (1991) and Scott (1999).

2. This practice is famously represented in Marlon Riggs's film, *Tongues Untied* (1989).

3. In the Black church, the minister of music oversees all the choirs and musical selections for worship service. This person is often the head musician and sometimes also serves as the choir director.

4. This information appeared on the website BeforeLastCall.com, which has been discontinued as of August 2020. This description was accessed in August 2018.

Keeping It on the Download

The Viral Afterlives of *Paris Is Burning*

Jih-Fei Cheng

The US documentary film classic *Paris Is Burning* (1990) is often discussed in terms of how it celebrated, or exploited, the subcultural lives of those who are queer and trans Black, Indigenous, and people of color (QTBIPOC).[1] What if we instead consider today's digital downloads of *Paris* as the viral transfers of embodied knowledges and strategies of survival for QTBIPOC across time and space?

Rashaad Newsome (2015), a New York City–based multimedia artist and Father of the House of Arms, addresses the impact that ball culture has had on popular culture, in terms of language, performance, and kinship systems: "Voguing is a practice that was created out of the community that I'm a part of as a black, queer man. Voguing and breakdancing were born in the same place at the same time. Breaking came into prominence but Voguing did not because so many people, including the leaders of the voguing community, were lost to the HIV/AIDS crisis." Citing *Paris*, Newsome (2015) explains why voguing has nonetheless persisted beyond this crisis of the 1980s and 1990s: "The internet plays such a huge role. The thing about vogue is that it's an open source . . . I was thinking about black vernacular and how that's associated with the black female and how in some way it has also become an open source. I'm really interested in the complications of that."

With its reverberations of a Black female vernacular, ball culture—and, in this specific case, voguing—has developed in different ways in New York City, as exhibited by the documentary film *Kiki* (2016). Yet, ball culture has also traveled beyond the context of queer nightlife in the postindustrial city and its representation through the AIDS-influenced style of independent filmmaking that B. Ruby Rich (1992) called New Queer Cinema (NQC). As an urtext through which voguing entered mainstream culture, *Paris*, and the resounding Black women's vernacular that carried it to prominence, was further transmitted via internet-based popular media in the form of video-on-demand platforms, memes, gifs, and more. In describing vogue as an "open source," Newsome (2015) contends that the echoes of Black women's vernacular in voguing coalesces various racialized subjectivities and identities. Simultaneously, Newsome points out, white cisgender gay men who "share" Black women's vernacular do not share the stigma and violence that continue to be levied against people of color, *especially* Black (cis)women and Black transfeminine peoples.

Elsewhere, I focus on the silencing of Black women in today's popular representations of historical and ongoing AIDS activism. I analyze how Black feminist and queer strategies of representation intervene into systems of violent erasure by transforming that silence into powerful critiques of science and media.[2] Here, I offer an understanding of how such Black feminist and queer strategies encounter and collaborate with other radical and anticolonial visions across time and space to generate ball culture as a decentralized and collaborative open-source model for QTBIPOC survival. To do so, I historicize and track downloads of AIDS media, focusing on those that have "gone viral" in contemporary popular culture, particularly the mass media distribution of the foundational NQC film *Paris*, which has achieved global recognition while casting the influences of ball culture in ways immeasurably far and wide.

DUAL PANDEMICS: HIV/AIDS AND COMPUTER VIRUSES

Although AIDS is only vaguely mentioned in *Paris*, many of the film's interviewees died from illnesses related to HIV/AIDS, or they were brutally murdered (Hilderbrand 2013; Kinser 2014; Faye 2016). *Paris*'s interviewees point to the connection between the epidemic harassment and murder of trans women of color and the emergent US AIDS epidemic. Marlon Bailey (2013, 4–7, 204) observes that ball culture has reached mainstream through *Paris* and proliferated through new media, while the community's strategies of survival "based on their own knowledge and ingenuity," or HIV "intraventions," are knit into its social fabric and events.[3] Ball culture offers its members significant protection from the everyday and systemic violences they must otherwise face alone, and which make them vulnerable to HIV infection. The specific contexts and sites of ball culture's emergence garners a kind of "opacity" that preserves its community while keeping the "cool hunters forever sniffing around the ball scene." As Tavia Nyong'o (2015) has pointed out, the "public performance and dramatic display" of these strategies for survival against quotidian and spectacular violence "is the openness of the secret" that keeps others "clueless and forever guessing." How might we understand the capacity of ball culture to remain "open source" yet protective against mainstream exploitation at the historical juncture of HIV/AIDS and new media at the turn of the millennium? How does this embodied practice of open source knowledge re-route our preoccupation with surveilling individual cases of HIV infection and instead magnify our address of HIV/AIDS as a pandemic conditioned by colonial and structural violence?

In 1981, acquired immunodeficiency syndrome (AIDS) and computer viruses simultaneously emerged into the public consciousness. This historical coemergence threw into stark relief how flesh and technology have fused a global circulatory system that regulates a collectively embodied sense of intimacy and pleasure, but with differential chances for survival. Initially thought to affect only a cluster of North American white gay men—and thus first identified as gay-related immune deficiency (GRID)—the illness was renamed AIDS after epidemiologists accounted for Haitian-born immigrants in Florida who had shown symptoms as early as 1980, as well as hemophiliacs and intravenous drug users who were affected (Centers for Disease Control 1982a, 1982b). Meanwhile, fifteen-year-old Rich Skrenta, of the largely white and affluent township of Mount Lebanon, Pennsylvania, designed the Elk Cloner to use games transferred via floppy disk to introduce code that would rewrite computer memory.[4] The causal agents for AIDS and the Elk Cloner were later traced, respectively, to the human immunodeficiency virus (HIV) and the first known computer virus to circulate beyond computer labs (Manjoo 2007). Little attention has been paid to the historical confluence of HIV/AIDS and computer viruses, although today we understand that their existence and effects long preceded the 1980s (Kerr 2016; Filiol 2005, 19–38). This juncture within the late twentieth-century global technoscientific landscape, I argue, reveals crucial reconfigurations of bodies, space, time, and memory that can best be understood through the medium and execution of what came to be termed in the age of networked devices as the *download*.

To address the historical relationship between *Paris*, HIV/AIDS, computer viruses, and the download, I draw on Alexandra Juhasz's (1995, 31–51) contention that AIDS media artist-activists were the first to integrate the analog camcorder into widespread direct action. Tapes were distributed in VHS format to educate the public and to politicize new activists. Producers of independent AIDS media, like *Paris*, used the relatively new handheld medium and drew from earlier Third, Black, and Indigenous Cinema, as well as feminist and anticolonial film/video movements, to forge techniques and representations that countered the US state and mainstream media's stigmatization of AIDS. Simultaneously, the popularization of personal computers (PCs) since the 1970s, and especially by IBM in the 1980s, placed mainframe technology into individual users' hands. The increase in PCs and computer programmers meant that software functions could be changed by more people and that PCs could be used to "create [local] visions [of the world] that go elsewhere" (Chun 2011, xi). The floppy disk became the format for the delivery of new software. As video and computer technology began to merge, and VHS and floppy disks became obsolete, the circulation of media transmitted via binary code through the digital sphere mapped out the viral networks that form the globalized routes for technoscience and commerce. *Paris,* which has been converted from analog VHS to downloadable digital form, reveals the "roots and routes" (Gilroy 1995) of early AIDS media that has "gone viral" to proliferate alternative stories, create new social attachments, and galvanize cultural and social movements.

"Virality" in the age of digital networks, Tony Sampson (2012, 4) asserts, names today's capacity to circulate media among countless users, generate affective impact, and induce change in the social field. These entanglements between bodies and representations constitute the "cybernetic organism [that is] . . . our social reality"—our "cyborg" reality (Haraway 1991, 149). The term *download*—first used as a noun in 1977 and then as a verb in 1980 (*Online Etymology Dictionary,* n.d.)—designates the cyborg reserves and performative acts that facilitate viral transfer. If one were to type "Paris Is Burning" into an online search engine, they would find the film, its participants, and the nightlife of ball culture live beyond the repurposed banquet halls and warehouses, while their dance floors and runways made out of stretches of sidewalks and piers extend farther than the imagination. We see hyperlinks to on-demand viewing, past and present news articles and blogs, and endless video clips, gifs, memes, and social media pages dedicated to the film and its performers. *Paris* is, and is also more than, the residue left on the floor from dance battles: it denotes the flourishing dynamism of contemporary ball culture, and it is the sweat and ecstasy that are continuously relived through digital popular media.

In *Paris,* the idiomatic expressions, embodied performances, gender transgressions, and kinship systems of the largely queer, gender nonconforming, and trans Black and Brown ball circuit participants during the early AIDS crisis form a reservoir of iconic representations, verbal expressions, and gestures. They circulate as an interactive and ever-expanding audiovisual archive that introduces through popular media the evolving practices of "queer worldmaking" (Muñoz 1999, 40), specifically "Blacktino" or "Blacktinx" queer performance (Bailey 2013, 5–8; Johnson & Rivera-Servera 2016, 4).[5] Interactivity also includes classroom and community-based screenings, the reality television show *RuPaul's Drag Race* (2009–present), YouTube clips of white children competitively "voguing" in Russia, and most recently the television series *Pose* (2018–present), to list a few.

Patterns of QTBIPOC kinship are reflected in the life of African American, Kanaka ʻŌiwi (Native Hawaiian), and trans activist and writer Janet Mock (2014, 115–16). Mock was born in Honolulu in 1983, a journalist in New York City by the mid-2000s, and eventually a writer, director, and producer for the hit television series *Pose* (2018–present). *Pose* is not only inspired by the ball scene in *Paris*; it involves significant participation from the film's interviewees. Mock remarks,

> [I]t introduced me to a world and to people who were very much like me. I saw it when I was in high school at my friend's house on VHS and it was powerful to be introduced to Octavia, to Venus, and to Corey. And for me, I think it's a gift that [Jennie Livingston] was there at the time, because we know that many of those people are not here today. The remaining survivors are very much involved on our series. Yeah, there's a complicatedness of whose gaze? Who controls the camera, who's behind it? (Dry 2019)

Pose, and Mock's pivotal involvement, route through the encounters between Black, Latinx, and Pacific Islander communities which cannot be explained by linear histories or accounted for by the maps and social categories employed by epidemiology.

Kathryn Xian and Brent Anbe's 2001 documentary film *Ke Kulana He Māhū: Remembering a Sense of Place* depicts the enduring Kanaka ʻŌiwi practices of precolonial kinships and nonbinary gender and sexual systems in the Hawaiian archipelago at the turn of the new millennium. As well, their interactions with ball culture underscore QTBIPOC mutual recognition as a crucial practice of collective survival in and through the AIDS pandemic. These cross-identity representations demonstrate the geopolitical distances achieved through the media transfers of *Paris* and its participants. A comparative approach to *Paris* and *Ke Kulana* outlines how virality is networked through HIV/AIDS, interactive media, and the performative acts of ball culture. This viral network transmits queer, gender nonconforming, and trans of color embodied knowledges through downloads of ball culture, a Blacktinx and Pacific Islander queer and trans repertoire (Taylor 2003). The sensuous dimensions conjured between these films—verbal cues, gender excesses, music, and dance—detail a constellation of performative acts and citational practices that José Esteban Muñoz (2009, 67) calls "queer gesture." By considering how *Paris* is kept on the download through queer gestures that move through *Ke Kulana*, and further on, we can trace the networked histories and local specificities of racialized, Indigenous, queer, gender nonconforming, and trans vulnerabilities to "premature death" (Gilmore 2006, 28), as well as the tactics of "resistance to and perseverance in the face of these structural forms of domination [that] mark these histories and futures of intimacy" (Johnson & Rivera-Servera 2016, 4). These viral networks underscore how QTBIPOC utilize the global circulatory system to traverse transatlantic and transpacific geohistorical divides, forging collective strategies for sustaining "livable lives" (Bailey 2013, x) across the ends and eras of AIDS and Euro-American empire.

THE VIRAL NETWORKS OF NEOLIBERALISM: AIDS AND INTERACTIVE MEDIA

> It's like crossing into the looking glass. Wonderland. You go in there and you feel . . . you feel 100 percent right being gay. . . . That's not what it's like in the world. You know, it should be like that in the world.
>
> —David DePino, House of Xtravaganza, *Paris Is Burning*

Paris emerged during, and despite, the late twentieth-century neoliberalization of media. This included the increased government censorship of art, film/video, and internet content addressing race, gender, sexuality, and HIV/AIDS. Government surveillance of media "obscenity" and regulation of "decency" across the 1980s and 1990s diminished the potential of the internet to serve as a public utility for widespread access. Infrastructural development of the internet was left in the hands of corporations (McKinney 2020). Internet privatization restricted public access while consolidating telecommunications industries and converging telephones, television, film/video, and computers online (Chun 2006, 77–98, 118–20). Thus, neoliberalization has come to funnel all media interactivity through corporate social networking platforms, including YouTube, Facebook, and "hookup" apps like Grindr, where HIV/AIDS public health information, services, and treatment access have concentrated. While users feel personally empowered, they trade their online behaviors as data for commercial exploitation and state monitoring (Chun 2006, 6–11; Banet-Weiser 2012, 67–69). As Wendy Hui Kyong Chun (2006, 40) mentions, *cybernetics* derives from the Greek term *kybernete* for "steersman, governor." IBM got its start in 1890 by producing machines that could more efficiently analyze census data. Such technoscientific innovations in computing advanced the Industrial Revolution as well as population genetics, public health, eugenics, and nuclear weapons.[6] The field of information has come to shape ontologies and life chances. At the same time, bioinformatics and media have become crucial terrain for the negotiation of power by nonstate and noncorporate actors, like those ball culture participants and performers who appear in *Paris* and *Ke Kulana*.

While the mainstreaming and profitability of *Paris* attest to the simultaneous neoliberalization of HIV/AIDS and media, they also tell of how queer gestures *always already* infect the system of bioinformatics and its representations. During the onset of the HIV/AIDS crisis, media activists utilized representation to critically intervene into the demonizing depictions forged by the US state and mainstream media. Alongside global structural adjustments, the moralistic and criminalizing representations of AIDS fanned the flames of violence that made the pandemic possible. *Paris* was an early experiment with a style of representing AIDS before a language and mode of expression existed to name its most devastating effects—which then shaped the independent filmmaking movement, including NQC, with fluctuating political promise. The film and its participants generated a downloadable source code for facing the most intense vulnerability to, vilification for, and violence of AIDS, despite barely muttering the acronym in the edited footage that was included in the feature-length version.

Paris's Black and Brown queer, gender nonconforming, and trans ball participants were not simply "captured" on film by director Jennie Livingston. Rather, these cultural performers transformed media and delivered an arsenal of *intraventions* into HIV/AIDS and media neoliberalization. The assumption is that the late 1980s New York City queer and trans Black and Brown ball performers had less access to medical care and media technologies to survive HIV/AIDS and direct their own representations. However, as *Paris* indicates, they had already fashioned their existence despite, and at a distance to, the institutions and compulsory measures for individualized "empowerment." Their performances of cultural labor appear as on-screen flashes of queer gestures, which move virally through an economy of collective care that remains off- and between screens (Bailey 2013, 16–20).

While seated before a swing-arm mirror, *Paris*'s featured interviewee and femme queen performer Dorian Corey waxes before the video camera about ball circuit history and its latest participants (see figure 1). Contemplating her reflection and applying makeup, Corey muses, "Liz Taylor is famous. So is Pepper LaBeija. In a sense, so am I. But, a very much different quantity.... But it's still a fame. It's a small fame." According to Corey, the "small fame" cultivated by the ball circuit is what maintains the competition, but also the collectivity and community. Seemingly well aware of and yet unmoved by the camera's presence, Corey narrates with her gaze fixed into the looking glass—gesturing and luring the audience toward the off-screen, virtually networked dimension of the download economy.

I first encountered *Ke Kulana* in 2002 while working at the Asian & Pacific Islander Coalition on HIV/AIDS in New York City. I was approached by Kathryn Xian, who codirected the film with Brent Anbe, to screen the film as part of the bimonthly Queer Asian & Pacific Islander Film Series that I curated. Immediately, I noticed that *Ke Kulana*'s interviews with lesbian, gay, bisexual, trans, and/or intersex māhū performers were filmed with the subjects' mirror reflections,[7] or the filmed interviews revealed mirrors in the background. Similar to Corey's performance in *Paris*, performer Lynda Brown is interviewed in *Ke Kulana* while facing the dressing room mirror and preparing a femme look for the night (see figure 2). Brown wisely remarks, "Sometimes it's so dark.... You can't really get to know people. You know, gay people have a tendency to just . . . if they're not always looking down on the ground . . . their head is too high."[8]

Ke Kulana's interviews with māhū performers Skeeter Mariah Crackseed and Araya Sunshine are also featured before mirrors. These scenes gesture at moments in *Paris* where Dorian Corey and Pepper LaBeija are each seated before or next to dressing room mirrors. These mirrors in *Ke Kulana* and *Paris* seem to endlessly reflect each other across the films, creating the effect of cascading, interminably nested, and multivalent representations for QTBIPOC relationality.

Arguing for a queer and decentered gaze, Muñoz (1999, 28) follows Frantz Fanon's critique of psychoanalytic traditions that treat film from the vantage point of white heterosexual men, specifically the Lacanian theory that insists that film "mirrors" oneself and facilitates identification. Instead, Muñoz asserts that "a minority spectator" engages in *disidentification*, "resist[ing] and confound[ing] socially prescriptive patterns of identification." Lynda Brown's comments register an identification with and against the Anglophone term *gay*. Meanwhile, Corey's discussion of ball culture's "small fame" asserts an identification with and against popular culture. Both interactions with the camera denote overlapping yet distinctive strategies for disidentifying with Euro-American representations in popular media. The cameras in both *Ke Kulana* and *Paris* are drawn to their interviewees' mirror images, or the interviewees' gazes into the mirror, not simply to facilitate the audience's identification. Rather, they fix the audience's fascination onto the specific yet myriad QTBIPOC performances of disidentifications.

These remarkable moments also mirror each other as they designate the potential loss of mutual recognition, connectivity, and kinship in a culture of neoliberal individualism where one's gaze is cast "too high" or "too low." The mirrors do not reflect or make equivalences between the two films' subjects and experiences. Neither do they suggest that interactive media designed the routes for collaboration and coalition.[9] Instead, they gesture at the multiple visual interfaces—the innumerable screens—that transmit audiovisual images, as well as their local and subjugated histories. As these images usurp the screens of contemporary media platforms, they reinforce *already existing* embodied knowledges and disidentifications. The femme queen's mirror gaze, then, is a queer gesture within the repertoire of ball culture that directs our attention not just to the image, but to the download—the corridor of visual interfaces that stoke the reservoir for otherworldliness, or what David DePino of the House of Xtravaganza refers to as "the looking glass" that infinitely reflects what the world "should be like."[10]

THE DOWNLOAD: MEMORY AND THE AFTERLIVES OF VIRAL MEDIA

> A change in memory, it seems, a change in machine.
>
> —Wendy Hui Kyong Chun, *Programmed Visions*

As recorded queer gestures, the gifs, memes, and video clips of Dorian Corey and Pepper LaBeija constitute the disidentificatory performances in *Paris* that "go viral," through projections of light passed along reflective and refractive surfaces, in our cyborg circulatory system. Queer gestures exist as "atomize[d] movements" that "transmit ephemeral knowledge of lost queer histories and possibilities within a phobic majoritarian public culture" (Muñoz 2009, 67). They move relatively undetected across screens, inserting and transmitting bits of stowed QTBIPOC memory to mutate and transform popular culture. Put simply, queer gestures function as viruses.

Chun (2011, 55) identifies a late nineteenth-century historical relationship between the fields of genetics and computing, which have both shaped the notion of "software" to mean the programmable aspects of life and machines in opposition to "hardware," or nature. Given the simultaneous late nineteenth-

Fig. 1. The camera gazes at ball culture performer Dorian Corey as she gazes into the mirror. (Still from the 1990 film *Paris Is Burning*.)

century advent of motion pictures, Chun's argument suggests that bodies and data converge as malleable objects on the grounds of cinematic memory. That is, queer gestures in cinema transmit subjugated histories as stored cultural and embodied source code, or what Chun (2011, 177) calls "'undead' writing." As "afterlives," the viral transfers of recorded queer gestures of ball culture infect biological and/or technological hosts. Their digital downloads transmit and enliven in popular culture the coded memories for QTBIPOC collective survival in the face of HIV/AIDS and neoliberal media.

Muñoz theorized disidentification while analyzing *Paris* in the late 1990s, around the same time that "viral" became a popular designation for widespread internet distribution.[11] Drawing on notions of encoding and decoding by Stuart Hall, Muñoz (1999, 31) states,

> Disidentification scrambles and reconstructs the encoded message of a cultural text in a fashion that both exposes the encoded message's universal-

Fig. 2. The camera gazes at the mirror image of māhū nightclub performer Aiko (Lynda Brown) as she prepares her look for the evening. (Still from the 2001 film *Ke Kulana He Māhū.*)

> izing and exclusionary machinations and recircuits its workings to account for, include, and empower minority identities and identifications. Thus, disidentification is a step further than cracking open the code of the majority; it proceeds to use this code as raw material for representing a disempowered politics or positionality that has been rendered unthinkable by the dominant culture.

As demonstrated in this passage, the language and imagery for software codes, HIV/AIDS, and disidentification are fused in *Paris* as an urtext, or source code. The retooling of the machine, the majority, the body, and power involves a common, even if distinct, usage of a simultaneously embodied and technological language—a queer code.[12]

Reading queer code, then, actively downloads the afterlives of queer gestures and induces their viral potential. As these downloads "go viral," the afterlives of queer gestures crisscross global media and capital to prompt mutations that turn the network into iterative disidentificatory practices that yield countless possibilities for QTBIPOC solidarities. The viral circulations of *Paris*'s queer gestures denote a popular longing for the kinds of connectivity and collective survival sustained by ball culture. Yet, reading queer code requires the embrace of "risk" otherwise stigmatized and criminalized by the juridical, biomedical, public health, and consumer models of HIV/AIDS. The former compels political and economic change through social and intimate vulnerability, while the latter set preaches individual empowerment through personal behavior change.

READING THE AFTERLIVES OF QUEER GESTURE: (INTER)FACE AND TOUCH

Downloading *Paris* from any number of online platforms prompts capricious encounters with the recorded queer gestures of Dorian Corey's facial expressions. In *Paris*, Corey reminds us that "reading" is the "art of insult" in which someone's social and embodied differences are made legible vis-à-vis the "face." Reading can be a mechanism for paying heed to the forms of difference that are violently targeted. State surveillance, too, relies on reading: faces and bodies are racialized, gendered, and tracked to be made legible through the circulatory system of our cyborg reality.

Yet, "reading" in ball culture vernacular is a strategy that preceded and anticipated the digital world.[13] It moves beyond merely pinpointing differences to, instead, take stock of and intervene in the asymmetry of surveillance and power.[14] Reading in ball culture vernacular articulates how vulnerability and risk are inherent to fleshly encounters in shared physical space as well as in the corporeal intimacies staged across media screens and settings. Specifically, the figuration and reading of faces, alongside a sense of touch, illuminate and even extend the *already existing* embodied connectivities across social identities that are immanent to media platforms. The virally circulated memes, gifs, and video clips suggest that the downloaded afterlives of ball culture's performative acts, such as Corey's queer facial gestures, reorganize language, space, time, and bodies off- and between screens (see figure 3). An economy of queer lexical, spatiotemporal, and collective embodiments exists through *Paris*, beyond the representations manifested on the visual interfaces of the machine.

The figure of the face and the material surface of the screen co-constitute the cyborg interface, wherein the afterlives of queer gestures are downloaded and executed through a series of linguistic commands. Popular memes of Corey explaining the difference between "reading" and "shade" rely not merely on the definitions Corey provides, but also on the distinctive looks she conveys to activate the viewer's reception: a raised brow, a knowing glance,

Fig. 3. A meme downloaded from the internet, where it circulates virally, an afterlife of queer gestures performed by Dorian Corey in the 1990 film *Paris Is Burning.*

a double nod, a smirk.[15] Yet, even as today's machines use algorithmic programming or facial recognition software to presumably determine and direct future consumer behaviors, they cannot verify "truth" about the past in ways that would accurately predict desires and future choices (Cheney-Lippold 2017). Media technologies cannot anticipate how stored memory might be virally activated by a multitude of viewers and their corporeal and affective exchanges in their encounter with the afterlives of downloaded queer gestures. In short, ball culture has virally and massively transformed languages, representations, bodies, technologies, and societies in ways that violate the consumer grid by which algorithms track, calculate, and extract identities and behavior as data.

For instance, in the parlance of drag, queer, and trans of color cultures that interact through and beyond the screen, "clocking" (versus "outing" a person as gay) is the moment in which, through a critical look or comment that musters potential violence, someone who is presumably normatively gendered renders the drag queen, queer, or trans person of color as out of place. Unlike outing, clocking does not involve a revelation of the "real"; what is highlighted is the problematic conditioning of time and place. Attention is drawn to the manner in which race, gender, and sexuality are synchronized with the face of the clock. Like many queer and trans homeless youth of color in urban settings like New York City, those who lack place (who lack a residence and do not belong) are also out of time (unemployed, barred access to health care). Yet, the face is also the focal point of expression for the loss of time and place. The modern clock has a face that directs time. One reads a clock to know what time it is. When we read a clock, we must stop to look at and question time, all the while producing a wrinkle in the logic of a single temporal duration. Being out of place and time—or being in "queer time," which emerged at least alongside the late twentieth-century advent of AIDS—invites other "willfully eccentric modes of being" (Halberstam 2005, 1–2).

"Giving face" is when a subject in ball culture features their face as the aesthetic center of their look. It is a consciousness regarding the ways in which forms of proper presentation and social mobility pivot on faciality. When one performs in drag, giving face also has the effect of effacing the logics of faciality. During a drag performance, lip-synching draws attention to the movement of the face, and in particular the lips, dislodging sound from oration. What is also produced in the process is an injunction between affect and temporality in the sense that the singer is not present, but the emotions of the imagined singing subject are constituted excessively and coterminously by the staging of the drag performer alongside the recorded music.

In *Ke Kulana*, the focus on the performers' facial expressions conjures a sense of both loss (of the precolonial world that gave way to modernity and identity) and resilience (of performances that code against settler-colonial narratives). Shortly after *Ke Kulana* begins, a montage sequence of Sami LA Akuna's nightclub performances depicts him dressed in drag that is neither clearly "feminine" nor clearly "masculine," yet presents as more feminine than we see him during sit-down interviews.[16] In the film, Akuna discloses that he is HIV-positive and goes by several other names, including Cocoa Chandelier and Pinka Lush.

For this scene, Akuna is shown lip-synching and moving to a somber version of Madonna's "Open Your Heart," with several other dancers following his lead (see figure 4). One might read this as a typical drag show at a club. Arguably, the sincerity and gravity of the performance turns drag on its head. Overlaying the scene are dressing room interviews with several māhū performers whom Akuna describes as his "adopted children" or "illegitimate child." They remark upon Akuna's character and, in turn, pay deference to him as "mother." The comments pause in time for the viewer to hear a line of the song: "one is such a lonely number." Now seated on the floor with the other dancers, Akuna closes his eyes. His lips cease to move during this line in the song. With an index finger raised and extended above his head, he leads the other dancers to bow in a silent reverie. Gazing at first directly into the cam-

Fig. 4. Sami LA Akuna in a cross-gender performance set to a rendition of Madonna's song "Open Your Heart." (Still from the 2001 film *Ke Kulana He Māhū*.)

era's frame, he brings his finger close to the camera as if to stroke the camera lens. He then lowers his head and angles his finger until it almost points at the screen, gesturing toward the viewer (see figure 5).

Like a person running their hands down a photograph as they turn the pages of an album, Akuna brushes the viewer's face with his finger, feeling the texture of the intersubjective and collectively embodied space between the viewing frame and the audience. The image of Akuna's finger starts by grazing the wrinkles on what we imagine as the surface of the viewer's face, indexing their age.[17] The finger moves further to puncture the screen and conjure the fleshly and affective encounters between the films' subjects and viewers across the modern grid of space-time.

This finger invokes a sensuous response from the viewer. According to Elizabeth Freeman (2010, 105–23), in literary and filmic tropes, fingers are a means of "indexing" time. The image hooks the audience's attention, and they, in turn, latch onto the image. Together, they crease space and time into

Fig. 5. Sami LA Akuna caresses the camera frame. He touches and multiply bends time. (Still from the 2001 film *Ke Kulana He Māhū.*)

wrinkles that seek sensuous apprehension in the folds of their skin. In "queer vision," Freeman submits, wrinkles represent how time folds when "our sexually impoverished present suddenly meets up with a richer past, or as the materials of a failed and forgotten project of the past find their uses now, in a future unimaginable in their time" (Freeman 2007a, 163). Across the screen, they grab each other's fingertips and graze each other's faces, feeling the texturization of many spacetimes fill between them. Here, looming large, are Gilles Deleuze's (1989, 12–13) notions of the "prehensile" cinematic images of hands, those that grip the viewer, and the "haptique,"—optics that grab the image—or what Laura U. Marks (2002, xvi–xvii, 1–20) calls "haptic visuality." Images and haptic vision stretch toward each other across time, tugging at, caressing, pressing up against, fingering each other.

Akuna's finger stretches to greet the fingers of the viewer in a haptic encounter. Time is bent multiply. These fingerings investigate what is around time's manifold bends. In the grammar of the film, Akuna and the viewer trace queer histories through these visually tactile, performative gestures, or what Freeman (2005, 57–68) calls *erotohistoriography*. Tacitly, Akuna turns to touch what time took. In the age of cyborg reality, time touches infinitely, and it does so temptingly. With his finger gesturing at "you," the viewer, he breaks the fourth wall, filling the space of the viewing experience with multiple times. Fingers that are used to count the capitalist, linear progression of time instead gather together mediated subjectivities across myriad milieu. The image of Akuna with his finger extended, indicating "one," then lowered to gesture at "you," implicates at least "two," or duplicity, and the interminable unfurling of time across the interstices of queer and trans Black, Indigenous, and people of color lifetimes. There is at once an implication of, and an invitation to, the viewer.

Akuna and his dancers' performances transmit and transform the afterlives of queer gesture, changing the past as well as the future. They challenge the viewer to reconsider how an individual subject occupies time and space. The viewer interfaces with the continual download and transmissions of queer gestures and glimpses what is around times' bends. These multiply shared and localized performances *intravene* into the neoliberal idealization of individualism and consumerism. Akuna's role as "mother" invokes a networked connectivity through māhū kinship, raveling around the viewing experience. This also recalls the pronouncement of Pepper LaBeija in *Paris* as "house mother" to all the "children" who are alienated from their blood kin. The recorded performances of precolonial māhū kinships in the presence of the viewer entwine with QTBIPOC kinships of *Paris*, other queer pasts, and innumerable queer utopian futures.

QUEER WORLDMAKING: BEYOND SOCIAL NETWORKS

The filmic embodiments and performances of māhū subjects move beyond the social networks imagined by epidemiologists, e-commerce, and state surveillance. Akuna and his dancers' performance beseeches the viewer to imagine a kinship that is not managed or mediated by government-driven institutions and consumer oriented ventures like marriage and gay tourism. As explained by *Ke Kulana*'s participants, māhū performances draw attention to the displacements of Kanaka ʻŌiwi by the US military, and the settler occupation that imposes marriage and other civil rights frameworks to the exclusion of the islands' original inhabitants.[18] Although it stops short of depicting the crucial and ongoing movement for Hawaiian sovereignty (Teves 2014, 10–11), the film highlights the damaging impact of the tourist economy that directs social and physical violence toward māhū peoples while proliferating HIV/AIDS in the archipelago. References to Akuna's close bond to his own mother and siblings, alongside his chosen kin, denote a reconfiguration of the idealized heterosexual family. No longer is family built strictly on romantic love and the sharing of a privatized and exclusive space. These relationships are instead fostered through a variety of intimacies, off- and on-screen, and in rehearsals and performances, that are meant for the stage as much as for life itself. Māhū kinships in the film are exercises in affective, embodied, and material redistribution set against settler colonialism, white supremacy, heteropatriarchy, and capitalist consumption.

Chandan Reddy's (1998, 367) analysis of *Paris* underscores how QTBIPOC—who share complicated histories and experiences with the homespace and the architecture of the house as a "structure of dominance"—appropriate notions of house and home to refashion a kinship network and sense of belonging. For QTBIPOC, whose relationship to this normativizing architecture of dominance is tenuous, the house must take on a different structure and meaning such that a house is not that which embodies, but instead is a place anchored in the embodiments of QTBIPOC kinships. In other words, as *Ke Kulana* explores and the film title suggests, being māhū is "a sense of place" maintained in the Hawaiian archipelago and Kanaka ʻŌiwi contexts despite dispossession, as well as within a global network of QTBIPOC kinships.

In *Ke Kulana*, queer gestures reference other virally networked kinships across geohistorical configurations. They also point to ellipses in popular texts. In the early 1990s, Madonna's song, music video, and performances of "Vogue" appropriated the house music and ball culture featured in *Paris* to instead use lyrics, movements, and imagery that celebrated mid-twentieth-century Hollywood beauty. Akuna disidentifies with Madonna by reappropriating her performances to infinitely code, instead of whiteness, the mutual constitution of Black, Latinx, and Pacific Islander subjects through and in the face of AIDS and Euro-American conquest. "Open Your Heart" is recast: no longer about a universal desire for love, it conveys the anxiety in the white imaginary at the sense of loss felt as a result of global capitalism's unmet promise to bind. It is love unrequited. Through a performance of QTBIPOC erotohistoriography between *Paris* and *Ke Kulana*, time is at once indexed, wrinkled, and ceaselessly bent. What is enabled, in Reddy's (1998, 367) words, are "other subjective logic mappings of 'home'" that boundlessly and seamlessly traverse a QTBIPOC imaginary—a queerworld kept on the download, a queerworld in the making.

Acknowledgments

Early drafts benefited from the comments of mentors and confidants. My thanks to dissertation committee members Dorinne K. Kondo, Macarena Gómez-Barris, Kara Keeling, J. Jack Halberstam, and Akira Mizuta Lippit, as well as writing group members Crystal Mun-hye Baik and Ho'esta Mo'e'hahne. Special thanks to Gladys Nubla, Nic John Ramos, Feng-Mei Heberer, Jennifer DeClue, the anonymous reader, copyeditor Jessica Hinds-Bond, press editors, and volume editors Kemi Adeyemi, Ramón H. Rivera-Servera, and especially Kareem Khubchandani for such spirited and inspiring engagement. All missteps and errors are my own.

Notes

1. I use QTBIPOC as an open and fluctuating signifier, and political referent, for racialized subjects whose gender and/or sexuality do not conform to Western categories and identities, including the oft-used umbrella term LGBT.

2. My monograph in progress is tentatively titled "Queer Code: HIV/AIDS and the History of Virology."

3. I thank Claudia Sofía Garriga-López for reminding me of Bailey's concept "intravention."

4. Reports differ regarding whether the Elk Cloner emerged in 1981 or 1982.

5. I first encountered the use of the term "Blacktinx" by Victor Bene (Ultra Omni).

6. Chun (2011, 7) maintains, "Historically, computers, human and mechanical, have been central to the management and creation of populations, political economy, and apparatuses of security."

7. According to the film, māhū is historically defined as someone who is Kanaka 'Ōiwi (Native Hawaiian) and intersex. Today, it also refers to locals, especially Kanaka 'Ōiwi and other Pacific Islanders, who are "practicing homosexuality" and/or who are "transgender." Yet, the film stresses that māhū is a precolonial designation that refers to a system of kinship that exceeds contemporary categories for gender and sexuality.

8. This scene is missing a title that clearly identifies the performer as Lynda Brown. However, cross-referencing the closing credits for *Ke Kulana* with a more recent documentary film that is still in production as of 2020, Connie M. Florez's *The Glades Project*, reveals a potential match with "Linda Brown" (or Lynda Brown). See Florez (2013) and Hula Girl Productions (n.d.).

9. Feng-Mei Heberer (2017, 208) describes the video recording and internet broadcasting of queer performance as "affinities and affiliations that are not yet thought through by nationalist logics and global capital."

10. As Kareem Khubchandani (pers. comm., 2017) reminded me, in *Paris*, performer Willy Ninja stages an elegant and elaborate dance while miming the use of a handheld compact mirror. Meanwhile, Willy Ninja explains through voice-over narration how "reading" and "shade" are performed through vogue.

11. For instance, Muñoz's (1999) writing about performance artist Vaginal Davis examined the convergence of Davis's zine-making and their VHS recordings that Davis produced and distributed to friends. My gratitude to Kareem Khubchandani for pointing this out.

12. Kara Keeling (2014) might describe queer code as part of a "queer operating system," or queer OS.

13. Fatimah Tobing Rony (1996) might describe reading as the deployment of the "third eye," while Kara Keeling (2003) might theorize this concept using Fanon's "interval."

14. According to Anjali Nath (2013, 185), "What truly makes warfare 'asymmetric'—aside from the sheer amount of soldiers, weaponry, and tactics of engagement—is the ways in which different sides see each other, what technologies each has available to view the other, and the ways each side can make themselves unseen."

15. Faciality, according to Gilles Deleuze and Félix Guattari (1987, 167–82), is "the form of the signifier in language, even its units, [that] would [otherwise] remain indeterminate if the potential listener did not use the face of the speaker to guide his or her choice ('Hey, he seems angry . . .'; 'He couldn't say it . . .'; 'You see my face when I'm talking to you . . .'; 'look at me carefully . . .')."

16. I follow the pronouns *him* and *he* used by the other film informants to refer to Akuna.

17. In Laura U. Marks's (2002, 1–20) discussion of "haptic vision," the viewer's face is often the imagined site in which tactility is produced.

18. Stephanie Nohelani Teves (2014, 12) argues, "The māhū communities shown in *Ke Kulana He Māhū* also possess a radical potentiality because they strategically evade the ways in which neoliberalism seeks to solidify new subjects and communities for the proliferation of capitalism. This film honors the history of Hawai'i by centering the actual experiences of Kānaka Maoli and, for those of us who see ourselves reflected in the film—whether we are māhū or not—it allows us to connect to its expressions of visual sovereignty." For a discussion of anticolonial feminist Indigenous remapping by the film's participants, see Hall (2009, 30–31). For a discussion of anticolonial cinematic traditions that appear in *Ke Kulana*, see Leung (2004, 160–63). In the chapter version of this essay for the book length project, I examine my involvement in HIV/AIDS social services and the tendency of the umbrella categorization of "Asian and Pacific Islander" to skew attention toward East Asian and, to a lesser extent, South Asian cis-gender men. This narrow focus variously reproduces colonial gender norms and settler occupation. It leaves unaddressed the lived realities and politics of Pacific Islanders, as well as West, Central, and Southeast Asians, especially Indigenous subjects across the regions subsumed under "Asia Pacific."

After the Eighties . . . A Queer Afterlife

An Interview with Eduardo Alegría

José Álvarez-Colón and Ramón H. Rivera-Servera

Eduardo Alegría is a Puerto Rican indie musician and performance artist active in San Juan arts and music since the 1990s. An iconic figure in Puerto Rico's queer scene, he is the mastermind and lead performer for Súperaquello and Alegría Rampante, both concept bands with highly developed performance concerts, often incorporating experimental dance and performance aesthetics and indie music platforms.

JOSÉ: What is queer nightlife? How did it begin for you?

EDUARDO: Escaping home with a bunch of a performative, flamboyant peacocks, starting to get our faces painted, and well, actually buying the clothes during the afternoon at the Salvation Army. I was young. I could still buy things at the Salvation Army. Basically, just spending the whole day and night preparing to go out. That's sort of the beginnings of queer nightlife for me for many years. I think I started to go out in 1985. I started to sneak out.

RAMÓN: Where were you living then?

EDUARDO: Home with my parents.

RAMÓN: Where was that?

EDUARDO: Guaynabo, Puerto Rico.

RAMÓN: And then where did you start going out to?

EDUARDO: It was basically the eighties in Puerto Rico. There wasn't anything, it was a very, very different time here in terms of the queer offerings and culture. Neons, that was it. Neons and then maybe some little bars like the Factory, which was where there was no entrance fee. So we could sort of get the club fantasy without having to pay because we were very young. None of us worked.

Fig. 1. Alegría Rampante in concert. Eduardo Alegría interpreting "Pedazo de Luna" by Sylvia Rexach in the 2019 concert series March Is Music at the Pregones Theater, Bronx, New York. (Photograph by Marisol Díaz-Gordon.)

RAMÓN: And both of these are in Old San Juan?

EDUARDO: Yeah. Old San Juan both of them. Yeah. Those were the old San Juan days. It was when San Juan was the hub of nightlife. Also Condado but I mainly hung out in San Juan. Well, in Condado there was the disco Souvenirs, where I met Jean Paul Gaultier and I had a lengthy conversation with [him] in 1987. He liked my outfit.

RAMÓN: Tell us more about Neons.

EDUARDO: We weren't any kind of a majority. We were a minority of people. Sometimes our looks were too hardcore and they wouldn't let us in. If we were looking too outlandish, we wouldn't be let in, because they would freak out. Basically, Neons was a very douchey place. It was just the closest thing that there was to listen to good music. In the eighties there wasn't access to a lot.

So basically in the eighties, if you wanted to sort of be where the good stuff is, you needed to hang out with douchey people who had money. It was the only option. So basically in the eighties, I used to hang out with a lot of rich kids from Condado, but those were the kids that had access to the good music. So the underground stuff that was happening in the United States and in Europe, that was how we were getting it here.

Neons wasn't great, but it was the only place where there were some VJs because this is the VJ area, meaning the video DJ who knew about the good stuff, and very late at night he would sort of wink, wink, nod, nod at us freaks, and he would bypass the Debbie Gibson and he would play us some Siouxsie and the Banshees.

RAMÓN: Would you say Neons was experienced as queer space? Was it queer?
EDUARDO: No, no it wasn't, but it was the closest thing.

RAMÓN: Was it mainstream?
EDUARDO: I mean, it was the place where we were allowed to be performative, like the way we were in terms of . . . because I always think that in the eighties, my dressing up and makeup thing, which I don't do now. I do it now onstage, if anything, but that was like my first performance. I used to get dressed to go to the disco and freak everybody out and annoy everybody.

Neons had that eighties vibe where there was a lot of gay people, a lot, but it wasn't like an openly gay space. It was supposed to be very neutral. But because it was very in vogue, well you had to let in all the hair stylists and the fashion designers of the time and the models.

JOSÉ: About how long did that scene sustain for you?
EDUARDO: Well, I met the experimental choreographer Viveca Vázquez in '87 or '88 and started moving my body with her. My body started changing. I became interested in other things, and I just left. My focus went into body-based performance, and I just sort of lost interest in that world. I just basically stopped going out to clubs. Then it became more about private parties, private parties at Viveca's house, parties at whoever's house, all kinds of fun. Where I guess queer people could get together. Queer in the very, sort of a contemporary sense.

RAMÓN: So was it an easy kind of natural transition out of the Neon scene into the Taller de Otra Cosa scene?
EDUARDO: I think it was easy. It was easy. When you're young, we're still full of energy, and we're just like exploding. We are like a volcano of energy and creativity. So when I discovered that I could be a part of this world of per-

forming, and creating, not just being an interpreter in somebody's work, but I immediately gravitated to creating and writing ideas, and making drawings, and coming up with things. It was a very natural process to me. It was like, "Okay, this is it, this is it. This is what I've been waiting for all my life."

So I was already very put off by the frivolity of the eighties and the douche bagginess of the eighties, which Neons very much encapsulates: that sort of yucky class thing. Actually, I feel like what we're living right now historically feels like the eighties. It's like back to "we're wealthy, we have money, and you don't, hahaha. We laugh in your face." Kind of like an eighties high school film.

RAMÓN: Is there anything about that eighties experience that you've found instructive, pleasurable, that you carried forth through to the next stage, and what was it?

EDUARDO: Yeah. Because I am hopelessly marked by the excitement of the eighties because there was no script. And so that meant that it wasn't only underground. In the eighties, when I was a kid, I would turn on the radio and something would start playing that you would be like, "What the fuck is this? Where is this coming from?" It was like a constant surprise of aesthetic sounds. I mean, I don't want to go like old pop culture on this, but even if you think about iconic eighties, let's say bands, which is like very sort of commercial radio, each band was very unique. You have the Police, you have the Cure, you had U2. Everybody had something that was very unique and very particular. The Smiths, et cetera, because there was no script. Nobody was following any kind of a formula. So it was just surprise after surprise, after surprise, after surprise. It was incredibly exciting. And I think that marked me, and I'm kind of still addicted to the idea that I could somehow provide something like that throughout my work.

RAMÓN: So in terms of the aesthetics, Eduardo, I'm wondering if you could describe maybe how those two worlds—the experimental dance scene and the queer nightlife—how they coexist in your work.

EDUARDO: Well, that's the question that I was fearing from this interview because I don't know or maybe I just have never thought about it.

JOSÉ: Maybe getting to the tension between each other?

EDUARDO: Tension? The thing is that the eighties were about going to the disco to perform myself and my queerness, and then when I enter the world of performance and the postmodern dance theory realm, everything got transferred there. All my creativity and my desire to, oh God, my desire to create and have an impression on the world is something that I started to do then through performance art because I've always been hopelessly like, I don't like to use this word, but I like to cause an impression . . . in this big way. I hate saying this, I hate admitting it on record, but I've always enjoyed art that is sort of aware that is being consumed and. . . . You know me, you know this because it's what I like. In a way, I'm doing what I want people to do because I want to consume it myself.

I haven't mentioned the pop thing that is sort of mixed up in the more sort of political and social view of the world that I have through performance and dance. There's also that need to entertain.

RAMÓN: Did the experimental scene become a kind of nightlife? Did that have qualities of nightlife for you?

EDUARDO: It was all about parties. Parties at somebody's house in the country, or on the beach, late-night parties. It was like being a part of this environment of having access to other artists and other like-minded people through these parties.

I was already working with my body. I was sort of getting into my body, so I was starting to look cute. I was getting ready for love and romance. It took me a long time, but there was a lot of that, like going out to finally get some action. Because I grew up very insecure, chubby kid, and then when I entered college and I started moving, I had like a complete life transformation of body and mind. So sexuality and an interest in sex becomes like a moving force too that has you going to these parties and stuff like that. So it was a mixture of wanting to be with other artists, but there was also like a sexual energy.

RAMÓN: What I think I'm trying to get at is the way in which that same impetus and investment in self presentation and desire carries across both scenes—the club and the avant-garde art party. You can go to a disco, but you can also go to the avant-garde party that has become a scene. What things about that scene continue to fuel the very same hunger that you had in going to nightlife?

EDUARDO: I've never thought about this the way you're describing it. I think the similar thing for me, and this is why I became very disenchanted by the eighties. That eighties "I'm cool" attitude and I was all about "I'm going to change the world through fashion." You know what I mean? That was the eighties, but it was like this horrible . . . the environment was really ugly and yucky, so whatever. At some point, I realized that it was just a very frivolous environment that wasn't any good for me.

JOSÉ: And what was the experimental scene proposing?

EDUARDO: The whole postmodern. I mean, just the whole like postmodern dance theory, which became like a spinal cord for me. That was the whole thing. Like, well, who is the correct body or the wrong body for something? Why can't I be represented as the body that I am? All my sort of political wanting to shape things and change things, got transferred into my body without having to get dressed.

It became about the fact that I was a body that wasn't meant to dance, and all of a sudden like having access to this theory and understanding how it really sort of spoke to me, which maybe I should think about more. But yeah, it was a very freeing experience, and I immediately transferred this thing up. This is something that needs to be shared, that needs to be pulled out there. I'm part of a revolution. This is something great.

The work and also the scene in Puerto Rico was very much led by women. So it was very easy for me to do the transition from the clubs and the performance of androgyny and all this sort of antipatriarchal thing that I was doing without knowing what I was doing in the eighties. It was very easy for me to transition into this sort of world that was led by women. It was refreshing, liberating, and I had just been waiting for it.

So it was like, those early years it felt like they had that feeling of like everything was just moving, almost like a plan. Like things were just sort of unraveling in front of me.

JOSÉ: How did the transitions from nightlife to experimental dance and performance and finally to music work for you in terms of your aesthetic?

EDUARDO: Well, I feel tempted to just say a phrase that I've used often, which is that I . . . so I always say that Súperaquello was my dream of the eighties. That I actually just made it happen at the end of nineties. If you look at my notebooks from when I was a kid, which I still have here in my office, I have drawings of myself in high school as a singer and as a performer. So it was like this, the whole music thing was always there. I always wanted to be a part of that. So, yeah, the pop dream of the eighties.

But I also went through, I mean a huge transformation in my life. This was in the midnineties, so Súperaquello, the band, is now the psyche as the new realm where Taller de Otra Cosa, the dance and performance collective, was the body. Then Súperaquello became the mind and the inner world, which the whole postmodern dance thing moves you toward because it has that whole like mind-body connection, and social, and political vision. But then when this happened, the whole thing about the world of the psyche became like a new playground, and it's no surprise.

I went to New York City for some years, and then I decided to move back to Puerto Rico in '97 to make Súperaquello happen. I had a dream of sort of retaking where I was there in a way because I wasn't seeing a disconnect because the body, and the thinking of the body, and the embodiment that you go through when you're improvising, when you're dancing was very, to me, analogous to my interests in music, which were very atmospheric. I'm interested in atmosphere, especially at that time I was very much interested in atmosphere and the contemplation of sonic atmosphere.

RAMÓN: What remains of that earlier experience with queer nightlife in these now earlier concerts and events? Like what remains for you in your aesthetic platform that you think you first discovered or learned in queer nightlife?

EDUARDO: I think it's the excitement of finding a place to be together as queer people, as multicolored, multifaceted kinds of people. Providing that space, I think it sounds a little romantic, but I think that's it. I'm kind of a loner. I'm a little bit of a loner. I didn't know this until I realized many years ago, but it was kind of a surprise for me. Like, "Oh, I'm not like Mr. Out There with everybody all the time." So, the performance space is kind of like a church thing. I love the idea of church, even though I'm atheist or whatever. Yeah, there's like the joy of creating a space to sort of revel in surprise and in otherness, perhaps. Something like that.

Bibliography

Aaron, Michele, ed. 2004. *New Queer Cinema: A Critical Reader*. New Brunswick, NJ: Rutgers University Press.

Abd'Allah-Álvarez Ramírez, Sandra. 2016. "Some Questions about a Post-Blockade Cuba." *Black Diaspora Review* 5 (2): 7–11.

Adeyemi, Kemi. 2019. "The Practice of Slowness: Black Queer Women and the Right to the City." *GLQ: A Journal of Lesbian and Gay Studies* 25 (4): 545–67.

Aguhar, Mark. 2011. *My First Denim Vest*. Posted November 9, 2011. Vimeo video, 13:25. https://vimeo.com/31834670

Aguirre, Valentin, and Augie Robles, dirs. 1994. *¡Viva 16!* Film.

Agustín, Laura María. 2007. *Sex at the Margins: Migration, Labour Markets and the Rescue Industry*. London: Zed Books.

Ahmed, Sara. 2004. *The Cultural Politics of Emotion*. New York: Routledge.

Ahmed, Sara. 2006. *Queer Phenomenology: Orientations, Objects, Others*. Durham, NC: Duke University Press.

Alexander, M. Jacqui. 1997. "Erotic Autonomy as a Politics of Decolonization: An Anatomy of Feminist and State Practice." In *Feminist Genealogies, Colonial Legacies, Democratic Futures*, edited by M. Jacqui Alexander and Chandra Mohanty, 63–100. New York: Routledge.

Allen, Jafari S. 2009. "For 'the Children' Dancing the Beloved Community." *Souls* 11 (3): 311–26.

Allen, Jafari S. 2011. *¡Venceremos? The Erotics of Black Self-Making in Cuba*. Durham, NC: Duke University Press.

American Realness Festival. 2013. *Antigone Sr. / Twenty Looks or Paris Is Burning*. Festival Program. Abrons Arts Center, New York, January 11, 2013.

Anderson, Ben. 2009. "Affective Atmospheres." *Emotion, Space and Society*. 2 (2): 77–81.

Aruquipa Pérez, David. 2012. *La China Morena: Memoria histórica travesti*. La Paz, Bolivia: Comunidad Diversidad.

Aruquipa Pérez, David. 2016. "Placer, deseo y política: La revolución estética de La Familia Galán." *Bulletin de l'institut français d'études andines* 45 (3): 451–61.

Aruquipa Pérez, David. 2017. (Danna Galán, La Familia Galán member), in discussion with the author. June. La Paz, Bolivia, June.

Aruquipa Pérez, David, Paula Estenssoro, and Pablo C. Vargas. 2012. *Memorias Colectivas: Miradas a la historia del Movimiento TLGB de Bolivia*. La Paz, Bolivia: Conexión Fondo de Emancipación.

Bacchetta, Paola. 1999. "When the (Hindu) Nation Exiles Its Queers." *Social Text* 61: 141–66.

Bailey, Marlon. 2013. *Butch Queens Up in Pumps: Gender, Performance, and Ballroom Culture in Detroit.* Ann Arbor: University of Michigan Press.

Banet-Weiser, Sarah. 2012. *Authentic™: The Politics of Ambivalence in a Brand Culture.* New York: New York University Press.

Barbará, Anna Marina. 2007. *As meninas da Daspu.* Teresópolis, Brazil: Novas Ideias.

Barker, Joanne. 2018. "Territory as Analytic: The Dispossession of Lenapehoking and the Subprime Crisis." *Social Text* 36 (2): 19–39.

Beliso-De Jesús, Aisha. 2015. *Electric Santería: Racial and Sexual Assemblages of Transnational Religion.* New York: Columbia University Press.

Benedicto, Bobby. 2014. *Under Bright Lights: Gay Manila and the Global Scene.* Minneapolis: University of Minnesota Press.

Berlant, Lauren. 1997. *The Queen of America Goes to Washington City: Essays on Sex and Citizenship.* Durham, NC: Duke University Press.

Berlant, Lauren. 2011. *Cruel Optimism.* Durham, NC: Duke University Press.

Berlant, Lauren, and Michael Warner. 1998. "Sex in Public." *Critical Inquiry* 24 (2): 547–66.

Berry, Maya. 2016. "'Salvándose' in Contemporary Havana: Rumba's Paradox for Black Identity Politics." *Black Diaspora Review* 5 (2): 24–54.

Bersani, Leo. 2010. "Is the Rectum a Grave?" In *Is the Rectum a Grave? And Other Essays,* 3–30. Chicago: University of Chicago Press.

Bérubé, Allan. 2003. "The History of Gay Bathhouses." *Journal of Homosexuality* 44 (3–4): 33–53. https://doi.org/10.1300/J082v44n03_03

Biles, Roger. 2001. "Race and Housing in Chicago" *Journal of the Illinois State Historical Society* 94 (1): 31–38.

Bodenheimer, Rebecca. 2015. *Geographies of Cubanidad: Music, Place, and Racialized Identity in Contemporary Cuba.* Jackson: University Press of Mississippi.

Bollen, Jonathan. 2001. "Queer Kinesthesia: Performativity on the Dance Floor." In *Dancing Desires: Choreographing Sexualities On and Off the Stage,* edited by Jane Desmond, 285–314. Madison: University of Wisconsin Press.

Bondi, Liz. 2004. "10th Anniversary Address for a Feminist Geography of Ambivalence." *Gender, Place & Culture* 11 (1): 3–15.

Boone, Joseph A. 1995. "Vacation Cruises; or, the Homoerotics of Orientalism." *PMLA* 110 (1): 89–107.

Bowe, Rebecca. 2015. "S.F. Study Documents Sharp Decline in Mission's Latino Population." *KQED,* October 28, 2015. https://www.kqed.org/news/10736143/s-f-study-documents-sharp-decline-in-missions-latino-population

Bridgforth, Sharon. 2004. *love conjure/blues.* Washington, DC: Redbone Press.

Brim, Matt, and Amin Ghaziani. 2016. "Introduction: Queer Methods." *WSQ: Women's Studies Quarterly* 44 (3): 14–27.

Broadus, Kylar. 2006. "The Evolution of Employment Discrimination Protections for

Transgender People." In *Transgender Rights*, edited by Paisley Currah, Richard M. Juang, and Shannon Price Minter, 93–101. Minneapolis: University of Minnesota.

Brooks, Daphne A. 2011. "Nina Simone's Triple Play." *Callaloo* 34 (1): 176–97.

Brown, Jayna. 2008. *Babylon Girls: Black Women Performers and the Shaping of the Modern*. Durham, NC: Duke University Press, 2008.

Browne, Kath. 2009. "Imagining Cities, Living the Other: Between the Gay Urban Idyll and Rural Lesbian Lives." *Open Geography Journal* 1 (1): 25–32.

Browne, Kath, and Catherine J. Nash. 2010. *Queer Methods and Methodologies: Intersecting Queer Theories and Social Science Research*. New York: Ashgate.

Brown-Saracino, Japonica. 2011. "From the Lesbian Ghetto to Ambient Community: The Perceived Costs and Benefits of Integration for Community." *Social Problems* 58 (3): 361–88.

Brown-Saracino, Japonica. 2018. *How Places Make Us: Novel LBQ Identities in Four Small Cities*. Chicago: University of Chicago Press.

Buckland, Fiona. 2002. *Impossible Dance: Club Culture and Queer World-Making*. Middletown, CT: Wesleyan University Press.

Butler, Judith. 1990a. *Gender Trouble: Feminism and the Subversion of Identity*. London: Routledge.

Butler, Judith. 1990b. "Performative Acts and Gender Constitution: An Essay in Phenomenology and Feminist Theory." In *Performing Feminisms: Feminist Critical Theory and Theatre*, edited by Sue-Ellen Case, 270–82. Baltimore, MD: Johns Hopkins University Press.

Butler, Judith. 1993. *Bodies That Matter: On the Discursive Limits of "Sex."* New York: Routledge.

Butler, Judith. 2002. *Antigone's Claim*. New York: Columbia University Press.

Byrd, Jodi A., Alyosha Goldstein, Jodi Melamed, and Chandan Reddy. 2018. "Predatory Value: Economies of Dispossession and Disturbed Relationalities." *Social Text* 36 (2): 1–18.

Camp, Stephanie. 2004. *Closer to Freedom: Enslaved Women and Everyday Resistance in the Plantation South*. Chapel Hill: University of North Carolina Press.

Campt, Tina. 2017. *Listening to Images*. Durham, NC: Duke University Press.

Campuzano, Giuseppe. 2008. *Museo Travesti del Perú*. Lima: Institute of Development Studies.

Carrillo, Héctor. 2004. "Sexual Migration, Cross-Cultural Sexual Encounters, and Sexual Health." *Sexuality Research & Social Policy* 1 (3): 58–70.

Carrington, Christopher. 1999. *No Place Like Home Relationships and Family Life among Lesbians and Gay Men*. Chicago: University of Chicago Press.

Carter, Julian. 2018. "Sex Time Machine for Touching the Transcestors." *Transgender Studies Quarterly*. 5 (4): 691–706.

Case, Sue-Ellen. 1988. "Towards a Butch-Femme Aesthetic." *Discourse* 11 (1): 55–73.

Centers for Disease Control and Prevention (CDC). 1982a. "Epidemiologic Notes and Reports Pneumocystis carinii Pneumonia among Persons with Hemophilia A." *Morbidity and Mortality Weekly Report* 31 (27): 365–67.

Centers for Disease Control and Prevention (CDC). 1982b. "Opportunistic Infections and Kaposi's Sarcoma among Haitians in the United States." *Morbidity and Mortality Weekly Report* 31 (26): 353–54, 360–61.

Chambers-Letson, Joshua Takano. 2018. *After the Party: A Manifesto for Queer of Color Life.* New York: New York University Press.

Chauncey, George. 2008. *Gay New York: Gender, Urban Culture, and the Making of the Gay Male World, 1890–1940.* New York: Basic Books.

Cheney-Lippold, John. 2017. *We Are Data: Algorithms and the Making of Our Digital Selves.* New York: New York University Press.

Cheng, Jih-Fei, Alexandra Juhasz, and Nishant Shahani, eds. 2020. *AIDS and the Distribution of Crises.* Durham, NC: Duke University Press.

Chibbaro, Lou, Jr. 2013. "Glory Days." *Washington Blade,* April 25, 2013.

Cho, Alexander. 2018. "Default Publicness: Queer Youth of Color, Social Media, and Being Outed by the Machine." *New Media & Society* 20 (9): 3183–200.

Chun, Wendy Hui Kyong. 2006. *Control and Freedom: Power and Paranoia in the Age of Fiber Optics.* Cambridge: MIT Press.

Chun, Wendy Hui Kyong. 2011. *Programmed Visions: Software and Memory.* Cambridge: MIT Press.

Clarin.com. 2015. "Escándalo por una performance porno en una facultad de la UBA." *Clarin.com,* January 7, 2015. https://www.clarin.com/sociedad/Escandalo-performance-porno-facultad-UBA_0_Bytb0UFvQe.html

Cohen, Cathy J. 1997. "Punks, Bulldaggers, and Welfare Queens: The Radical Potential of Queer Politics?" *GLQ: A Journal of Lesbian and Gay Studies* 3 (4): 437–65.

Cohen, Cathy J. 2004. "Deviance as Resistance: A New Research Agenda for the Study of Black Politics." *Du Bois Review* 1 (1): 27–45.

Cohen, Lawrence. 1995. "Holi in Banaras and the Mahaland of Modernity." *GLQ: A Journal of Lesbian and Gay Studies* 2 (4): 399–417.

Cohen, Lawrence. 2005. "The Kothi Wars: AIDS Cosmopolitanism and the Morality of Classification." In *Sex in Development: Science, Sexuality, and Morality in Global Perspective,* edited by Vincanne Adams and Stacy Leigh Pigg, 269–303. Durham, NC: Duke University Press.

Cohen, Lawrence. 2007. "Song for Pushkin." *Daedalus* 136 (2): 103–15.

Crawford, Lucas. 2014. "A Transgender Poetics of the High Line Park." *TSQ: Transgender Studies Quarterly* 1 (4): 482–500.

Cvetkovich, Ann. 2001. "White Boots and Combat Boots: My Life as a Lesbian Go-Go Dancer." In *Dancing Desires: Choreographing Sexualities On and Off the Stage,* edited by Jane Desmond, 315–48. Madison: University of Wisconsin Press.

D'Agostino, Rosanne. 2009. "Dona da Daslu é condenada pela Justiça Federal a 94 anos e meio de prisão." *Folha Online,* March 26, 2009. https://noticias.uol.com.br/cotidiano/2009/03/26/ult5772u3388.jhtm

Daniel, Yvonne Payne. 1991. "Changing Values in Cuban Rumba, a Lower Class Black Dance Appropriated by the Cuban Revolution." *Dance Research Journal* 23 (2): 1–10.

Daniel, Yvonne Payne. 1995. *Rumba: Dance and Social Change in Contemporary Cuba.* Bloomington: Indiana University Press.

Dasgupta, Rohit K. 2014. "Parties, Advocacy, and Activism: Interrogating Community and Class in Digital Queer India." In *Queer Youth and Media Cultures*, edited by Christopher Pullen, 265–77. London: Palgrave Macmillan.

David, Emmanuel. 2018. "Transgender Archipelagos." *TSQ: Transgender Studies Quarterly* 5 (3): 332–54.

Dean, Tim. 2009. *Unlimited Intimacy: Reflections on the Subculture of Barebacking.* Chicago: University of Chicago Press.

Decena, Carlos Ulises. 2011. *Tacit Subjects: Belonging and Same-Sex Desire among Dominican Immigrant Men.* Durham, NC: Duke University Press.

Delany, Samuel R. 1999. *Times Square Red, Times Square Blue.* New York: New York University Press.

Deleuze, Gilles. 1989. *Cinema-2: The Time-Image.* Minneapolis: University of Minnesota Press.

Deleuze, Gilles, and Félix Guattari. 1987. *A Thousand Plateaus: Schizophrenia and Capitalism.* Minneapolis: University of Minnesota Press.

Delgado, Celeste Fraser, and José Esteban Muñoz. 1997. "Rebellions of Everynight Life." In *Everynight Life: Culture and Dance in Latin/o America*, edited by Celeste Fraser Delgado and José Esteban Muñoz, 9–32. Durham, NC: Duke University Press.

Deshmukh, Ganesh. 2013. "Amravati Becoming a National-Level Den for Homosexual Activities." *Lokmat*, August 13, 2013.

Domínguez Ruvalcaba, Héctor. 2016. *Translating the Queer: Body Politics and Transnational Conversations.* London: ZED Books.

Drysdale, Kerryn. 2015. "When Scenes Fade." *Cultural Studies* 29 (3): 345–62.

DuComb, Christian. 2017. *Haunted City: Three Centuries of Racial Impersonation in Philadelphia.* Ann Arbor: University of Michigan Press.

Dudrah, Rajinder Kumar. 2006. *Bollywood: Sociology Goes to the Movies.* New Delhi: Sage.

Duggan, Lisa. 2002. "The New Homonormativity: The Sexual Politics of Neoliberalism." In *Materializing Democracy: Toward a Revitalized Cultural Politics*, edited by Russ Castronovo and Dana D. Nelson, 175–94. Durham, NC: Duke University Press.

Duggan, Lisa. 2003. *The Twilight of Equality? Neoliberalism, Cultural Politics, and the Attack on Democracy.* Boston: Beacon Press.

Dyer, Richard. 1979. "In Defence of Disco." *Gay Left* 8: 20–23.

Echols, Alice. 2010. *Hot Stuff: Disco and the Remaking of American Culture.* New York: W. W. Norton.

Edelman, Lee. 1994. *Homographesis: Essays in Gay Literary and Cultural Theory.* New York: Routledge.

Edelman, Lee. 1998. "The Future Is Kid Stuff: Queer Theory, Disidentification, and the Death Drive." *Narrative* 6 (1): 18–30.

Elias, Ana Sofia, Rosalind Gill, and Christina Scharff. 2017. *Aesthetic Labour: Rethinking Beauty Politics in Neoliberalism.* London: Palgrave Macmillan.

Eltit, Diamela. 2007. "La Familia Galán." In *Cruce de lenguas: Sexualidades, diversidad y ciudadanía*, edited by Kathya Araujo, 121–25. Santiago: LOM Ediciones.

Ernsberger, Paul. 2009. "Does Social Class Explain the Connection between Weight and Health?" In *The Fat Studies Reader*, edited by Esther Rothsblum and Sondra Solovay, 25–36. New York: New York University Press.

Falconí Trávez, Diego, Santiago Castellanos, and María Amelia Viteri. 2014. *Resentir lo queer en América Latina: Diálogo desde/con el sur*. Barcelona: EGALES.

Fatzick, Josh. 2015. "DC Uses Eminent Domain to Seize Land for New Soccer Stadium." *Daily Caller*, October 1, 2015. https://dailycaller.com/2015/10/01/dc-uses-eminent-domain-to-seize-land-for-new-soccer-stadium/

Faye, Shon. 2016. "Looking at *Paris Is Burning* 25 Years after Its Release." *Dazed*, August 23, 2016. http://www.dazeddigital.com/artsandculture/article/32530/1/looking-at-paris-is-burning-25-years-after-its-release

Feliciano, Omar. 2015. "Memoria y traición en el Museo del Chopo." *Animal Politico*, August 11, 2015. http://www.animalpolitico.com/blogueros-blog-invitado/2015/08/11/memoria-y-traicion-en-el-museo-del-chopo/

Ferguson, Roderick A. 2004. *Aberrations in Black: Toward a Queer of Color Critique*. Minneapolis: University of Minnesota Press.

Fernandes, Deepa. 2017. "Cuba's Transformistas Bring Their Drag Performances Out in the World." *PRI's The World*, March 20, 2017. https://www.pri.org/stories/2017-03-20/cubas-transformistas-bring-their-drag-performances-out-open

Filiol, Eric. 2005. *Computer Viruses: From Theory to Applications*. Paris: Springer.

Flores, Juan, and George Yúdice. 1992. "Living Borders/Buscando América: Languages of Latino Self-Formation." In *Divided Borders: Essays on Puerto Rican Identity*, by Juan Flores, 199–224. Houston, TX: Arte Publico Press.

Florez, Connie M. 2013. "The Glades Project (Re-Enactment Filming behind the Scenes)." Posted November 21, 2013. Vimeo video, 3:05. https://vimeo.com/79960605

Forstie, Clare. 2020. "Theory Making from the Middle: Researching LGBTQ Communities in Small Cities." *City & Community* 19 (1): 153–68.

Foster, Susan. 2003. "Choreographies of Protest." *Theatre Journal* 55 (3): 395–412.

Foucault, Michel. 2000. "For an Ethic of Discomfort." In *The Essential Works of Michel Foucault*, vol. 3, *Power*, edited by James D. Faubion, translated by Robert Hurley, 443–48. New York: New Press.

Foucault, Michel. 2005. *Society Must Be Defended: Lectures at the Collège de France*. Translated by David Macey. New York: Picador Press.

Freeman, Elizabeth. 2005. "Time Binds, or, Erotohistoriography." *Social Text* 23 (3–4): 57–68.

Freeman, Elizabeth. 2007a. Introduction to "Queer Temporalities." Special issue, *GLQ: A Journal of Lesbian and Gay Studies* 13 (2–3): 159–76.

Freeman, Elizabeth. 2007b. "Queer Belongings: Queer Theory and Kinship Theory." In *A Companion to Lesbian, Gay, Bisexual, Transgender, and Queer Studies*, edited by George E. Haggerty and Molly McGarry, 295–314. Malden, MA: Blackwell.

Freeman, Elizabeth. 2010. *Time Binds: Queer Temporalities, Queer Histories*. Durham, NC: Duke University Press.

Freespirit, Judy, and Aldebaran. 1973. "The Fat Liberation Manifesto." Fat Underground, November 1973. Association for Size Diversity and Health (ASDAH). Accessed November 16, 2017. https://www.sizediversityandhealth.org/content.asp?id=205&articleID=111

Geertz, Clifford. 1973. "Deep Play: Notes on the Balinese Cockfight." In *The Interpretation of Cultures*, 412–53. New York: Basic Books.

Ghaziani, Amin. 2014. *There Goes the Gayborhood?* Princeton, NJ: Princeton University Press.

Gill, Lyndon Kamaal. 2018. *Erotic Islands: Art and Activism in the Queer Caribbean*. Durham, NC: Duke University Press.

Gilmore, Ruth Wilson. 2006. *Golden Gulag: Prisons, Surplus, Crisis, and Opposition in Globalizing California*. Berkeley: University of California Press.

Gilroy, Paul. 1995. *The Black Atlantic: Modernity and Double-Consciousness*. Cambridge, MA: Harvard University Press.

Goltz, Dustin Bradley. 2014. "'We're Not in Oz Anymore': Shifting Generational Perspectives and Tensions of Gay Community, Identity, and Future." *Journal of Homosexuality* 61 (11): 1503–28.

Gopinath, Gayatri. 2018. *Unruly Visions: The Aesthetic Practices of Queer Diaspora*. Durham, NC: Duke University Press.

Gould, Deborah B. 2009. *Moving Politics: Emotion and ACT UP's Fight against AIDS*. Chicago: University of Chicago Press.

Gray, Mary L. 2009. *Out in the Country: Youth, Media, and Queer Visibility in Rural America*. New York: New York University Press.

Grazian, David. 2008. *On the Make: The Hustle of Urban Nightlife*. Chicago: University of Chicago Press.

Greene, Theodore. 2014. "Gay Neighborhoods and the Rights of the Vicarious Citizen." *City & Community* 13 (2): 99–118.

Griffin, Hollis. 2008. "Your Favorite Stars, Live on Our Screens: Media Culture, Queer Publics, and Commercial Space." *Velvet Light Trap* 62 (1): 15–28.

Guerrero, Gubidxa. 2014. "¿Quién fue José Gregorio Meléndez?" *Comité Melendre* (blog), March 17, 2014. http://comitemelendre.blogspot.com/2014/03/quien-fue-jose-gregorio-melendez.html

Gupta, Alok. 2011. "Moral Order of Blackmail." In *Law Like Love: Queer Perspectives on Law*, edited by Arvind Narrain and Alok Gupta, 466–79. New Delhi: Yoda Press.

Ha, Kim Chi. 2010. "Is a Gay Strip Club Too Close to Nationals Park for D.C.'s Comfort?" *Washington City Paper*, July 2, 2010. https://www.washingtoncitypaper.com/news/article/13039176/is-a-gay-strip-club-too-close-to-nationals-park

Hae, Laam. 2012. *The Gentrification of Nightlife and the Right to the City: Regulating Spaces of Social Dancing in New York*. New York: Routledge.

Hage, Ghassan. 2009. Introduction to *Waiting*, edited by Ghassan Hage, 1–12. Melbourne: Melbourne University Press.

Halberstam, Judith. 2003. "What's That Smell? Queer Temporalities and Subcultural Lives." *International Journal of Cultural Studies* 6 (3): 313–33.

Halberstam, J. Jack. 2005. *In a Queer Time and Place: Transgender Bodies, Subcultural Lives.* New York: New York University Press, 2005.

Hall, Lisa Kaheleole. 2009. "Mapping Our Own 'Sea of Islands': Remapping Theoretical Space for Hawaiian Women and Indigenous Feminism." *Wicazo Sa Review* 24 (2): 15–38.

Hamera, Judith. 2007. *Dancing Communities: Performance, Difference, and Connection in the Global City.* New York: Palgrave Macmillan.

Han, C. Winter. 2015. *Geisha of a Different Kind: Race and Sexuality in Gaysian America.* New York: New York University Press.

Hanhardt, Christina B. 2013. *Safe Space: Gay Neighborhood History and the Politics of Violence.* Durham, NC: Duke University Press.

Haraway, Donna. 1991. "A Cyborg Manifesto: Science, Technology, and Socialist-Feminism in the Late Twentieth Century." In *Simians, Cyborgs, and Women: The Reinvention of Nature*, 149–82. New York: Routledge.

Harrell, Trajal. 2011. "Trajal Harrell in Conversation with Thomas DeFrantz." *Critical Correspondence*, January 14, 2011. http://old.movementresearch.org/criticalcorrespondence/blog/?p=3123

Harris, Craig G. 1986. "Cut Off from among Their People." In *In the Life: A Black Gay Anthology*, edited by Joseph Beam, 63–67. Boston: Alyson.

Hartman, Saidiya V. 1997. *Scenes of Subjection: Terror, Slavery, and Self-Making in Nineteenth-Century America.* New York: Oxford University Press.

Hartman, Saidiya V. 2008. "Venus in Two Acts." *Small Axe* 26: 1–14.

Hartman, Saidiya V. 2016. "The Belly of the World: A Note on Black Women's Labors." *Souls* 18 (1): 166–73.

Hatherly, Frances. 2015. "Against 'Good Taste': Class, Corpulence, and Subversive Pleasure of 'Unfit' Femininities." In *Fat Sex: New Directions in Theory and Activism*, edited by Helen Hester and Caroline Walters, 67–84. Farnham, Surrey: Ashgate.

Haynes, Nell, and David Aruquipa Pérez. 2017. "Making Histories of Bolivian Sexual and Gender Diversity Legible in the Twenty-First Century." *Notches: (re)marks on the history of sexuality* (blog), September 19, 2017. http://notchesblog.com/2017/09/19/making-histories-of-bolivian-sexual-and-gender-diversity-legible-in-the-twenty-first-century/

Heap, Chad. 2003. "The City as a Sexual Laboratory: The Queer Heritage of the Chicago School." *Qualitative Sociology* 26 (4): 452–87, https://doi.org/10.1023/B:QUAS.0000005052.77181.51

Heap, Chad. 2009. *Slumming Sexual and Racial Encounters in American Nightlife, 1885–1940.* Chicago: University of Chicago Press.

Heberer, Feng-Mei. 2017. "The Asianization of *Heimat*: Ming Wong's Asian German Video Works." In *Asian Video Cultures: In the Penumbra of the Global*, edited by Joshua Neves and Bhaskar Sarkar, 198–214. Durham, NC: Duke University Press.

Herring, Scott. 2010. *Another Country: Queer Anti-Urbanism*. New York: New York University Press.

Hesmondhalgh, David, and Sarah Baker. 2011. *Labour: Media Work in Three Cultural Industries*. London: Routledge.

Hilderbrand, Lucas, dir. 2013. *Paris Is Burning: A Queer Film Classic*. Vancouver: Arsenal Press.

Höchtl, Nina. n.d. "Archivos desclosetados: Espectros y poderes disidentes." *Nina Höchtl* (website). Accessed August 2, 2020. http://www.ninahoechtl.org/works/archivos-desclosetados-espectros-y-poderes-disidentes/

Hodge, G. Derrick. 2001. "Colonization of the Cuban Body: The Growth of Male Sex Work in Havana." *NACLA Report on the Americas* 34 (5): 20–28.

Hodge, G. Derrick. 2014. "'Dangerous' Youth: Tourism Space, Gender Performance, and the Policing of Havana Street Hustlers." *Journal of Latin American and Caribbean Anthropology* 19 (3): 441–72.

hooks, bell. 1992. *Black Looks: Race and Representation*. Boston: South End Press.

Horton-Stallings, LaMonda. 2007. *Mutha' Is Half a Word: Intersections of Folklore, Vernacular, Myth, and Queerness in Black Female Culture*. Columbus: Ohio State University Press.

Hostetler, Andrew J. 2009. "Generativity and Time in Gay Men's Life Stories." In *The Story of Sexual Identity: Narrative Perspectives on the Gay and Lesbian Life Course*, edited by Phillip M. Hammack and Bertram J. Cohler, 397–424. New York: Oxford University Press.

Huizinga, Johan. 1949. *Homo Ludens: A Study of the Play-Element of Culture*. London: Routledge.

Hula Girl Productions. n.d. "The Glades Project Reveals an Integral Part of Hawaii's Culture and History That Has Been Kept in the Dark until Now." *HulaGirlProductions.com*. Accessed September 5, 2018. http://www.hulagirlproductions.com/glades

Humphreys, Laud. 1970. *Tearoom Trade: Impersonal Sex in Public Places*. New Brunswick, NJ: Aldine Transaction.

Irving, Dan. 2012. "Elusive Subjects: Notes on the Relationship between Critical Political Economy and Trans Studies." In *Transfeminist Perspectives in and beyond Transgender and Gender Studies*, edited by Anne Enke, 153–69. Philadelphia, PA: Temple University Press.

Jackson, Christina, and Nikki Jones. 2012. "Remember the Fillmore: The Lingering History of Urban Renewal in Black San Francisco." In *Black California Dreamin': The Crisis of California's African American Communities*, edited by Ingrid Banks, Gaye Johnson, George Lipsitz, Ula Taylor, Daniel Widener, and Clyde Woods, 57–73. Santa Barbara, CA: Center for Black Studies Research.

Johnson, Colin R. 2013. *Just Queer Folks: Gender and Sexuality in Rural America*. Philadelphia, PA: Temple University Press.

Johnson, E. Patrick. 1998. "Feeling the Spirit in the Dark: Expanding Notions of the Sacred in the African-American Gay Community." *Callaloo* 21 (2): 399–416.

Johnson, E. Patrick. 2001. "'Quare' Studies, or (Almost) Everything I Know about Queer Studies I Learned from My Grandmother." *Text and Performance Quarterly* 21 (1): 1–25.

Johnson, E. Patrick. 2008. *Sweet Tea: Black Gay Men of the South—An Oral History.* Chapel Hill: University of North Carolina Press.

Johnson, E. Patrick, and Ramón H. Rivera-Servera. 2016. "Introduction: Ethnoracial Intimacies in Blacktino Queer Performance." In *Blacktino Queer Performance,* edited by E. Patrick Johnson and Ramón H. Rivera-Servera, 1–20. Durham, NC: Duke University Press.

Jordenö, Sara, dir. 2016. *Kiki.* New York: Sundance Selects. Film, 96 min.

Joseph, Miranda. 2002. *Against the Romance of Community.* Minneapolis: University of Minnesota Press.

Joseph, Miranda. 2017. "Community, Collectivity, Affinities." In *A Companion to Critical and Cultural Theory,* edited by Imre Szeman, Sarah Blacker, and Justin Sully, 205–21. Oxford: Wiley-Blackwell.

Juhasz, Alexandra. 1995. *AIDS TV: Identity, Community, and Alternative Video.* Durham, NC: Duke University Press.

Kant, Immanuel. 1997. *Lectures on Metaphysics.* Edited by Karl Ameriks and Steve Naragon. Cambridge: Cambridge University Press.

Katyal, Akhil. 2013. "Laundebaazi: Habits and Politics in North India." *International Journal of Postcolonial Studies* 15 (4): 474–93.

Kazyak, Emily. 2012. "Midwest or Lesbian? Gender, Rurality, and Sexuality." *Gender & Society* 26 (6): 825–48.

Keeling, Kara. 2003. "'In the Interval': Frantz Fanon and the 'Problems' of Visual Representation." *Qui Parle* 13 (2): 91–117.

Keeling, Kara. 2009. "Looking for M—Queer Temporality, Black Political Possibility, and Poetry from the Future." *GLQ: A Journal of Lesbian and Gay Studies* 15 (4): 565–82.

Keeling, Kara. 2014. "Queer OS." *Cinema Journal* 53 (2): 152–57.

Ke Kulana He Māhū: Remembering a Sense of Place. Dir. Kathryn Xian and Brent Anbe, 2001.

Kelley, Robin D. G. 1993. "'We Are Not What We Seem': Rethinking Black Working-Class Opposition in the Jim Crow South." *Journal of American History* 80 (1): 75–112.

Kennedy, Elizabeth Lapovsky, and Madeline D. Davis. 1993. *Boots of Leather, Slippers of Gold: The History of a Lesbian Community.* New York: Routledge.

Kerr, Theodore (Ted). 2016. "AIDS 1969: HIV, History, and Race." In "AIDS and Memory," special issue, *Drain* 13 (2). http://drainmag.com/aids-1969-hiv-history-and-race/

Khubchandani, Kareem. 2020. *Ishtyle: Accenting Gay Indian Nightlife.* Ann Arbor: University of Michigan Press.

Kinser, Jeremy. 2014. "What Would the *Paris Is Burning* Legends Think about 'Transphobia'?" *Queerty.com,* June 30, 2014. https://www.queerty.com/what-would-the-paris-is-burning-legends-think-about-transphobia-20140630

Kourlas, Gia. 2012. "Stop and Vogue: 'Antigone' Meets the Postmodern." *New York Times*, April 20, 2012.

Lady Chablis, with Theodore Bouloukos. 1996. *Hiding My Candy*. New York: Pocket Books.

La Fountain-Stokes, Lawrence. 2008. "Trans/Bolero/Drag/Migration: Music, Cultural Translation, and Diasporic Puerto Rican Theatricalities." *WSQ: Women's Studies Quarterly* 36 (3–4): 190–209.

Lal, Ruby. 2013. *Coming of Age in Nineteenth-Century India: The Girl-Child and the Art of Playfulness*. Cambridge: Cambridge University Press.

Lanuza, Fernando, and Raúl Carrasco. 2015. *Queer & Cuir: Políticas de lo Irreal*. Mexico City: Fontamara.

Lavers, Michael K. 2017. "Mariela Castro: Marriage Does Not Stop Hate Crimes." *Washington Blade*, March 13, 2017. http://www.washingtonblade.com/2017/03/13/mariela-castro-marriage-not-put-end-hate-crimes/

Lawrence, Tim. 2006. "'I Want to See All My Friends at Once': Arthur Russell and the Queering of Gay Disco." *Journal of Popular Music Studies* 8 (2): 144–66.

Lawrence, Tim. 2009. "Beyond the Hustle / 1970s Social Dancing, Discotheque Culture, and the Emergence of the Contemporary Club Dancer." In *Ballroom, Boogie, Shimmy Sham, Shake: A Social and Popular Dance Reader*, edited by Julie Malnig, 199–215. Urbana: University of Illinois Press.

Lawrence, Tim. 2011. "Disco and the Queering of the Dance Floor." *Cultural Studies* 25 (2): 230–43.

LeBesco, Kathleen. 2001. "Queering Fat Bodies/Politics." In *Bodies Out of Bounds: Fatness and Transgression*, edited by Jana Evans Braziel and Kathleen LeBesco, 74–87. Berkeley: University of California Press, 2001.

LeBesco, Kathleen. 2004. *Revolting Bodies? The Struggle to Redefine Fat Identity*. Amherst: University of Massachusetts Press.

LeBesco, Kathleen. 2009. "Quest for a Cause: The Fat Gene, the Gay Gene, and the New Eugenics." In *The Fat Studies Reader*, edited by Esther Rothblum and Sondra Solovay, 65–74. New York: New York University Press.

Lee, Summer Kim. 2019. "Staying In." *Social Text* 37 (1): 27–50.

Lefebvre, Henri. 1970. *The Production of Space*. Oxford: Blackwell.

Leigh, Carol. 2004. *Unrepentant Whore: Collected Works of Scarlot Harlot*. San Francisco: Last Gasp.

Leung, Helen Hok-Sze. 2004. "New Queer Cinema and Third Cinema." In *New Queer Cinema: A Critical Reader*, edited by Michele Aaron, 155–70. New Brunswick, NJ: Rutgers University Press.

Livermon, Xavier. 2014. "Soweto Nights: Making Black Queer Space in Post-Apartheid South Africa." *Gender, Place & Culture* 21 (4): 508–25.

Livingston, Jennie, dir. 1990. *Paris Is Burning*. New York: Off White Productions. Film, 71 min.

Long, Alecia P. 2004. *The Great Southern Babylon: Sex, Race, and Respectability in New Orleans, 1865–1920*. Baton Rouge: Louisiana State University Press.

Lorde, Audre. 1978. *The Black Unicorn: Poems.* New York: Norton, 1978.

Lorde, Audre. 1993. "The Uses of the Erotic: The Erotic as Power." In *The Lesbian and Gay Studies Reader*, edited by Henry Abelove, Michèle Aina Barale, and David M. Halperin, 339–43. New York: Routledge.

Lorde, Audre. 2007. "The Master's Tools Will Never Dismantle the Master's House." In *Sister Outsider: Essays and Speeches by Audre Lorde*, rev. ed., 110–13. New York: Ten Speed Press.

Love, Heather. 2009. *Feeling Backward: Loss and the Politics of Queer History.* Cambridge, MA: Harvard University Press.

Luna, Caleb. 2018. "The Gender Nonconformity of My Fatness." *The Body Is Not an Apology.* August 10, 2018. https://thebodyisnotanapology.com/magazine/the-gender-nonconformity-of-my-fatness/

Malaby, Thomas. 2007. "Beyond Play: A New Approach to Games." *Games and Culture* 2 (2): 95–113.

Malaby, Thomas. 2009. "Anthropology and Play: The Contours of Playful Experience." *New Literary History* 40 (1): 205–18.

Malinda, Ato. 2015. "Kenyan Queer Identification as a Globalized Endeavor." In *Boldly Queer: African Perspectives on Same-Sex Sexuality and Gender Diversity*, edited by Theo Sandfort, Fabienne Simenel, Kevin Mwachiro, and Vasu Reddy, 117–24. The Hague, Netherlands: Hivos.

Manalansan, Martin F. 1995. "In the Shadows of Stonewall: Examining Gay Transnational Politics and the Diasporic Dilemma." *GLQ: A Journal of Lesbian and Gay Studies* 2 (4): 425–38.

Manalansan, Martin F. 2003. *Global Divas: Filipino Gay Men in the Diaspora.* Durham, NC: Duke University Press.

Manalansan, Martin F. 2005. "Race, Violence, and Neoliberal Spatial Politics in the Global City." *Social Text* 23 (3–4): 141–55.

Manjoo, Farhad. 2007. "The Computer Virus Turns 25." *Salon.com*, July 17, 2007. http://www.salon.com/2007/07/12/virus_birthday/

Marino, Angela. 2016. "Fiesta Time: The 'In-Time' of Durational Art and Festival Performance." *Representations* 136 (1): 157–60.

Marino, Angela. 2018. *Populism and Performance in the Bolivarian Revolution of Venezuela.* Evanston, IL: Northwestern University Press.

Marks, Laura U. 2002. *Touch: Sensuous Theory and Multisensory Media.* Minneapolis: University of Minnesota Press.

Mattson, Greggor. 2015. "Style and the Value of Gay Nightlife: Homonormative Placemaking in San Francisco." *Urban Studies* 52 (16): 3144–59.

Mattson, Greggor. 2019. "Are Gay Bars Closing? Using Business Listings to Infer Rates of Gay Bar Closure in the United States, 1977–2019." *Socius* 5 (1–2). https://doi.org/10.1177/2378023119894832

Matus, Macario. 2010. "Macario Matus, la Nación Zapoteca." Posted December 22, 2010, by Noe Yamahata. YouTube video, 6:00. https://www.youtube.com/watch?v=W5IBQ4pkARg

McAllister, John. 2015. "LGBT Activism and 'Traditional Values': Promoting Dialogue through Indigenous Cultural Values in Botswana." In *Boldly Queer: African Perspectives on Same-Sex Sexuality and Gender Diversity*, edited by Theo Sandfort, Fabienne Simenel, Kevin Mwachiro, and Vasu Reddy, 41–48. The Hague Netherlands: Hivos.

McBride, Dwight A. 2005. *Why I Hate Abercrombie & Fitch: Essays on Race and Sexuality*. New York: New York University Press.

McCoy-Torres, Sabia. 2017. "'Love Dem Bad': Embodied Experience, Self-Adoration, and Eroticism in Dancehall." *Transforming Anthropology* 25 (2): 185–200.

McCoy-Torres, Sabia. 2018. "Alternative Spatiality and Temporality: Diasporic Mobilities and Queer West Indian Inclusion." *Global South* 12 (1): 59–88.

McCune, Jeffrey Q. 2004. "Transformance: Reading the Gospel in Drag." *Journal of Homosexuality* 46 (3–4): 151–67.

McKinney, Cait. 2020. "Crisis Infrastructures: AIDS Activism Meets Internet Regulation." In *AIDS and the Distribution of Crises*, edited by Jih-Fei Cheng, Alexandra Juhasz, and Nishant Shahani, 162–82. Durham, NC: Duke University Press.

McPherson, Miller, Lynn Smith-Lovin, and James M. Cook. 2001. "Birds of a Feather: Homophily in Social Networks." *Annual Review of Sociology* 27: 415–44.

Melamed, Jodi. 2006. "The Spirit of Neoliberalism: From Racial Liberalism to Neoliberal Multiculturalism." *Social Text* 24 (4): 1–24.

Mendoza, Zoila. 2000. *Shaping Society through Dance: Mestizo Ritual Performance in the Peruvian Andes*. Chicago: University of Chicago Press.

Merabet, Sofian. 2004. "Disavowed Homosexualities in Beirut." *Middle East Report* 34 (1): 30–33.

Merton, Robert K. 1976. *Sociological Ambivalence & Other Essays*. New York: Free Press.

Miller, Daniel. 1991. "Absolute Freedom in Trinidad." *Man* 26 (2): 323–41.

Mitchell, Gregory. 2016. *Tourist Attractions: Performing Race and Masculinity in Brazil's Sexual Economy*. Chicago: University of Chicago Press.

Mock, Janet. 2014. *Redefining Realness: My Path to Womanhood, Identity, Love and So Much More*. New York: Atria Books.

Moon, Michael, and Eve Kosofsky Sedgwick. 2001. "Divinity." In *Bodies Out of Bounds: Fatness and Transgression*, edited by Jana Evans Braziel and Kathleen LeBesco, 292–328. Berkeley: University of California Press.

Moore, Madison. 2018. *Fabulous: The Rise of the Beautiful Eccentric*. New Haven, CT: Yale University Press.

Moore, Robin. 1997. *Nationalizing Blackness: Afrocubanismo and Artistic Revolution in Havana, 1920–1940*. Pittsburgh, PA: University of Pittsburgh Press.

Morcom, Anna. 2013. *Illicit Worlds on Indian Dance: Cultures of Exclusion*. London: Hurst.

Morgensen, Scott Lauria. 2011. *Spaces between Us: Queer Settler Colonialism and Indigenous Decolonization*. Minneapolis: University of Minnesota Press.

Muñoz, José Esteban. 1996. "Ephemera as Evidence: Introductory Notes to Queer Acts." *Women & Performance: A Journal of Feminist Theory* 8 (2): 5–16.

Muñoz, José Esteban. 1999. *Disidentifications: Queers of Color and the Performance of Politics*. Minneapolis: University of Minnesota Press.

Muñoz, José Esteban. 2000. "Feeling Brown: Ethnicity and Affect in Ricardo Bracho's *The Sweetest Hangover (and Other STDs)*." *Theatre Journal* 52 (1): 67–79.

Muñoz, José Esteban. 2009. *Cruising Utopia: The Then and There of Queer Futurity*. New York: New York University Press.

Muñoz, José Esteban. 2020. *The Sense of Brown*. Edited by Joshua Chambers-Letson and Tavia Nyong'o. Durham, NC: Duke University Press.

Munuera, Ivan L. 2017. "An Organism of Hedonistic Pleasures: The Palladium." *Log* 41:102–12.

Murray, Laura. 2012. *A Kiss for Gabriela*. New York: Films Media Group. Film, 30 min.

Musser, Amber Jamilla. 2014. *Sensational Flesh: Race, Power, and Masochism*. New York: New York University Press.

Musser, Amber Jamilla. 2018. *Sensual Excess: Queer Femininity and Brown Jouissance*. New York: New York University Press.

Nath, Anjali. 2013. "Seeing Guantánamo, Blown Up: Banksy's Installation in Disneyland." *American Quarterly* 64 (1): 185–92.

Navarro-Yashin, Yael. 2012. *Make-Believe Space: Affective Geographies in a Postwar Polity*. Durham, NC: Duke University Press.

Negrón-Muntaner, Frances. 2008. "'Mariconerías' de Estado: Mariela Castro, los homosexuales y la política cubana." *Nueva Sociedad* 218: 163–79.

Nero, Charles. 1991. "Toward a Black Gay Aesthetic: Signifying in Contemporary Black Gay Literature." In *Brother to Brother: New Writings by Black Gay Men*, edited by Essex Hemphill, 229–52. Boston: Alyson Press.

Newsome, Rashaad. 2015. "Interview: Rashaad Newsome on Voguing, Heraldry, and FKA Twigs." By David Balzer. *Momus*, June 10, 2015. http://momus.ca/interview-rashaad-newsome-on-voguing-heraldry-and-fka-twigs/

Newton, Esther. 1993. "My Best Informant's Dress: The Erotic Equation in Fieldwork." *Cultural Anthropology* 8 (1): 3–23.

Nkabinde, Nkunzi Zandile. 2008. *Black Bull, Ancestors and Me: My Life as a Lesbian Sangoma*. Auckland Park, South Africa: Fanele Press.

North, Anna. 2009. "Short Skirt Sparks Mass Hysteria at Brazilian University." *Jezebel*. November 9, 2009. https://jezebel.com/short-skirt-sparks-mass-hysteria-at-brazilian-universit-5400255

Nyong'o, Tavia. 2008. "I Feel Love: Disco and Its Discontents." *Criticism* 50 (1): 101–12.

Nyong'o, Tavia. 2015. "After the Ball." *BullyBloggers* (blog), July 8, 2015. https://bullybloggers.wordpress.com/2015/07/08/after-the-ball/

Nyong'o, Tavia. 2018. *Afro-Fabulations: The Queer Drama of Black Life*. New York: New York University Press.

Ochoa, Marcia. 2014. *Queen for a Day: Transformistas, Beauty Queens, and the Performance of Femininity in Venezuela*. Durham, NC: Duke University Press.

Online Etymology Dictionary. n.d. "download." Accessed June 17, 2017. http://www.etymonline.com/word/download

Orne, Jason. 2017. *Boystown: Sex and Community in Chicago*. Chicago: University of Chicago Press.

Palmer, Bryan. 2000. *Cultures of Darkness: Night Travels in the Histories of Transgression*. New York: Monthly Press Review.

Parédez, Deborah. 2009. *Selenidad: Selena, Latinos, and the Performance of Memory*. Durham, NC: Duke University Press, 2009.

Parra, Carlos. 2017. (Paris Galán, La Familia Galán member), in discussion with the author. June. La Paz, Bolivia, June.

Parra-Bernal, Guillermo. 2005. "Brazil Raids Daslu Retailer, Arrests Owner in Tax Evasion Probe." *Bloomberg Businessweek*, July 13, 2005.

Pearl, Monica B. 2004. "AIDS and New Queer Cinema." In *New Queer Cinema: A Critical Reader*, edited by Michele Aaron, 23–35. New Brunswick, NJ: Rutgers University Press.

Pérez, Hiram. 2015. *A Taste for Brown Bodies: Gay Modernity and Cosmopolitan Desire*. New York: New York University Press.

Peterson, Grant Tyler. 2011. "Clubbing Masculinities: Gender Shifts in Gay Men's Dance Floor Choreographies." *Journal of Homosexuality* 58 (5): 608–25.

Pineda, Irma. 2001. "La Pared." *La Jornada*, April 23, 2001. http://www.jornada.unam.mx/2001/04/23/oja48-poemas.html

Piscitelli, Adriana. 2006. "Sujeição ou subversão: Migrantes brasileiras na indústria do sexo na Espanha." *Revista História & Perspectivas* 1 (35): 13–55.

Piscitelli, Adriana. 2007. "Sexo tropical em um país europeu: Migração de brasileiras para a Itália no marco do 'turismo sexual' internacional." *Revista Estudos Feministas* 15 (3): 717–44.

Preciado, Beatriz. 2013. *Testo Junkie: Sex, Drugs, and Biopolitics in the Pharmapornographic Era*. Translated by Bruce Benderson. New York: Feminist Press.

Probyn, Elspeth. 1996. *Outside Belongings*. New York: Routledge.

Puar, Jasbir K. 2007. *Terrorist Assemblages: Homonationalism in Queer Times*. Durham, NC: Duke University Press.

Quiroga, José. 2000. *Tropics of Desire: Interventions from Queer Latino America*. New York: New York University Press.

Qureshi, Abdullah. 2018. "Queer Migrations: The Case of an LGBT Cafe / Queers without Borders." In *Feminism and Queer in Art Education*, edited by Anniina Suominen and Tiina Pusa, 90–115. Espoo, Finland: Aalto ARTS Books.

Radcliffe-Brown, A. R. 1940. "On Joking Relationships." *Africa: Journal of the International African Institute* 13 (3): 195–210.

Ramos, Iván A. 2015. "The Dirt That Haunts: Looking at Esta Noche." *Studies in Gender and Sexuality*16 (2): 135–36.

Ramsay, Burt. 2001. "Dissolving in Pleasure: The Threat of the Queer Male Dancing

Body." In *Dancing Desires: Choreographing Sexualities On and Off the Stage*, edited by Jane Desmond, 209–42. Madison: University of Wisconsin Press.

Reddy, Chandan. 1998. "Home, Houses, Nonidentity: *Paris Is Burning*." In *Burning Down the House: Recycling Domesticity*, edited by Rosemary Marangoly George, 355–77. Boulder, CO: Westview Press.

Reddy, Chandan. 2011. *Freedom with Violence: Race, Sexuality, and the US State*. Durham, NC: Duke University Press.

Regnault, Chantal. 2011. *Voguing and the House Ballroom Scene of New York City 1989–92*. London: Soul Jazz Books.

Rich, B. Ruby. 1992. "New Queer Cinema." *Sight & Sound*, September 1992. https://www.bfi.org.uk/news-opinion/sight-sound-magazine/features/new-queer-cinema-b-ruby-rich

Rivera-Servera, Ramón H. 2012. *Performing Queer Latinidad: Dance, Sexuality, Politics*. Ann Arbor: University of Michigan Press.

Rivera-Servera, Ramón H. 2016. "Reggaetón's Crossings: Black Aesthetics, Latina Nightlife, and Queer Choreography." In *No Tea, No Shade: New Writings in Black Queer Studies*, edited by E. Patrick Johnson, 95–112. Durham, NC: Duke University Press.

Rivera-Servera, Ramón H. 2017. "History in Drag: Latina/o Queer Affective Circuits in Chicago." In *The Latina/o Midwest Reader*, edited by Omar Valerio-Jiménez, Santiago Vaquera-Vásquez, and Claire F. Fox, 185–96. Urbana: University of Illinois Press, 2017.

Roach, Tom. 2012. *Friendship as a Way of Life: Foucault, AIDS, and the Politics of Shared Estrangement*. Albany: State University of New York Press.

Rodríguez, Juana María. 2014. *Sexual Futures, Queer Gestures, and Other Latina Longings*. New York: New York University Press.

Rodríguez, Juana María. 2020. "Activism and Identity in the Ruins of Representation." In *AIDS and the Distribution of Crises*, edited by Jih-Fei Cheng, Alexandra Juhasz, and Nishant Shahani, 352–87. Durham, NC: Duke University Press.

Rohter, Larry. 2005. "Prostitution Puts U.S. and Brazil at Odds on AIDS Policy." *New York Times*, July 24, 2005.

Román, David. 2003. "Dance Liberation." *Theatre Journal* 55 (3): vii–xxiv.

Rony, Fatimah Tobing. 1996. *The Third Eye: Race, Cinema, and the Ethnographic Spectacle*. Durham, NC: Duke University Press.

Ross, Marlon B. 2005. "Beyond the Closet as Raceless Paradigm." In *Black Queer Studies: A Critical Anthology*, edited by Mae Henderson and E. Patrick Johnson, 161–89. Durham, NC: Duke University Press.

Saldana, Janel. 2015. "Meet the Muxes: Mexican Indigenous Community Where Sexual Diversity Is Celebrated since Birth." *Latin Times*, December 17, 2015.

Salkind, Micah E. 2019. *Do You Remember House? Chicago's Queer of Color Undergrounds*. New York: Oxford University Press.

Sampson, Tony. 2012. *Virality: Contagion Theory in the Age of Networks*. Minneapolis: University of Minnesota Press.

Saunders, Tanya. 2009. "Grupo OREMI: Black Lesbians and the Struggle for Safe Social Space in Havana." *Souls* 11 (2): 167–85.

Saunders, Tanya. 2015. *Cuban Underground Hip Hop: Black Thoughts, Black Revolution and Black Modernity*. Austin: University of Texas Press.

Saunders, Tanya. 2016. "Toward a Hemispheric Analysis of Black Lesbian Feminist Activism and Hip Hop Feminism: Artist Perspectives from Cuba and Brazil." In *No Tea, No Shade: New Writings in Black Queer Studies*, edited by E. Patrick Johnson, 147–65. Durham, NC: Duke University Press.

Schlör, Joachim. 1998. *Nights in the Big City: Paris. Berlin, London, 1840–1930*. London: Reaktion Books.

Scott, Darieck. 1999. "More Man Than You'll Ever Be: Antonia Fargas, Eldridge Cleaver, and Toni Morrison's *Beloved*." In *Dangerous Liaisons: Blacks, Gays, and the Struggle for Equality*, edited by Eric Brandt, 217–42. New York: New Press.

Seligman, Amanda I. 2005. *Block by Block: Neighborhoods and Public Policy on Chicago's West Side*. Chicago: University of Chicago Press.

Seymour, Craig. 2008. *All I Could Bare: My Life in the Strip Clubs of Gay D.C.* New York: Atria Books.

Shaffer, Andrew W. 2017. "A (Re)Turn to the Past: Memory and Movement in ¡Viva 16!" *Queer Studies in Media & Popular Culture* 2 (2): 243–54. https://doi.org/10.1386/qsmpc.2.2.243_1

Shah, Nayan. 2011. *Stranger Intimacy: Contesting Race, Sexuality, and the Law in the North American West*. Berkeley: University of California Press.

Shahani, Parmesh. 2008. *Gay Bombay: Globalization, Love and (Be)Longing in Contemporary India*. Thousand Oaks, CA: Sage.

Siegel, Paul. 2001. "A Right to Boogie Queerly: The First Amendment on the Dance Floor." In *Dancing Desires: Choreographing Sexualities On and Off the Stage*, edited by Jane Desmond, 267–84. Madison: University of Wisconsin Press.

Sierra Madero, Abel. 2014. "Del Hombre Nuevo al Travestismo de Estado." *Diario de Cuba*, January 25, 2014. http://www.diariodecuba.com/cuba/1390513833_6826.html

Sigl, Eveline, and David Mendoza. 2012a. *No se baila así no más*... Vol. 1, *Género, poder, política, etnicidad, clase, religión y biodiversidad en las danzas del altiplano boliviano*. La Paz: Self-published.

Sigl, Eveline, and David Mendoza. 2012b. *No se baila así nomás . . . Tomo II: Danzas autóctonas y folklóricas de Bolivia*. La Paz: Self-published.

Simon, Frank, dir. 1968. *The Queen*. New York: Grove Press. Film, 68 min.

Simpson, Paul. 2013. "Alienation, Ambivalence, Agency: Middle-Aged Gay Men and Ageism in Manchester's Gay Village." *Sexualities* 16 (3–4): 283–99.

Singh, Bhrigupati. 2015. *Poverty and the Quest for Life: Spiritual and Material Striving in Rural India*. Chicago: University of Chicago Press.

Smelser, Neil J. 1998. "The Rational and the Ambivalent in the Social Sciences: 1997 Presidential Address." *American Sociological Review* 63 (1): 1–16.

Smith, Andrea. 2010. "Queer Theory and Native Studies: The Heteronormativity of Settler Colonialism." *GLQ: A Journal of Lesbian and Gay Studies* 16 (1–2): 41–68.

Spade, Dean. 2011. *Normal Life: Administrative Violence, Critical Trans Politics, and the Limits of Law.* Durham, NC: Duke University Press.

Spatz, Ben. 2015. *What a Body Can Do: Technique as Knowledge, Practice as Research.* London: Routledge.

Spillers, Hortense J. 1987. "Mama's Baby, Papa's Maybe: An American Grammar Book." In "Culture and Countermemory: The 'American' Connection," special issue, *Diacritics* (17) 2: 64–81.

Stephen, Lynn. 2007. *Transborder Lives: Indigenous Oaxacans in Mexico, California, and Oregon.* Durham, NC: Duke University Press.

Stewart, Kathleen. 2011. "Atmospheric Attunements." *Environment and Planning D: Society and Space* 29: 445–53.

Stone, Amy L. 2018. "The Geography of Research on LGBTQ Life: Why Sociologists Should Study the South, Rural Queers, and Ordinary Cities." *Sociology Compass* 12 (11): e12638. https://doi.org/10.1111/soc4.12638

Stout, Noelle. 2014. *After Love: Queer Intimacy and Erotic Economies in Post-Soviet Cuba.* Durham, NC: Duke University Press.

Strey, Jacquelyn P. 2017. "Queerness's Domain? Queer Negotiations, Utopian Visions, and the Failures of Heterotopias in Bangalore." In *Urban Utopias: Excess and Expulsion in Neoliberal South Asia,* edited by Tereza Kuldova and Mathew A. Varghese, 247–67. Cham, Switzerland: Palgrave Macmillan.

Strings, Sabrina. 2019. *Fearing the Black Body: The Racial Origins of Fat Phobia.* New York: New York University Press.

Sublette, Ned. 2004. *Cuba and Its Music: From the First Drums to the Mambo.* Chicago: Chicago Review Press.

Suny, Ronald Grigor. 2015. *"They Can Live in the Desert but Nowhere Else": A History of the Armenian Genocide.* Princeton, NJ: Princeton University Press.

Suresh, Mayur. 2011. "'I'm Only Here to Do Masti': Sodomy Law and the Limits of Subjectivation." In *Law Like Love: Queer Perspectives on Law,* edited by Arvind Narrain and Alok Gupta, 466–79. New Delhi: Yoda Press.

Sutton-Smith, Brian. 2006. "Play and Ambiguity." In *The Game Design Reader: A Rules of Play Anthology,* edited by Katie Salen and Eric Zimmerman, 296–313. Cambridge: MIT Press.

Sylvester. 1978. "Dance (Disco Heat)." Written by Eric Robinson and Victor Osborn. Track 2 on *Step II.* Fantasy F-9556, LP.

Taylor, Diana. 2003. *The Archive and the Repertoire: Performing Cultural Memory in the Americas.* Durham, NC: Duke University Press.

Teves, Stephanie Nohelani. 2014. "A Critical Reading of Aloha and Visual Sovereignty in *Ke Kulana He Māhū.*" *International Journal of Critical Indigenous Studies* 7 (1): 1–17.

Thornton, Sarah. 1996. *Club Cultures: Music, Media, and Subcultural Capital.* Hanover, NH: University Press of New England.

Thorpe, Rochella. 1996. "'A House Where Queers Go': African-American Lesbian Nightlife in Detroit, 1940–1975." In *Inventing Lesbian Cultures in America*, edited by Ellen Lewin, 40–61. Boston: Beacon Press.

Tongson, Karen. 2011. *Relocations: Queer Suburban Imaginaries*. New York: New York University Press.

Torres Santana, Ailynn. 2020. "Regímenes de bienestar en Cuba: Mujeres y desigualdades." *Cuban Studies* 49: 6–31.

Tourmaline, and Sasha Wortzel, dirs. 2018. *Happy Birthday Marsha!* San Francisco: Frameline. Film, 15 min.

Trouillot, Michel-Rolph. 2003. *Global Transformations: Anthropology and the Modern World*. New York: Palgrave Macmillan.

Tsang, Wu, dir. 2012. *Wildness*. New York: Electronic Arts Intermix. Film, 74 min.

Tuck, Eve, and K. Wayne Yang. 2012. "Decolonization Is Not a Metaphor." *Decolonization: Indigeneity, Education & Society* 1 (1): 1–40.

US Census American Community Survey. 2018. "ACS Demographic and Housing Estimates." Accessed October 1, 2020. https://data.census.gov/cedsci/table?g=0400000US06_1600000US0667000&d=ACS%205-Year%20Estimates%20Data%20Profiles&tid=ACSDP5Y2018.DP05

Vaid-Menon, Alok. 2018. "Imp Queen and the Perpetually Problematic Erasure of Trans Drag Queens." *Them*, September 29, 2018. https://www.them.us/story/imp-queen-trans-drag-queens

Vaktania, Shirish. 2015. "Cops Used My Husband as Honey Trap to Extort Money from Gay Men." *Mid-Day*, April 16, 2015. http://www.mid-day.com/articles/cops-used-my-husband-as-honey-trap-to-extort-money-from-gay-men/16133184

Valencia Triana, Margarita Sayak. 2014. "Tijuana Cuir." In *Queer Geographies*, edited by Lasse Lau, Mirene Arsanios, Felipe Zúñiga-González, Mathias Kryger, and Omar Mismar, 90–95. Roskilde, Denmark: Museet for Samtidskunst.

Vargas, Deborah R. 2013. "Punk's Afterlife in Cantina Time." *Social Text* 31 (3): 57–73.

Vargas, Deborah R. 2014. "Ruminations on Lo Sucio as a Latino Queer Analytic." *American Quarterly* 66 (3): 715–26.

Vasquez Toral, Enzo E. 2020. "Queer Fiesta: Hybridity, Drag and Performance in Bolivian Folklore," *Performance Research* 25, no. 4: 96–104.

Vidal-Ortiz, Salvador. 2006. "Sexuality Discussions in Santería: A Case Study of Religion and Sexuality Negotiation." *Sexuality Research & Social Policy* 3 (3): 52–66.

Viteri, María-Amelia. 2014. *Desbordes: Translating Racial, Ethnic, Sexual, and Gender Identities across the Americas*. Albany: State University of New York Press.

Vogel, Shane. 2009. *The Scene of Harlem Cabaret: Race, Sexuality, Performance*. Chicago: University of Chicago Press.

Voss, Barbara L. 2008. *The Archaeology of Ethnogenesis: Race and Sexuality in Colonial San Francisco*. Berkeley: University of California Press.

Ward, Jane. 2010. "Gender Labor: Transmen, Femmes, and Collective Work of Transgression." *Sexualities* 13 (2): 236–54.

Warhurst, Chris, and Dennis Nickson. 2009. "'Who's Got the Look?': Emotional, Aesthetic and Sexualized Labour In Interactive Services." *Gender, Work & Organization* 16 (3): 385–404.

Warner, Michael. 1992. "The Mass Public and the Mass Subject." In *Habermas and the Public Sphere*, edited by Craig Calhoun, 377–401. Cambridge, MA: MIT Press.

Washington, Craig. 2013. "Fall Down on Me: Stories of the Club from Black Gay Men in the South." In *Queer South Rising: Voices of a Contested Placed*, edited by Reta Ugena Whitlock, 73–89. Charlotte, NC: Information Age.

Weston, Kath. 1991. *Families We Choose: Lesbians, Gays, Kinship*. New York: Columbia University Press.

Weston, Kath. 1995. "Get Thee to a Big City: Sexual Imaginary and the Great Gay Migration." *GLQ: A Journal of Lesbian and Gay Studies* 2 (3): 253–77.

White, Kerry P. 2017. "Cruising Havana: Affective Spaces, Public Gestures, and the Worlds They Make in a Contemporary Cuba." Master's thesis, University of Florida.

Whitesel, Jason. 2014. *Fat Gay Men: Girth, Mirth, and the Politics of Stigma*. New York: New York University Press.

Whittle, Stephen. 2000. *Employment Discrimination and Transsexual People*. Report. Melverley, Surrey: Gender Identity Research and Education Society. https://www.gires.org.uk/employment-discrimination-and-trans-people/

Wilson, Ara. 2004. *The Intimate Economies of Bangkok: Tomboys, Tycoons, and Avon Ladies in the Global City*. Berkeley: University of California Press.

Wilson, James F. 2010. *Bulldaggers, Pansies, and Chocolate Babies: Performance, Race, and Sexuality in the Harlem Renaissance*. Ann Arbor: University of Michigan Press.

Wolfe, Patrick. 2006. "Settler Colonialism and the Elimination of the Native." *Journal of Genocide Research* 8 (4): 387–409.

Wolff, Christian. 1963. *Preliminary Discourse on Philosophy in General*. Translated by R. J. Blackwell. Indianapolis, IN: Bobbs-Merrill.

Wynter, Sylvia. 2003. "Unsettling the Coloniality of Being/Power/Truth/Freedom: Towards the Human, after Man, Its Overrepresentation—an Argument." *CR: The New Centennial Review* 3 (3): 257–337.

Xian, Kathryn, and Brent Anbe, dirs. 2001. *Ke Kulana He Māhū: Remembering a Sense of Place*. Zang Pictures. Film, 67 min.

Zurbano, Roberto. 2014. "The Country to Come: And My Black Cuba." *Afro-Hispanic Review* 33 (1): 71–72.

Notes on Contributors

Kemi Adeyemi is assistant professor of gender, women, and sexuality studies and director of The Black Embodiments Studio at the University of Washington. Her writing and curatorial projects use performance as a site and methodology for theorizing the contours of contemporary Black queer life. Her book, *Feels Right: Black Queer Women's Choreographies of Belonging in Chicago* is under contract with Duke University Press. Recent writing has appeared in *GLQ*, *Women & Performance*, and the *Routledge Handbook of African American Art History*, and she has written on and for artists including Tschabalala Self, Jovencio de la Paz, Indira Allegra, Brendan Fernandes, and taisha paggett.

Eduardo Alegría is a multidisciplinary artist who since the 1990s has been working in experimental theater and dance as well as musical projects that merge post-pop music with electroacoustic sound. After training in his youth with theater director Maritza Pérez-Otero, he collaborated for more than twenty years with experimental dancer and choreographer Viveca Vázquez and her postmodern dance group Taller de Otra Cosa. His performance pieces were presented within the alternative performance circuit of New York City during the nineties, before he became one of the founding members of the iconic Puerto Rican indie band Súperaquello. Later he developed his own musical project, Alegría Rampante, which became one of the most emblematic alternative bands in Puerto Rico.

José Álvarez-Colón is a Puerto Rican interdisciplinary artist and scholar working across the disciplines of dance, theater, and performance art. He follows a practice-based research methodology to establish links between art practice, critical theory, and cultural history. He is currently a PhD candidate in the Department of Performance Studies at Northwestern University. His doctoral research project examines Puerto Rico's experimental dance history, particularly the practices, aesthetics, and sociopolitical frameworks of dance improvisation in the context of Puerto Rico's decades-long economic crisis. He is coprincipal investigator of the Puerto Rican Arts Initiative, sponsored by the Andrew W. Mellon Foundation.

Emily R. Bock is a PhD candidate in the Department of Anthropology at the University of Chicago. Her research is situated at the intersection of critical race theory, Black studies, queer theory, performance studies, and ethnographic methods/writing. Her dissertation, "Ordinary Queens: the ball, the streets, and the beyond of survival," is an ethnographic investigation of the everyday lives of members of the underground ballroom scene in Chicago and New York, tracking the diverse aesthetic and performative practices this community has developed for imagining, performing, and securing the "good life." Before securing an MA in anthropology from the University of Chicago, Bock danced for choreographers and performance artists in New York City including Douglas Dunn, Jin Ju Song-Begin, Hadley Smith, and Johanna Meyer. She continues to make dance in Chicago.

Andrea Bolivar is assistant professor of Women's and Gender Studies and faculty associate of the Latina/o Studies Program at the University of Michigan. She received her doctorate in Anthropology from Washington University in St. Louis, and held an LSA Collegiate Postdoctoral Fellowship at the University of Michigan. Her first book manuscript, tentatively titled *"We Are a Fantasy": Trans Latina Ways of Knowing, Being, and Loving*, ethnographically examines sex working trans Latinas' epistemologies and ontologies, especially concerning five interrelated themes: fantasía, life/death, the body, immigration, and race.

AB Brown is a performance artist and performance studies scholar. Their manuscript, "Staging Statelessness: Queer African Refugees and the Limits of Belonging," looks at aesthetic practices that expand legal definitions of statelessness in a South African context. They are assistant professor of contemporary performance at Colby College and received their PhD in performance studies from Northwestern University.

Jih-Fei Cheng is assistant professor of Feminist, Gender, and Sexuality Studies at Scripps College. He has worked in HIV/AIDS social services, been involved in media production and curation, and participated in queer and trans of color grassroots organizations in Los Angeles and New York City. He is co-editor, with Alexandra Juhasz and Nishant Shahani, of *AIDS and the Distribution of Crises* (Duke UP 2020). His first book project, tentatively titled *Queer Code: HIV/AIDS and the History of Virology*, examines the science, media, and activism of HIV/AIDS in relation to the colonial history of virology. A second research project addresses the roles of virology and genetics in developing the national identity of the People's Republic of China. It commences with an investigation of the HIV epidemic outbreak among blood plasma donors in his paternal grandfather's province of Henan.

Clare Croft is a dance historian and theorist, and sometimes a dramaturg and curator. She is the editor of *Queer Dance: Meanings and Makings* and the curator of the EXPLODE! Queer Dance Festival. She is also the author of *Dancers as Diplomats: American Choreography in Cultural Exchange*. She is associate professor of dance and American culture at the University of Michigan.

Meiver De la Cruz is a visiting assistant professor of dance and a Consortium for Faculty Diversity Fellow at Scripps College, where she teaches dance studies, feminist and performance theory, and Arab dance technique. She writes about Arab and Arab American movement practices (social, staged, and ritual dance) as well as Arab dance pedagogy. As an artist, she creates works addressing the intersections of globalization, racism, and sexual violence.

Clare Forstie is a staff member at the University of Minnesota's Center for Educational Innovation. Her research and teaching interests include gender and sexuality, community, identities, emotions, and technology, as well as queer and feminist theories and methodologies. Her research explores ambivalent LGBTQ community and queer friendships in small cities in New England and the rural Midwest.

Eddie Gamboa is an instructor of Communication and Gender and Sexuality Studies at Governors State University. Their current research explores the adaptation of sensorially-based pedagogies of pleasure among queer men of color into online mediated environments. They have been published in *Women in Performance*, *Liminalities*, *Text and Performance Quarterly*, and *Departures in Critical Qualitative Research*. Gamboa also serves as Director of Forensics at GSU, and is the founder of Homeplace: A Forensicator of Color Collective, which serves as an advocacy group for students and coaches of color within the forensics community.

Brian A. Horton is an anthropologist working at the intersections of queer of color critique, South Asian anthropology, and critical theory. His current research explores how queer aesthetics offer alternative forms of queer politics and labor as well as new repertoires of what might constitute unruly, ephemeral, and critical forms of queer life. Drawing on extensive fieldwork in India, he asks how queer lives in Global South and postcolonial contexts might be apprehended beyond a tethering to abjection, precarity, and suffering. He is currently an assistant professor of anthropology at Brandeis University.

Professional dominant, intuitive, and burlesque goddess **Ms. Briq House** is the founder and owner of Briq House Entertainment. Under this umbrella she produces all-POC burlesque revues, sexual healing through movement and body love workshops, spiritual gatherings, kink-based antiracism trainings, and kink events exclusively for people of color throughout the United States and abroad. Her monthly production (coproduced with Sin de la Rosa), Sunday Night Suga Shaq, is the longest running, monthly all-POC burlesque revue in the Pacific Northwest. Ms. Briq House is one of *21st Century Burlesque Magazine*'s 2018 Top 50 and *Autostraddle*'s 23 Black Queer & Trans Femmes to Follow, and she has been featured by The House of Knyle, the *Seattle Times*, *Time*, and *The Stranger*.

Karen Jaime (PhD, performance studies, New York University) is an assistant professor of performing and media arts and Latina/o studies at Cornell University. Her current monograph, *The Queer Nuyorican: Racialized Sexualities and Aesthetics in Loisaida*, argues for a reexamination of the Nuyorican Poets Café as a historically queer space, in terms of both sexualities and performance practices. Her critical writing has been published in: *Women and Performance: A Journal of Feminist Theory*, *e-Misférica*, *Small Axe: A Caribbean Journal of Criticism*, and in *TSQ: Transgender Studies Quarterly*. She is also an accomplished spoken word/performance artist who served as the host/curator for the Friday Night Poetry Slam at the world-renowned Nuyorican Poets Café. Her poems are included in: *The Best of Panic! En Vivo from the East Village*, *Flicker and Spark: A Queer Anthology of Spoken Word and Poetry*, *Sinister Wisdom*, and *Latinas: Struggles and Protests in 21st Century USA*.

E. Patrick Johnson is Dean of the School of Communication and Annenberg University Professor at Northwestern University. A member of the American Academy of Arts & Sciences, Johnson's work has greatly impacted African American Studies, Performance Studies, and Gender, and Sexuality Studies. He is the author of several books, including *Appropriating Blackness: Performance and the Politics of Authenticity* (2003); *Sweet Tea: Black Gay Men of the South—An Oral History* (2008); *Black. Queer. Southern. Women.—An Oral History* (2018); *Honeypot: Black Southern Women Who Love Women* (2019), in addition to a number of edited and co-edited collections, essays, and plays.

Kareem Khubchandani is the Mellon Bridge assistant professor in theater, dance, and performance studies, and women's, gender, and sexuality studies at Tufts University. He is the author of *Ishtyle: Accenting Gay Indian Nightlife*, and is working on other monographs titled "Decolonize Drag!" and "Auntologies: Queer Aesthetics and South Asian Aunties." He has published in *Scholar and Feminist Online*, *Transgender Studies Quarterly*, *Journal of Asian American Studies*, and the *Velvet Light Trap*. He is also a performance artist and has shown work at Queens Museum, Jack Theater, Bronx Academy of Arts and Dance, Links Hall, and A.R.T. Oberon.

Matthew Leslie Santana is a violinist and ethnomusicologist broadly interested the role of performance within movements toward racial, sexual, and economic justice throughout the Americas. They are currently at work on a book about gender performance in contemporary Cuba, and they have also conducted research on queer performance in their hometown of Miami and written about the reception of queer artists doing hip-hop in New York City. As a violinist, Leslie Santana was a New Fromm Player at the Tanglewood Music Center and has served on the faculty of the Sphinx Performance Academy. They received a DMA from the University of Michigan and a PhD from Harvard University, and they are currently an assistant professor of music at the University of California San Diego.

Noé López is a social anthropologist at the University of Texas at Austin. Their work is on Ñuu Savi (Mixtec) sovereignty in southern Mexico, specializing on the relationship between sexuality and legal claims of nationalism—a response to the radical formation of culture amid deliberate and structural subjugation in Mexico and the United States. López explores *sexuality* as the foundation to discuss radical politics of belonging, civic formation, and the philosophy of the Ñuu Savi (Mixtec) people.

Caleb Luna is a PhD student in theater, dance, and performance studies at the University of California, Berkeley. Luna is a working-class, fat, brown queer, living, writing and dancing in Oakland, California. Their work explores the intersections of fatness, desire, fetishism, white supremacy, and colonialism from a queer of color lens. Their writing appears in *Black Girl Dangerous*, *Everyday Feminism*, and *The Body Is Not An Apology*.

DJ Rekha/Rekha Malhotra is a DJ, producer, curator, and educator. They have been credited with pioneering bhangra music in North America via

Basement Bhangra club night (1997–2017). Rekha was the sound designer for the Tony Award–winning Broadway show *Bridge and Tunnel* and received a Drama Desk Award nomination for their work on the play *Rafta Rafta*. Rekha has done remixes for artists from Meredith Monk to Priyanka Chopra, and has performed at the White House during Obama's tenure and internationally. They are on the board of Queens-based Chhaya Community Development Corporation, serving New Yorkers of South Asian origin. They have a master's degree in comparative media studies from MIT and produce the weekly podcast *Bhangra and Beyond*.

Martin F. Manalansan IV is associate professor of American studies at the University of Minnesota, Twin Cities. He is the author of *Global Divas: Filipino Gay Men in the Diaspora*. He has coedited numerous anthologies including *Eating Asian America* and *Beauty and Brutality: Manila and Its Global Discontents*, and he is completing a book manuscript titled "Queer Dwellings."

Sabia McCoy-Torres is a sociocultural anthropologist and assistant professor of anthropology and Africana studies at Tulane University. Her research focuses on the English- and Spanish-speaking African diaspora, race, gender, sexuality, transnationalism, and popular music and performance in the circum-Caribbean and United States. Her current book project uses reggae (including dancehall) culture as an ethnographic lens to examine Afro-Caribbean migration to and between Brooklyn and Costa Rica, racial and cultural identity formations, pride, deconstructions of gender and sexuality, and creation of informal Caribbean cultural institutions with affective ties to other West Indian diasporic communities. McCoy-Torres has articles published in *Transforming Anthropology*, *Black Music Research Journal*, *Popular Music and Society*, and *Global South*. She is a proud native Bronx New Yorker and avid hip-hop, dancehall, house, salsa, and samba dancer.

Gregory Mitchell is associate professor of women's, gender, and sexuality studies at Williams College. He is the author of *Tourist Attractions: Performing Race and Masculinity in Brazil's Sexual Economy*. His work has appeared in *GLQ*, *American Ethnologist*, *Journal of Popular Music Studies*, *Brasiliana*, *Criminal Justice and Law Enforcement*, *Wagadu*, and many other journals and edited volumes in Brazil and the United States. His next book is tentatively titled "Panics Without Borders: Spectacles, Global Sporting Events, and the Production of Sex Trafficking."

Alexandre Paulikevitch is a dancer, choreographer and LGBT rights activist based in Beirut. He has taught and performed in Europe, the United States, and Lebanon.

Ramón H. Rivera-Servera is Dean of the College of Fine Arts and Professor of Theatre and Dance at the University of Texas at Austin. He is author and editor of several books, including *Performing Queer Latinidad: Dance, Sexuality, Politics*, *Blacktino Queer Performance*, and *Performance in the Borderlands*. He is founder and director of the Puerto Rican Arts Initiative (PRAI), a project supported by the Andrew W. Mellon Foundation to advance contemporary art practice in Puerto Rico.

Juana María Rodríguez is professor and chair of ethnic studies at the University of California, Berkeley, where she serves as faculty in gender and women's studies and the performance studies graduate group. She is the author of two books, *Queer Latinidad: Identity Practices, Discursive Spaces* and *Sexual Futures, Queer Gestures, and Other Latina Longings*, and served as coeditor for "Trans Studies *en las Américas*," a special issue of *TSQ: Transgender Studies Quarterly*. She is currently completing a new book project on visual culture and Latina sexual labor, entitled "*Puta* Life: Seeing Latinas, Working Sex."

Sable Elyse Smith is an interdisciplinary artist, writer, and educator based in New York. Using video, sculpture, photography, and text, she points to the carceral, the personal, the political, and the quotidian to speak about a violence that is largely unseen and potentially imperceptible. Her work has been featured at MoMA Ps1, New Museum, the Studio Museum in Harlem, and JTT Gallery, among numerous others. Smith has received awards from Creative Capital, Fine Arts Work Center, the Queens Museum, Skowhegan School of Painting and Sculpture, Rema Hort Mann Foundation, the Franklin Furnace Fund, and Art Matters. She is currently assistant professor of Visual Arts at Columbia University.

Jennifer Tyburczy is an associate professor of feminist studies at the University of California, Santa Barbara. She is the author of the Lambda Literary Award–winning book *Sex Museums: The Politics and Performance of Display*. Tyburczy is currently writing her second monograph, "Sex after NAFTA: The Queer Traffic of Free Trade."

Enzo E. Vasquez Toral is a Peruvian performer, scholar, theater director, and PhD candidate in Performance Studies at Northwestern University. His doctoral work focuses on contemporary queer and trans participation and interventions in Andean folklore through ritual cross-dressing in patron-saint fiestas, drag aesthetics, and performance art. His writings have appeared in *Modern Drama*, *El Alto*, *Ecumenica*, *Performance Research*, and *The Routledge Companion to Theatre and Performance Historiography*. Enzo holds an MA in Performance Studies from Northwestern University, an MA in Latin American Literature and Culture from Princeton University, and a BA in History and Literature and Brazilian Studies from Harvard University.

Index

Note: page numbers followed by *f* refer to figures.